Challenges of Diversity

Challenges of Diversity

Essays on America

WERNER SOLLORS

Rutgers University Press

New Brunswick, Newark, and Camden, New Jersey, and London

Library of Congress Cataloging-in-Publication Data
Names: Sollors, Werner, author.
Title: Challenges of diversity : essays on America / Werner Sollors.
Description: New Brunswick, New Jersey : Rutgers University Press, 2017. | Includes bibliographical references and index.
Identifiers: LCCN 2017016372 (print) | LCCN 2017037894 (ebook) | ISBN 9780813589343 (E-pub) | ISBN 9780813589350 (Web PDF) | ISBN 9780813589336 (hardback) | ISBN 9780813589329 (paperback)
Subjects: LCSH: National characteristics, American, in literature. | American literature—History and criticism. | Multiculturalism in literature. | Ethnicity in literature. | Race in literature. | Immigrants in literature. | BISAC: LITERARY CRITICISM / American / General. | LITERARY CRITICISM / American / African American. | SOCIAL SCIENCE / Ethnic Studies / General. | SOCIAL SCIENCE / Ethnic Studies / African American Studies. | SOCIAL SCIENCE / Discrimination & Race Relations. | HISTORY / United States / General.
Classification: LCC PS169.N35 (ebook) | LCC PS169.N35 S56 2017 (print) | DDC 810.9/358—dc23
LC record available at https://na01.safelinks.protection.outlook.com/?url=https%3A%2F%2Flccn.loc.gov%2F2017016372&data=02%7C01%7Cesm102%40press.rutgers.edu%7Cf322287ce9f742b86ac908d4de6caec4%7Cb92d2b234d35447093ff69aca6632ffe%7C1%7C0%7C636378005747504484&sdata=pCzTf4SB7IulCMbn7M66i%2B9TwG6CIxuGMaAO5rzeWOQ%3D&reserved=0

A British Cataloging-in-Publication record for this book is available from the British Library.

∞ The paper used in this publication meets the requirements of the American National Standard for Information Sciences—Permanence of Paper for Printed Library Materials, ANSI Z39.48-1992.

www.rutgersuniversitypress.org

Manufactured in the United States of America

Sacvan Bercovitch in memoriam

Contents

Challenges of Diversity

Introduction

Ah me, what are the people whose land I have come to this time,
and are they violent and savage, and without justice,
or hospitable to strangers, with a godly mind?
—Homer, *Odyssey* VI:119–121[1]

Migration has been a human experience since the earliest times, and epic stories of migrants have accompanied this experience. In the biblical book of Genesis, Adam and Eve are expelled from the Garden of Eden, and the three monotheistic religions have drawn on the story of paradise as an ideal place of origin that man forfeited because of his fallibility. Noah and his family are saved from the environmental disaster of the flood and can start a new life elsewhere. In the book of Exodus, Moses and the Israelites escape from oppressive slavery in Egypt. In Vergil's *Aeneid* the defeated Trojans leave their city in search of a new country. Such great stories have provided vivid and often heartrending scenes that writers, painters, and composers have returned to. They include scenes of departures, as when Aeneas carries his father Anchises out of the burning city and brings his son and the Penates along but loses his wife; of difficult journeys, as when the Israelites follow a pillar of fire at night and of cloud in the day and miraculously cross the Red Sea to reach the Promised Land; and of arrivals, as when Noah's ark lands on Mount Ararat after the dove he sent out returns with an olive leaf in her beak. Such epic stories tell tales of the hospitality that Nausikaa extends to Odysseus and that the inhospitable Polyphemus does not. They tell tales of the many obstacles along the way; of the sadness at the loss of family, friends, or homeland; of feeling *Fernweh*, the yearning for faraway and unknown places; of the hopefulness of new beginnings elsewhere; of the wish for a return from exile in what remains a strange location to the familiar place of origin; or of the migrants' peculiar sense of seeing the world through the eyes of two places.

Such stories resonate in a world characterized by vast global migrations. There were 244 million international migrants in the world in 2015, more than the population of Brazil, the fifth largest country. The United States was the most important host country with 47 million migrants living there, followed by Germany and Russia, with twelve million migrants each.[2] But for a very long time, Europe was a continent better known for sending migrants abroad, a good many of them to the Americas, than for receiving them. Hence the term "emigration" became more popular than "migration" in Europe. By contrast, American cultural history has been shaped, from colonial times on, by large-scale immigration (as well as by substantial internal migrations), and it is not surprising that some of the ancient migration stories have been invoked and adapted for the American experience.[3] Both the English Puritan settlers who arrived in order to practice their religion freely and the Africans who were enslaved and brought to America against their wills found in their experiences echoes of the Book of Exodus. Thus Cotton Mather wrote about New England: "This New World desert was prefigured long before in the howling deserts where the Israelites passed on their journey to Canaan."[4] And African Americans created and sang the spiritual "Go Down, Moses," claiming their freedom with the biblical exclamation, "Let my people go!" When the founding fathers discussed the design of the Great Seal of the United States, Benjamin Franklin proposed "Moses standing on the Shore, and extending his Hand over the Sea, thereby causing the same to overwhelm Pharaoh who is sitting in an open Chariot, a Crown on his Head and a Sword in his Hand. Rays from a Pillar of Fire in the Clouds reaching to Moses, to express that he acts by Command of the Deity. Motto, Rebellion to Tyrants is

Obedience to God."[5] Thomas Jefferson thought of choosing the scene of the "children of Israel in the wilderness, led by a cloud by day and a pillar of fire by night."[6] The final Seal promises a *novus ordo seclorum* (new order of the ages), an inscription adapted from Vergil's *Eclogues* 4:4–10. The motto *annuit coeptis* also derived from Vergil (*Aeneid* IX:625), and turned a supplication for Jupiter's assent into the claim that God already "prospered this undertaking."[7] And many an immigrant tale has been called an "American Odyssey."

The United States is a settler-dominated country, the product of a composite of waves of immigration and westward migration that have reduced the original inhabitants of the fourth continent to a small minority called Indians. In the mid-nineteenth century, Irish, German, and Scandinavian migrants joined the English settlers, as did the Spanish-speaking population of the parts of Mexico that the United States annexed. Toward the end of the nineteenth and the beginning of the twentieth century, the so-called new immigration of such south and east European groups as Slavs, Jews, Greeks, and Italians followed, transforming the country from a small English (and English-dominated) colonial offshoot into a polyethnic nation, a process that continued in the second half of the twentieth century with the still ongoing migratory mass movements of Latin Americans and Asians.

The United States has thus become a prototypical immigrant country in which ethnic diversity is a statistical fact as well as a source of debate, of anxiety, and of pride. The statistical fact, well documented by the US Census Bureau, is readily established: at the moment I am writing this, the ticking American population clock shows 324,420,496 inhabitants, with one immigrant arriving every thirty-three seconds. The American population grew from about 5 million in 1800 to 308 million in 2010, and the total foreign-born population as of 2009 was 38.5 million, among whom 20.5 million came from Latin America, 10.5 million from Asia.[8] Divided by race and Hispanic origin, 244 million (or 79 percent) classified themselves as white, 48 million as Hispanic, 39 million as black or African American, 14 million as Asian, and 3 million as American Indian; there were also about 5 million who described themselves as part of two or more races.[9] Divided by ancestry group, 50 million Americans claimed to have German roots, 36 million Irish origins, 27 million English heritage, and 18 million an Italian background.[10] Yet when looked at through the lens of languages spoken, it becomes apparent that language loyalty is rather weak for the older immigrant groups, with only a small fraction of German Americans speaking German and Italian Americans speaking Italian at home.[11]

Immigration thus brought an enormous population growth, a fact that made it a source of national pride, all the more so because it took place alongside vast territorial expansions by purchase, conquest, and treaty. Yet immigration also generated a national population of very diverse origins, and this created times of anxiety and fearfulness over diversity and assimilation. For the Puritans it was inconceivable that Quakers could become part of the Massachusetts Bay Company; for the free whites in a slave-holding country it was self-evident that African slaves and their descendants had no rights that a white man was bound to respect, and plans to resettle freed slaves in Africa became popular for some time. Cotton Mather feared that Satan was planning to create "a colony of Irish," and Benjamin Franklin wondered whether the "swarthy" Germans of Pennsylvania "will shortly be so numerous as to Germanize us instead of our Anglifying them, and will never adopt our language and customs, any more than they can acquire our complexion."[12] Alexander Hamilton, though he currently enjoys much fame in the world of musicals and is associated with such lines as "Immigrants (We Get the Job Done)" wondered whether, because "foreigners will generally be apt to bring with them attachments to the persons they have left behind," their influx to America "must, therefore, tend to produce a heterogeneous compound; to change and corrupt the national spirit; to complicate and confound public opinion; to introduce foreign propensities. In the composition of society, the harmony of the ingredients is all-important, and whatever tends to a discordant intermixture must have an injurious tendency."[13] Race and religion have often overlapped in calls for exclusion, from the nineteenth century to the present. For mid-nineteenth-century Protestant culture, it was the threat of the religious difference that Irish and German Catholic immigrants presented that led to the anti-immigrant Know Nothing movement. Racial anxieties stoked fears of Chinese immigrants and led to the passing of the Chinese Exclusion Act in 1882 and the Gentlemen's Agreement with Japan in 1907. The passing of the 1924 Johnson-Reed Act, in the name of US racial homogeneity, restricted each nationality to no more than 2 percent of its presence in the United States as of 1890 (that is, before the "new immigration" had peaked). And after half a century of high immigration figures, the current political mood, fomented by fears of terrorism, seems again to turn toward restricting the influx of immigrants, with a primary target of the religious difference of Muslims.

Diversity implies that it may be challenging to find the unifying elements that hold this heterogeneous population together in a Hamiltonian "harmony of the ingredients." Nationalisms are often based on myths of shared blood and soil, yet present-day Americans are not of one blood and hail from quite different terrains. Other settler countries chose racial mixing or interpreted figures that seemed to embody such mixing, like the Mexican Virgin of Guadalupe, as symbols of national unity. Mixing races was also common in the parts of Mexico that were annexed, as well as in New Orleans and other parts of formerly French Louisiana where the important category "free man of color" stood between black and white. For the English colonies and much of the later United States, however, mixing black and white remained a vexed issue through the twentieth century. Hence turning diversity into unity took different forms. "What is the connecting link between these so different elements," Alexis de Tocqueville asked in a letter. "How are they welded into one people?"[14] The first three essays in this book pursue this question in various ways and search for the answers given in American texts and symbols.

One answer was that enforced assimilation in an English mold, or Anglo-conformity, was the most promising pattern that would unify the population. It made English the dominant language and turned America into a graveyard of spoken languages other than English, except only among recent immigrants; currently that means speakers of Spanish and of Asian languages. Anglo-domination also meant that a historical consciousness of American culture as an offshoot of England had to be developed and instilled in the population. Though it may always have sounded somewhat odd to hear children with thick immigrant accents sing "Land where our fodders died," the assertion of Anglo-American patriotism by non-Anglo Americans could sound hollow, at times even duplicitous, when the United States was at war with the countries of origin of millions of immigrants, as was the case during World War I. Furthermore, racially differing groups, most especially blacks and Indians, were excluded or severely marginalized in Anglicization projects. Their status as citizens still needed to be fought for, even though they were clearly a continued and strong presence in American cultural productions. Could the invocation of shared English origins really serve as a "connecting link" between America's "different elements"?

Religious typology, examined in the opening essay "Literature and Ethnicity," was particularly adept in making sacred biblical stories prototypes of secular American tales that could then be seen as their fulfillment on Earth, and the Puritan method of reading migration history in the light of the biblical text has left many traces in the culture. Biblical stories could provide answers to such questions as: Why did we leave? What did we come here to find? And how may we still be connected to the people and places we left behind? For nonadherents to messianic religions and even for nonbelievers, American "civil religion" (Robert Bellah) helped to transfer religious to political sentiments, leaving the meaning of "God" relatively unspecific in the formula "In God We Trust."

Invoking New World Puritan, Pilgrim, and Virginian beginnings—also by people who were not descended from any such group—thus became a way of imagining a cultural connecting link. Feeling like a fellow citizen of George Washington or reciting the founding fathers' revered political documents could create a feeling of national cohesion that each Fourth of July celebration reenacted. Yet the Declaration of Independence, the subject of the third essay, "Dedicated to a Proposition," was interpreted and invoked and parodied in heterogeneous ways, sometimes quite irreverently, in Massachusetts freedom suits, by immigrants, by Abraham Lincoln and Martin Luther King, and it was echoed differently in the suffrage and labor movements and in the musical *Hair*. Frederick Douglass's rhetorical question "What to the Slave is the Fourth of July?" stands for many other vantage points from which such documents could be cited for the purpose of demanding urgent changes of the status quo and not yet for celebrating the country's unity. The "American Creed" was often less a firm set of beliefs in an existing system than a promise that would still need to be fulfilled through struggles and hard work.

Beyond Anglo-conformity, religious typology, and invocation of founding fathers and their texts, making arrival points stand for ultimate origins could provide some form of family resemblance and American inclusiveness. As the second essay, "National Identity and Ethnic Diversity," suggests, instead of tracing one's roots back to different places on the globe, one only had to go back to such heterogeneous arrival points as the *Mayflower* at Plymouth Rock; a slave ship in Jamestown; and the steerage of a steamship at Castle Garden, Ellis Island, or Angel Island and thus settle on comparable threshold symbols in America. Some immigrants regarded their moment of arrival on American shores as their true birthday. They sometimes celebrated that birthday with fellow passengers, now christened "ship brothers" or "ship sisters." The shared feeling that a pre-American past had been transcended, that even the Hamiltonian "attachments to the persons they have left behind" had been severed, could thus paradoxically turn diversity with its "foreign propensities" into another source of unity.

This origin story could also lead to an eradication of any past and a reorientation toward the future of things to come. Thus the narrator of one of Edgar Allan Poe's short stories introduces himself: "Of my country and of my family I have little to say. Ill usage and length of years have driven me from one, and estranged me from the other."[15] "All the past we leave behind," Walt Whitman proclaimed in "Pioneers! O Pioneers!" and he continued: "We debouch upon a newer mightier world, varied world, / Fresh and strong the world we seize, world of labor and the march, / Pioneers! O pioneers!"[16] Willa Cather used Whitman's poem in a title of one of her novels of immigrant life, while the Norwegian immigrant Ole E. Rølvaag invoked the text of the poem in one of the volumes of his saga of the settlement by Norwegians in the prairies. What a reader of Herman Melville's novel *Moby-Dick, or, The Whale* learns about Captain Ahab's background is only that he had a "crazy, widowed mother."[17] In his *White-Jacket,* Melville wrote that the "Past is, in many things, the foe of mankind," but that the "Future" is "the Bible of the Free."[18] If the past is dead, then migration could be like a rebirth experience. Thus the immigrant Mary Antin begins her memoir, *The Promised Land* (1912): "I was born, I have lived, and I have been made over. Is it not time to write my life's story? I am just as much out of the way as if I were dead, for I am absolutely other than the person whose story I have to tell. [. . .] My second birth was no less a birth because there was no distinct incarnation."[19]

Ethnicity as ancestry could thus lead to the denial, forgetting, or in any event, the overcoming of the past. Here, again, racial difference created an odd counterweight because though self-monitored rebirth, renaming, and other ethnic options were open to the diverse immigrant population that the US Census Bureau considered "white," "non-whites" were often believed to remain immutably tied to their past. When a black passenger seated in the white section of a segregated train tells the conductor, "I done quit the race," he is saying something that is believed to be so impossible as to make his statement funny, even at a time when Jim Crow rules were sadistically enforced throughout the society. The nameless narrator-protagonist of Ralph Ellison's *Invisible Man* fits well into the American "all-the-past-we-leave-behind" camp because we learn little about his parents, and he only refers to his grandfather's one-sentence deathbed maxim, to "overcome'em with yeses, undermin'em with grins, agree'em to death and destruction"—yet the identity shifts of this urban migrant never cross the color line.[20] The color line was crossed, of course, in the extensive literature on racial passing. The word "passing" itself was an Americanism that names the supposed impossibility for characters of mixed-race ancestry to successfully define themselves by their white ancestors and as white, except by deception. In a country that believes in social mobility and worships the upstart as self-made man, racial passing was often a tragic affair. And for a racially passing person, success furthermore meant abandoning past attachments with a vengeance, for even just acknowledging a colored relative could mean the immediate end of passing, as characters in Jessie Fauset's or Nella Larsen's novels rightly fear.

Can all Americans perhaps share a form of double consciousness, as their deep history points to other continents? That we are all immigrants could be the answer here, and one finds even the migration across the Bering Strait of the people who would become American Indians merged into this unifying story of a nation of immigrants. The migratory background could be folded into a neatly harmonized family metaphor, as when the Danish immigrant Jacob Riis wrote in his autobiography, *The Making of an American* (1901): "Alas! I am afraid that thirty years in the land of my children's birth have left me as much of a Dane as ever. . . . Yet, would you have it otherwise? What sort of a husband is the man going to make who begins by pitching his old mother out of the door to make room for his wife? And what sort of a wife would she be to ask or to stand it?"[21] Mother country and country of marriage partner are thus reconciled as unchangeable parts of one single family story. One can surely be proud of both one's parent and one's spouse, and spouses should not demand the discarding of their mothers-in-law. One also notices Riis's weighty phrase, "land of my children's birth." As the dominant cultural outlook may have subtly shifted from following the example of one's parents to imagining a better future for one's children, the importance of success stories of upward mobility is not negligible for this reorientation to work. And the fact that American-born children may be the first American citizens in immigrant families intensifies this forward-looking identification.

Yet in situations of war or other great conflicts, the immigrants' parentage or former citizenship, their "foreign propensities" and "attachments to the persons they have left behind," could matter again. Public anxieties could emerge and be stoked by rhetoric, culminating in strong majoritarian beliefs in the incompatibility of some groups who are believed to tend to "change and corrupt the national spirit." Attempts to stress and normalize hyphenated double identities as family stories did become particularly troubling during World War I, when national loyalty had to be reinforced and seemed to demand "pitching one's old mother out of the door." Hence the fast-track abandonment of the hyphens in Americanization campaigns, the Ford Motor Company Melting Pot rituals, and the slogans promising "Americans All!" Yet the more melting-pot catalogs listed the heterogeneous pasts with the intention of making sure that they would be left behind, the more these differing pasts could also be reclaimed now that they had been named.

It is thus telling that Randolph Bourne's utopian-cosmopolitan notion of a "Transnational America" as well as Horace Kallen's concept of cultural pluralism emerged in opposition to the wartime assimilation project of the Americanizers. Bourne thought Americanization would lead to the dominance of vapid, lowest-common-denominator popular culture of cheap magazines and movies and eradicate the country's vibrant cultural-linguistic diversity. Kallen believed that assimilation was a violation of the democracy of ethnic groups that a country like Switzerland realized more fully than melting-pot America, for assimilationists fail to recognize that "men cannot change their grandfathers."[22] As Philip Gleason showed, this belief in the immutability of ethnoracial origins was a feature that early pluralist thinking shared with that of racists, and neither believed in assimilation. Did pluralists, to use Kwame Anthony Appiah's formulation, simply "replace one ethnocentrism with many"?[23] The complex and somewhat surprising story of the origins of cultural pluralism is the subject of the fourth essay, "A Critique of Pure Pluralism."

From such beginnings, there slowly emerged a new sense of Americanness that emphasized more and more the aspects of ethnic diversity as constitutive and hopefully unifying features of the country. Rather than generating anxiety, diversity could now become a source of national pride, generating the belief that the inhabitants' "heterogeneous compound" was, in fact, the answer to the quest for national unity. The process was interrupted by World War II, when the search for "common ground" (also the title of a magazine edited by the Slovenian immigrant Louis Adamic) summoning national unity out of diversity was challenged by the fear of new sets of US relatives of wartime enemies: fifth columnists from the European Axis countries, but most especially West Coast Japanese Americans who were held in detention camps for the duration of the war, even though the majority of them held US citizenship. During the Cold War, new fears were targeted toward immigrants who had Communist backgrounds and affiliations or who were merely suspected of Communist sympathies.

Big changes in race relations and in immigration policies came in the course of the 1960s. Neither the Americanizers' assimilation project nor Bourne and Kallen's pluralism had paid much attention to African Americans and Indians in their models of transnational or pluralist America; they remained "encapsulated in white ethnocentrism," as John Higham put it.[24] However, the successes of the civil rights movement forced a new recognition of the privilege of whiteness that earlier models of Americanness had quietly taken for granted or simply ignored in their reflections. The example of African Americans' struggle for equality inspired the American Indian movement, women's liberation, the struggle for gay rights, and other movements and led to more vocal demands for a more universally egalitarian country, measured by its inclusiveness of previously excluded groups. This was reflected in the 1965 Immigration and Naturalization Act that abolished racially motivated national origins quotas. The recognition also gained dominance that past discriminations on the basis of categories like race, gender, and religion needed not just corrections on the individual level but "affirmative action" toward groups that had been discriminated against as groups. This recognition required strenuous attacks on exclusionary practices of the past and generated a new hopefulness that stressing what had divided Americans in the past could become the connecting link of the present. This emphasis on group rights is what became known in the

1980s as multiculturalism to its advocates and, a decade later, as identity politics to its critics.

The transformation of an Anglo-American settler country into a polyethnic and self-consciously multicultural nation may thus appear as a story of great progress toward the fulfillment of egalitarian ideals in a more and more inclusive society. When seen through the lens of multiculturalism, one could imagine a success story: that a slow equalization process among different status groups had affirmed the "American Dream" of high social and economic mobility. There are more women in leadership positions than before the 1960s, and African Americans and Latinos have a far stronger representation in governmental bodies and educational structures, in business, health care, law, and the military. Discrimination on the grounds of race, sex, national origin, or sexual orientation is being monitored, and nasty jokes or spiteful comments about minorities are no longer common currency or politely tolerated in many areas of American life.[25]

Yet it is also the case that classes have been drifting apart in America. The status and share in income of poor people has been declining, while that of the highest-earning strata has increased dramatically. Whereas the bottom half made 19.9 percent of the pretax national income in 1980, their share has declined to a mere 12.5 percent in 2014, while that of the top 1 percent has risen from 10.7 percent in 1980 to 20.2 percent in 2014.[26] And this American situation has global relevance, as nowadays the world's eight richest men—among them six Americans—own as much as the world's bottom half, or 3.6 billion people.[27]

Economic equalization is not in evidence, then, and multiculturalism's focus on group rights may have made it harder for the poorer half of Americans to form intergroup alliances, while antisocial tax and healthcare legislation can be advanced in the name of opposing identity politics, thus further deepening the class divide and accelerating the movement toward a multiculturally styled plutocracy. How could social movements be built, Richard Rorty asked, that would attempt to fight the crimes of social selfishness with the same vigor that multiculturalists have focused on the crimes of sadism against minority groups?[28] Group divisions, reinforced by the bureaucratic procedures of what David Hollinger criticized as America's "ethnoracial pentagon," a "rigidification of exactly those ascribed distinctions between persons that various universalists and cosmopolitans have so long sought to diminish," seemed to assume a much more permanent and quasi-natural status, obscuring more malleable connections by choice and around shared interests.[29] Pluralism also alienated radical young intellectuals, as Higham observed, "from the rank and file of the American working people—that is, from all the people except the culturally distinctive minorities."[30] And those nonminority working people could now be mobilized by populist politicians as "forgotten Americans" who consider themselves free of the racisms of the past but express forceful, and even spiteful, resentment against those minority groups who were singled out for policies of collective redress or benefit, and against the political and educational elites as well as the liberal press they hold responsible for devising and defending these policies. Multiculturally oriented intellectuals in turn register and indict this reaction as racism, xenophobia, and anti-intellectualism. In the face of growing class inequality, multiculturalism may no longer serve as the "connecting link" between the "different elements of America," but might instead enable potentially explosive group divisions and help to create that "discordant intermixture" with "an injurious tendency" that Hamilton feared. Perhaps it is no coincidence that the debate about multiculturalism was drawn to the dystopian imagination of George Orwell's *Nineteen Eighty-Four*, a novel that has again moved to the center of public attention. (Erich Fromm's use of the term "mobile truth" in his 1961 afterword to Orwell's novel also has assumed a new relevance at the present moment.) The last essay in this volume, "The Multiculturalism Debate as Cultural Text," focusing on the so-called culture wars, includes the sentence, "There may now be many multicultural men and women who are completely disconnected from any proletariat anywhere, and multicultural internationalism may even serve as the marker that separates these intellectuals from people, making multiculturalists instead part of a global ruling class." Multiculturalism may thus need a strong infusion of social consciousness and a steady, active attention to economic inequalities. But what other model of integration could we turn to now, when an immigrant arrives every thirty-three seconds in the United States, than multiculturalism's affirmation of diversity as a sign of strength?

Which tales of hospitality toward refugees and strangers will the current moment generate in the United States or, as a matter of fact, anywhere in the world, since the United States is no longer exceptional as a host country to large numbers of immigrants. Many other countries have become the destination of global flows of refugees and migrants. More than 140 countries, among them the United States, signed the 1951 United Nations Convention Relating to the Status of Refugees, an important international treaty that was expanded by the 1967 Protocol and reaffirmed by the 2016 New York Declaration.[31] That most recent declaration stipulates "a shared responsibility to manage large movements of refugees and migrants in a humane, sensitive, compassionate and people-centred manner." It continues:

> Large movements of refugees and migrants must have comprehensive policy support, assistance and protection, consistent with States' obligations under international law. We also recall our obligations to fully respect their human rights and fundamental freedoms, and we stress their need to live their lives in safety and dignity. We pledge our support to those affected today as well as to those who will be part of future large movements. [. . .]
>
> We strongly condemn acts and manifestations of racism, racial discrimination, xenophobia and related intolerance against refugees and migrants, and the stereotypes often applied to them, including on the basis of religion or belief. Diversity enriches every society and contributes to social cohesion.

One can only hope that the governments of member countries will live up to the language and spirit of the United Nations and that the stories that dominate our time will resemble Nausikaa's caring hospitality and not Polyphemus's violence.

The Illustrations

Each essay is accompanied by an image, inviting the reader to ponder how one might be able to visualize multicultural America in a single telling image. Edward A. Wilson, critically casting America as *El Dorado* (1913; see Figure 1, the opening image of the first essay), imagined the arrival of an immigrant family in the harbor of New York not with the Statue of Liberty but with a golden Fortuna-like goddess who rolls the dice of chance toward the newcomers, thus casting a critical question mark on the myth of America. The representational shortcomings of such artwork as Howard Chandler Christy's poster *Americans All!* (1917, see Figure 2, the frontispiece to the second essay) are immediately apparent, as the Christy girl is a poor allegorical embodiment of the varieties of physical features that the list of ethnic names suggests. The Enlightenment-inspired egalitarian promise of "All Men Are Created Equal" remains an ideological foundation of any multicultural sensibility, but John Trumbull's 1819 painting *Declaration of Independence* (in its two-dollar bill adaptation, the frontispiece of the third essay, Figure 3) does little to give visual expression to American ethnic diversity. Grant E. Hamilton's cartoon *Uncle Sam Is a Man of Strong Features* (1898, Figure 4, the image opening the fourth essay) is a valiant, Arcimboldo-style attempt to transform a virtual catalogue of all major ethnic groups—not only English, German, Irish, Swede, French, Italian, Greek, and Russian, but also Indian, Negro, Hebrew, Cuban, Esquimaux, Hawaiian, Turk, and Chinese—into the facial features of the familiar Uncle Sam figure. Uncle Sam's beard, composed by the only female figure, a stout Quaker woman with piously folded hands, forms a comic counterpoint to the rather worrisome male specimens. Whether a twenty-first-century viewer is more startled by the Negro and Hawaiian as thick-lipped dark pupils of the eyes, by the big-nosed Hebrew and shiftless Italian as ears, or by the stoic Indian with his outstretched arms as nose and eyebrows, one simply has to wonder about Grant's employment of grossly stereotypical ethnic features and his need to give captions to all those figures in order to make the heterogeneous ingredients of America more readily legible. The fifth and last essay opens with a diagram (Figure 5) adapted from Stewart G. and Mildred Wiese Cole's *Minorities and the American Promise* (1954) rather than an image, in order to highlight the significance of the now forgotten history of mid-century research about cultural diversity and intercultural education. In the absence of a single trademark-like image that would recognizably signal America in all its diversity, the cover designer arranged ten of Francis Augustus Sherman's Ellis Island portrait photographs from the years 1905 to 1920.[32] Sherman worked as chief registry clerk with the Immigration Division of Ellis Island and thus had ample opportunity to get migrants who passed through, or were detained at Ellis Island to pose for him. Starting with the image at the top center of the cover, "Three Women from Guadeloupe," the photographs represent, in clockwise direction, "Greek soldier," "Ruthenian Woman," "Slovakian Women," "Algerian Man," "Danish man," "Protestant Woman from

Zuid-Beveland, The Netherlands," "Greek Woman," "Russian Cossacks," and "Bavarian Man." Dressed in traditional costumes, many of Sherman's subjects stand in front of recognizable Ellis Island buildings, often look straight at the camera, and thus manage to prompt the viewer to wonder about their individual stories, the meaning of migration, and the challenges of diversity.

FIGURE 1 Edward A. Wilson. *El Dorado*. Cover of *Life*, December 18, 1913. Widener Library, Harvard University.

1

Literature and Ethnicity

The Roots of Ethnicity: Etymology and Definitions

On October 9, 1854, Nathaniel Hawthorne, then serving as the American consul to Liverpool, made a curious entry in his journal: "My ancestor left England in 1635. I return in 1853. I sometimes feel as if I myself had been absent these two hundred and eighteen years." During his years in England, Hawthorne became fascinated by the idea of tracing his roots, made genealogical enquiries, and was hopeful of finding "a gravestone in one of these old churchyards, with my own name upon it; although for myself, I should wish to be buried in America. The graves are too devilish damp here."

Hawthorne's search for genealogical facts remained fruitless, but his literary curiosity was intensified by his inability to trace his real ancestors. Ready to embrace an imaginary ancestry, he was intrigued by the

SOURCE *The Harvard Encyclopedia of American Ethnic Groups*, ed. Stephan Thernstrom, Ann Orlov, and Oscar Handlin. Cambridge, MA, and London: Belknap Press of Harvard University Press, 1980, 647–665. Used by permission of Harvard University Press.

legend of a bloody footmark, which a sixteenth-century clergyman, George Marsh, had miraculously left on the stone pavement of Smithills Hall in Lancashire. When martyr Marsh was arrested, he "stamped his foot in earnest protest against the injustice with which he was treated. Blood issued from his foot, which slid along the stone pavement of the hall, leaving a long footmark printed in blood; and there it remained ever since, in spite of the scrubbings of all after generations." *The Ancestral Footstep*, one of Hawthorne's fragmentary attempts at creating an English-American romance, is an excellent image for Hawthorne's sense of what is now known as "ethnicity." It refers to a specific tradition, born out of protest against another tradition; it is as thick as blood; and it defies "scrubbing" descendants. It is embedded in myth and invites faith rather than critical scrutiny. Hawthorne reasons: "Of course, it is all humbug—a darker vein cropping up through the gray flagstone," but concludes that "the legend is a good one."

The dark-brown stain of the footprint also defied Hawthorne's endeavors to use it as an emblematic center of a novel. Despite numerous efforts, he could not make the legend functional in the story of an American's return to his Old World roots. Hawthorne tried to make the American the missing heir of the English manor house, but realized that an English title would compromise the hero's Americanness. Hawthorne then changed the plot and made the English inheritance invalid and unreal, thus making ethnicity imaginary, but again he ran into new problems. On the one hand, the English manor house represented for Hawthorne the structured social life Americans had left behind in the Old World. On the other hand, it was the doomed shell of a class structure that had left its bloody footprint on the pavement of time.

In another unfinished romance, *Septimius Felton*, Hawthorne returned to the bloody footmark, but sketched a different American protagonist with a "wild genealogy," a descendant of an old witch on one side and "an Indian prophet and powwow" on the other. This strange and exceptional man had "brooded upon the legends that clung around his line, following his ancestry, not only to the English universities, but into the wild forest, and into hell itself. [. . .] His mind and character had a savage and fiendish strain, intermixed with its Puritan characteristics." But this multiethnic prototypical American carried Hawthorne no further than did his imaginary New England descendant of martyr Marsh. The author could not finish the tale of *The*

Ancestral Footstep. Hawthorne's love-hate for his ancestors, his understanding of the "humbug" of good genealogical legends, and finally, his difficulties in finding a precise literary use of ethnicity are indicative of a persistent problem in American literature and culture. The memory of diverse pre-American pasts has instilled a pervasive sense of ethnicity into the minds and imaginations of American writers.

If American culture symbolizes man's entry into fragmented modernity, then "ethnicity" functions as a formidable expression of a countervailing yearning for history and community. The tension between these forces is a persistent theme in American literature. Tocqueville described American society as one "which comprises all the nations of the world—English, French, German: people differing from one another in language, in beliefs, in opinions; in a word a society possessing no roots, no memories, no prejudices, no routine, no common ideas, no national character," and inquired, "What is the connecting link?" More than a century later Margaret Mead concluded that "however many generations we may actually boast of in this country, however real our lack of ties in the old world may be, we are all third generation, our European ancestry tucked away and half forgotten, the recent steps in our wanderings over America immortalized and overemphasized." Ethnicity as a tenuous ancestry and as the interplay of different ancestries may be the most crucial aspect of the American national character.

The word "ethnicity" itself has an interesting past with etymological contexts of its own. In the modern sense of "differentiation based on nationality, race, religion, or language," "ethnicity" is an Americanism, first used in 1941 in W. Lloyd Warner's *Yankee City Series* as one category—along with age, sex, and religion—that separates "the individual from some classes of individuals and identifies him with others." In 1953 David Riesman extended the dimensions of the word "ethnicity" in a famous *American Scholar* debate about McCarthyism. Riesman suggested that the struggle between ethnicity and modernity was at the root of the problem: "There is a tendency for the older 'class struggles,' rooted in clear hierarchical antagonisms, to be replaced by a new sort of warfare: the groups who, by reason of rural or small-town location, ethnicity, or other parochialism, feel threatened by the better educated upper-middle-class people (though often less wealthy and politically powerful) who follow or create the modern movements in science, art, literature, and opinion generally." Riesman furthermore argued that the shift from class to ethnicity in America created outlets for fears and hatreds of Indians, Mexicans, and other ethnic groups but that ethnic diversity and regional and religious pluralism tended to confine the dangerous potential of a fanatical fascist leader to "his" ethnic group or section. Whereas Warner did not always include the descendants of English migrants under the term "ethnicity," Riesman applied it to *all* Americans, denying the validity of "ethnicity minus one."

"Ethnicity" is, of course, derived from the older adjective and noun "ethnic," which in turn goes back to a Greek root comprising the word field "nation" and "heathen." The word *ethnikos* was thus used in the Greek Bible to render the Hebrew goyim (non-Israelites, Gentiles). In the Christianized context of the English language, the word "ethnic" (sometimes spelled "hethnic") recurred, from the fourteenth through the nineteenth centuries, in the sense of "pagan, heathen, non-Christian." Only in the mid-nineteenth century did the more familiar meaning of "ethnic" as "peculiar to a race or nation" reemerge. However, the English language has retained the memory of "ethnic" as "heathen," often secularized in the sense of ethnic as "other," as "nonstandard," or in the United States, as somehow "un-American." This connotation gives the opposition of "ethnic" and "American" the additional religious dimension of the contrast between "heathens" and "chosen people." Therefore, the relationship between "ethnicity" and "American identity" parallels that of "heathenish superstition" and "true religion," and it is in the sense of "heathendom" that the word ethnicity was once recorded in 1772. But this instance is described as obsolete and rare in the *Oxford English Dictionary*.

"*Ethnics*"—originally just "people"—are etymologically the "others," "they" as opposed to "us." "Ethnicity" as "otherness" refers to self-definitions of one group of people through an opposition against other groups: we are not like them, they are not like us. Puritans liked to distinguish their own religious practice from heathenish customs. In 1702, Cotton Mather wrote that the "custom of preaching at funerals may seem ethnical in origin."

The negative separation from heathens has had its counterpart in a more or less hidden envy and admiration for the "other," which reached a high point with romantic racialism in the mid-nineteenth century. Thus, Harriet Beecher Stowe's *Uncle Tom's Cabin* (1852) expostulated that Negroes make better Christians than whites. The Anglo-Saxons, on the other hand, a "cool, logical, and practical" race, should remember that God gave the Bible "to them in the fervent language and with the glowing imagery of the more susceptible and passionate Oriental races." And in one of James Fenimore Cooper's last novels, *The Oak Openings* (1848), the Indians are "the chosen people of the Great Spirit." Frank Forrester (William H. Herbert) wrote of the slave woman Tituba, in *The Fair Puritan, an Historical Romance of the Days of Witchcraft* (1844–1845), that there was "more of the true, the lowly, and the grateful spirit of the Christian, in that poor, overtasked, despised, scourged heathen, than in her haughty master."

Ethnicity as otherness evoked disparagement and emulation in American writing. In order to attain full selfhood one has to experience otherness; and in that sense, ethnicity is not only in others but also in ourselves. Perhaps a latent fascination with the other in ourselves may account for the great popularity of autobiographical narratives of conversions from heretic to true believer, from criminal to social hero, or from ethnic to American. The affinities of ethnicity and heathendom are focused most clearly in conversion stories. Mary Antin's immigrant autobiography, *The Promised Land* (1912), begins: "I was born, I have lived, and I have been made over. Is it not time to write my life's story? I am just as much out of the way as if I were dead, for I am absolutely other than the person whose story I have to tell." It is obvious that the imagery of progressive change, of a transformation from a pre-American past to an American identity—Edward Steiner's *From Alien to Citizen* (1914) or Michael Pupin's *From Immigrant to Inventor* (1923)—is patterned on the symbolism of religious conversions. There is a heathenish dimension to the past, to *any* past, in American literature and a sacred quality to the future in America. American writers of the most diverse ancestries perceived America in religious terms, whether they sided with the saving grace of an American future ("Reborn in the Promised Land!") or with the adversary ethnicity of a "heathenish" past ("A Curse Upon Columbus!").

Horace Bushnell instructed his parishioners in 1859 that regeneration is "the naturalization of a soul in the kingdom of heaven" and thus related the process of becoming a true Christian with that of becoming an American. In 1873, Chamberlain Cummings preached that not only the "others" must be regenerated, or "naturalized," but that Jew and Gentile, Christian and heathen must be born again. If the completion of Cummings's metaphor means that all Americans, whether immigrant or native born, have to be naturalized in order to become true Americans, then this expanded use of the idea of a rebirth anticipated the rhetoric of the ethnic "revival"; however, in the 1960s, the relationship of ethnicity and American identity was inverted. Traditionally, the struggle was toward a true Christian, or later, a truly American identity; now many Americans yearn for an *ethnic* identity. Ethnicity has been transformed from a heathenish liability into a sacred asset, from a trait to be overcome in a conversion and rebirth experience to an identity to be achieved through yet another regeneration.

The rhetoric of ethnicity thus comes out of the tradition of American revivalism and awakenings: American literature is a rich repository of the footprints of ethnicity. American writers from Cotton Mather to Richard Wright, from Charles Brockden Brown to Pietro di Donato, from William Faulkner to Hisaye Yamamoto have developed such a systematic religious symbolism of ethnicity and American identity that American literature as a whole can be read as the ancestral footstep or coded hieroglyph of ethnic group life of the past and ethnic tensions in the present.

In this sense, "literature and ethnicity" in America refers to nothing less than the whole range of American culture, from classics to commercials, from seventeenth-century migrants' letters (as collected and edited by Everett Emerson) to nineteenth and twentieth-century black folk rhetoric (definitively analyzed in Lawrence Levine's *Black Culture and Black Consciousness*); from the first stage Yankee and ancestor of "Uncle Sam" in Royall Tyler's *The Contrast* (1787) to the first Ibsen productions on Scandinavian and Yiddish stages in America; from *Uncle Tom's Cabin* to *Dr. Fu Man Chu* serial movies; from Japanese-American detention-camp newspaper editorials to Mutt and Jeff and the Katzenjammer Kids; from T. S. Eliot to T. A. Daly; from *The Birth of a Nation* to *Roots*; from the *Bay Psalm Book* to *Rhymin' Paul Simon*. In his introduction to *The Uprooted* (1951), Oscar Handlin made the famous statement: "Once I thought to write a history of the immigrants in America. Then I discovered that the immigrants *were* American history." Analogously, one may say that ethnic literature *is* American literature.

Ethnicity is a pervasive theme in all American literature, whether in the shape of ethnicity as ancestry or ethnicity as diversity. The relationship of an American identity with pre-American pasts, the interaction of people with different pre-American pasts, and the emergence of an American character are among the central themes of American writing. And the very forms of American literature are also partly shaped by the forces of "ethnicity," from the first emergence of Americanized genres to the highest achievements of the American Renaissance, from the opposition of "romance" and "novel" to the rise of modernism and proletarian writing, from the growth of a mass culture to the literature of alienation and to the writings of the ethnic revival of the 1970s.

Promised Land and Melting Pot: Typology and Ethnicity

The most important source of literary ethnicity in North America is in the application of biblical images to the colonists' new experiences. Biblical analogies to the drama of seafaring and settling in new worlds are common in colonial literatures; in Puritan New England, however, a systematic religious symbology was applied to the transatlantic crossing—a theme of primary importance in American literature—and to a New World consciousness. The religious thought of seventeenth-century New England was thus an important source of the most widespread literary treatments of American ethnicity. Especially that aspect of Protestant theology known as typology has influenced diverse ethnic literary traditions in America.

Whereas traditional Christian typological exegesis was restricted to an interpretation of Old Testament characters and events as "types" that foreshadowed the redemptive history of the New Testament, Puritan typology related the secular history of the American colonists to biblical types. American writing from the seventeenth to the twentieth centuries abounds with characters who, in Sacvan Bercovitch's phrase, reveal the "Puritan origins of the American self" and who appear to be, as Ursula Brumm suggested, "based on fixed models, of which the most important are Adam and Christ." The events of early American history were, with the help of typology, rhetorically transformed into the biblical drama, as New Englanders interpreted their transatlantic voyage as a new exodus, their mission as an errand into the wilderness, and their role as that of a new Israel. American literature is exceptionally religious in its imagery, and this is true for mainstream as well as for minority writers. These anomalous religious tendencies advanced by the literature of a modern, postrevolutionary, bourgeois culture that so often invokes the ideals of the Enlightenment were ironically reinforced by the fact of immigration.

The continuous history of immigration strengthened the typological imagination in America. Marcus Lee Hansen wrote about the "process of Puritanization" among immigrant groups when he observed how familiar the records of seventeenth-century Massachusetts sounded to a historian of nineteenth-century immigration. The potential divisiveness of a multiethnic culture could be softened by a widespread acceptance of a modified typological framework for the American literary imagination. Roman Catholic, Jewish, and continental Protestant forms of worship had little in common with Puritan theology; yet the participants of the new immigration, along with African Americans, share a surprising concern with typology in their writings. Among the most prevalent typological elements are the imagery of a continued exodus from Egyptian–Old World bondage to the shores of an American promised land, the creation of American protagonists as Adamic and Christic figures, and the related notion of the welding of an American "new man." The image of the new exodus provides a sacral meaning to a secular migration. In the view of Puritan ministers in New England, God had carried the first settlers "by a mighty hand, and an out-stretched arm, over a sea greater than the Red Sea." Cotton Mather described both William Bradford and John Winthrop as a "new Moses"; and according to Winthrop's famous dictum, New England was the biblical "Citty vpon a Hill." Following the book of Revelation, colonists viewed America as a typological "new Jerusalem" and a "new Canaan," an association that remained powerful and alive in New England place names as well as in American literature.

Philip Freneau and Hugh Henry Brackenridge's "Poem, On the Rising Glory of America" (1771) views America typologically: "A Canaan here, / Another Canaan shall excel the old." In Timothy Dwight's patriotic poem *The Conquest of Canaan* (1785), the motif of the New World as a "last retreat for poor, oppress'd mankind" is part of a providential view of the history of America as the history of fulfillment: "And a new Moses lifts the daring wing / Through trackless seas, an unknown flight explores, / And hails a new Canaan's promis'd shores." It is no exaggeration to say that the exodus is one of America's central symbols. When the choice of an official seal for the United States was discussed in 1776,

Franklin suggested as the device "Moses lifting up his wand and dividing the Red Sea while Pharaoh was overwhelmed by its waters, with the motto, 'Rebellion to tyrants is obedience to God'"; and "Jefferson proposed the children of Israel in the wilderness 'led by a cloud by day and a pillar of fire at night.'" The eagle that was used for the seal is not just the classical emblem, but also the eagle of Revelation (12:13–17), an image of exodus and emigration.

Isaac Mitchell's novel *The Asylum* (1811), again viewed America as a promised land and as a haven for the oppressed: "The new land is the poor man's Canaan; to him it is a land flowing with milk and honey." The belief in America as a promised land for what Emma Lazarus called the "huddled masses" and the "wretched refuse" (in her Statue of Liberty poem, "The New Colossus") may reflect the popularity of the exodus theme in the literature of non-English immigrants to America, and the association of the exodus with a deliverance from slavery may explain the widespread use of this theme in African American writing. The typological adaptation of the second book of Moses to varieties of secular migrations remains a characteristic trait of American literature.

Phillis Wheatley, for example, who had been captured and enslaved in Senegal and sold to a Boston tailor in 1761, paradoxically described her own enslavement as a typological deliverance from Egypt in the poem "To the University of Cambridge, in New England." Absorbing the American rhetoric, she also claimed a full American identity as a Christian in "On Being Brought from Africa to America" and enjoined her compatriots: "Remember, Christians, Negroes black as Cain / May be refined, and join the angelic train." Similarly, Mary Antin, in *The Promised Land*, took a position of apparent self-effacement only to proudly proclaim a sense of equality. Antin continued the portraiture of America as a New Canaan for oppressed immigrants, while leaving no doubt that the metaphor of the promised land was especially suited to Jewish immigrants, whom she all but equated with the Pilgrim Fathers in *They Who Knock at Our Gates* (1914).

The pervasive adaptation of a typological view of America also reflected a deeper need for a spiritualization of collective experiences. To see a journey as a spiritual pilgrimage was, moreover, part of the cultural background of many people who became Americans. The very titles of ethnic books often suggest their affinities to the exodus theme: Sholem Asch, *Uncle Moses* (1918); Stoyan Christowe, *My American*

Pilgrimage (1947); Margaret Marchand, *Pilgrims on the Earth* (1940); Chaim Potok, *The Chosen* (1968); Mario Puzo, *The Fortunate Pilgrim* (1965); Claude Brown, *Manchild in the Promised Land* (1965); Robert Laxalt, *Sweet Promised Land* (1957); and Martin Wendell Odland, *The New Canaan* (1933).

The rhetoric of the new exodus also permitted writers to treat the providential deliverance as a continual process. Thus, the westward movement, especially across the prairie, is often compared with the exodus; and in James Fenimore Cooper's *The Prairie* (1827) or in Ole E. Rølvaag's *Giants in the Earth* (1927), the prairie becomes a new Atlantic Ocean and a typological extension of the Red Sea. The *Book of Mormon* similarly extended the exodus theme westward; but the patterns established by the Puritan settlers of the seventeenth century found even more amazing applications to other migrations. In much black literature, the "promised land" was not Phillis Wheatley's America but a transcendental realm of true liberty, somewhere "over Jordan," as the spiritual "Deep River" suggests. In some slave narratives "that promised land [. . .] where all is peace" became equated with the North; in other stories it could mean Canada or Africa. Following the North Star had a nautical and a messianic connotation in writings that abounded in descriptions of slaveholders as pharaohs or the South as Egypt. Even America's most ardent critics resorted to the exodus and promised land theme and simply inverted its use by casting the United States as Egypt. When the escaped slave, George Harris, toward the end of Harriet Beecher Stowe's *Uncle Tom's Cabin* (1852) outlines his plans for a "new enterprise, the colonization in Africa, his pioneer spirit is expressed in Winthrop's rhetoric: "As a Christian patriot [. . .] I go to *my country,*— my chosen, my glorious Africa!"

In *The Condition, Elevation, Emigration and Destiny of the Colored People of the United States* (1852), Martin Robison Delany, a radical nineteenth-century black nationalist, denounced the Liberian colonization plans in the strongest terms as an expression of a white American wish "to get rid of us." Delany adapted typological rhetoric to his own plans for a black nation in Central or South America, however: "That the continent of America seems to have been designed by Providence as an asylum for all the various nations in the world, is very apparent." Facing the problem of the aboriginal Americans as owners of the land, he noted the relative "consanguinity" of Africans and Indians as opposed to Europeans and used the myth of a lost African tribe in central America—a remnant of the Carthaginian expedition—in order to justify his colonization scheme.

In the twentieth century, Marcus Garvey and Elijah Muhammad adapted the chosen-people theme to an African American sense of mission; Martin Luther King consciously cast himself as a black Moses in his famous speech, "I've Been to the Mountaintop"; and even Amiri Baraka (LeRoi Jones) offered himself as a new Noah, ready to lead his chosen people out of American bondage in his new ark (the old place name Newark recaptured in its typological dimensions). Melvin Tolson planned his volume of poetry, *Harlem Gallery* (1965), as the first of five to follow black history from 1619 to the present; the projected volumes were to be entitled "Egypt Land," "The Red Sea," "The Wilderness," and "The Promised Land."

The exodus to the promised land also meant the return to a new paradise, an enclosed garden. The paradise image goes back to sixteenth-century travelers and seventeenthcentury colonists and accounts for the notion of an enclosure and gates. Having escaped from the "wicked land" of England, the colonists wrested from the American "wilderness" the pastoral ideal of "that blest land," the American garden. In 1629, Francis Higginson reported the desire "to see our new paradise of New England." John Cotton warned of the "weeds" of religious dissent growing so near that they might "easily creep into the Garden." In the mythic landscape of America, the "gates" often came to mean the ports through which immigrants entered; and the metaphors of closing, or guarding, or knocking at gates became commonplace in the literature of immigration and immigration restrictions. Thomas Bailey Aldrich's nativist poem, "Unguarded Gates" (1895), is typical: "Wide open and unguarded stand our gates, / And through them presses a wild motley throng." The Statue of Liberty, lighting the way to freedom in America, yet guards the entrance to Castle Garden. To pass through the gates into the garden, the neophyte had to demonstrate his garden qualities, his inner acculturation. Thomas Hooker made an important distinction between "a gracious and sanctifying knowledge, garden knowledge" that is characteristic of saints and "a wild and a common knowledge" typical of hypocrites. Much American literature is concerned with the transformation of "wild knowledge" into "garden knowledge," with the process of "civilization." And as in the case of the exodus theme, the notion of a return to paradise has remained effective even in writers critical of America. Lincoln Steffens, for instance, in 1914 described Mexico as a paradise and Americans as the serpent. And in the American counterculture of the 1960s, Bob Dylan and Joni Mitchell sang about the gates of Eden and getting back to the garden.

Of course, there was a secular parallel to the theme of the promised land, perhaps associated with the golden calf worshiped by the people while Moses was on the mountaintop. America could thus be both the new golden ark, which the Lord commanded Moses to build, and the pagan image of the land of gold, El Dorado (Figure 1). Columbus's hope that he had found Cathay in America and the Puritan belief that Christ's Second Coming was destined to occur in America clothed themselves in the imagery of gold. Cotton Mather's description of New England as the "golden candlestick" of Revelation, as well as Voltaire's image of the New World as a "land of [. . .] gold," inspired writers to sound the auric dimensions of America. The quest for gold, an obsession with European and American alchemists, could signify a spiritual search for purification and a material search for gain; and America could be seen as the philosopher's stone—which corresponded to Christ in Christian alchemy—and as the land of plenty, the location of abundant gold and of Ponce de Leon's fountain of youth. The two meanings of America's golden quality can be seen in Mark Twain's and Charles Dudley Warner's critique of *The Gilded Age* (1873) and in Van Wyck Brooks's description of the rift in American culture between Jonathan Edwards's tradition of visionaries and Benjamin Franklin's progeny of practical men. Finally, the rhetoric of America as a land of gold has also affected much metallurgical imagery in the writings concerned with the "fusion" or "welding" of a new American identity.

The pervasive sense of an *imitatio Christi* in American literature and the frequent use of melting-pot imagery may be more intimately connected than is usually assumed. Ethnicity is one source for the many Christ figures in American literature. Of course, an immediate reason for the strength of the Christic stream in the American imagination is the imagery of the Garden of Eden and an American Adam; Adam and Christ are typologically related—Christ is the "new Adam"—and the connection between America and Christ is thus established. Thomas Shepard combined the motif of the transatlantic voyage with the notion of a new, Christlike identity in New England; the migrants "passed through the waves [. . .] and stood many a week within six inches of death," he explained, "to see Christ here" (see Matt. 11:7–9). To the transatlantic migrants of diverse ethnic backgrounds, the New Testament references to Christ as the "new man," who has not only united the divine with the human nature in himself but who has broken down divisions between man and man as well, must have been significant. Christ's breaking down of the "partition wall" between us (Eph. 2:14) is explained in the Geneva Bible as making "one flocke . . . of the Iewes and the Gentiles." In order to find unity in Christ, Christians are asked to "put off the olde man and to put on Christ," the "new man," "after the image of him that created him, Where is neither Grecian nor Iewe, circumcision nor vncircumcision, Barbarian, Scythian, bonde, fre" (Col. 3:10–11). Paul's rhetoric is that of transcending segregation—symbolized by the inscriptions on the partition wall of the Temple that warned Gentiles on pain of death not to enter the inner sanctuary. It is a curious coincidence that the first occurrence of the word "ethnic" cited by the *Oxford English Dictionary* is in a Middle English hagiographical description of the destruction of the Temple: "A part of It fel done & made gret distruccione Of ethnykis" (1375). Michel-Guillaume-Saint-Jean de Crèvecœur's famous question, "What then is the American, this new man?" in the third of his *Letters from an American Farmer* (1782) alludes to Paul's "new man." Crèvecœur, who in America published under the name Hector St. John, defined the American as a man who, "leaving behind him all his ancient prejudices and manners, receives new ones from the new mode of life he has embraced." America's mission continues the transethnic demands of Paul's Christianity, and as Crèvecœur continues, the metallurgical imagery of forging a new man is brought close to the concept of the melting pot: "He becomes an American by being received in the broad lap of our great *Alma Mater*. Here individuals of all nations are melted into a new race of men, whose labours and posterity will one day cause great change in the world." New York governor DeWitt Clinton made the same association when he said in 1814 that "the triumph and general adoption of the english language have been the principal means of melting us down into one people, and of extinguishing those stubborn prejudices and violent animosities which formed a wall of partition between the inhabitants of the same land."

The motif of the melting pot has persisted in American writing, from religious adaptations of Ezekiel's parable of the "seething pot" and Edward Taylor's "fining pot, and Test, and melting fire" to Crèvecœur's new man, "melting" in the lap of an American Ceres; from Ralph Waldo Emerson's "smelting pot" to Francis Parkman's public school "crucible," Frederick Jackson Turner's frontier "crucible," and Woodrow Wilson's national "melting pot." The sociological meaning of the image is often less clear than its psychologically accurate implication of a self-renewal through a testing and refining, through a baptismal immersion, and through a rebirth. Thus, the melting pot appears not only in fictionalizations of the emergence of "the" American—sometimes from a mix of Europeans, sometimes from a fusion of all races—but also as a metaphor of the hardening of ethnic group consciousness in America.

Harriet Beecher Stowe thought that American slavery was a "furnace" for Negroes, a divine test from which they were to emerge as the best Christians of the world. In *Yekl* (1896), Abraham Cahan described the Lower East Side as an all-Jewish melting pot, "a seething human sea fed by streams, streamlets, and rills of immigration flowing from all the Yiddish-speaking centers of Europe." Despite the obvious differences between Cahan's realistic chapter "The New York Ghetto" and Israel Zangwill's visionary account of the alchemical workings of the melting pot in his play called *The Melting Pot* (1908), the rhetoric is amazingly similar. In another ethnic tradition, Alain Locke applied Crèvecœur's rhetoric of the "new man" to his own concept of *The New Negro* (1925). Locke saw Harlem as the place for an African American rebirth, the Harlem Renaissance, and as the "home of the Negro's 'Zionism'"—"the first concentration in history of so many diverse elements of Negro life," and Locke concludes, "as its elements mix and react, the laboratory of a great race-welding."

The imagery of the melting pot pervades even the essays of ardent critics of the supposed social meaning of the term, as Michael Novak's *Rise of the Unmeltable Ethnics* (1973) easily illustrates. And melting pots also appear in the often apocalyptic rhetoric of American revolutionaries. Thus, Mike Gold described the road "Towards Proletarian Art" in the classic terms of the religious and ethnic rebirth: "We cling to the old culture, and fight for it against ourselves. But it must die. [. . .] Let us fling all we are into the cauldron of the Revolution. For out of our death shall arise glories, and out of the final corruption of this old civilization we have loved shall spring the new race—the Supermen." Zangwill's anticipation of the birth of a new superman in America is another aspect of biblical exegesis that has been popular in the United States, culminating perhaps in Jerry Siegel's and Joe Shuster's comic-book protagonist *Superman* (1938) who, ironically, already is the new man but has to disguise himself among earthlings as mild-mannered Clark Kent.

Imitatio Christi was a duty for the "Western pilgrims." Thomas à Kempis's book of instruction in the imitation of Christ was reprinted in seventeenth-century New England, banned by the magistrates in 1669, but became extremely popular. Cotton Mather mentioned and commented on Kempis. This is not surprising because Mather struggled, throughout his writings, for a Christlike existence. "I thought, I was arrived unto the highest *Pinnacle of my Happiness*, if I might Represent and Exhibit, any Glory of my Lord JESUS CHRIST, unto the world," he wrote in *Paterna* (1699–1702). Then some "horrid people" threw anonymous libels at Mather's gate: "They drew ye Picture of a Man, hanging on ye *Gallowes*; They wrote *my Name* over it." Mather read this anonymous note as a "Token *for Good*" because it symbolized his own crucifixion: "Now, Now! my Soul was filled with *unspeakable Joy!* Now I had *Gain'd all my Point!* Now my Resemblance unto my Lord JESUS CHRIST, had a Glorious Addition made unto it." Cotton Mather wrote *Paterna* as a testament for his sons, but American literature as a whole seems to have inherited his imitation of Christ.

American protagonists are more likely than the heroes of non-American literature to be born on Christmas (as is Peder in Rølvaag's *Giants in the Earth*) or to die on Good Friday (like Geremia in Pietro di Donato's *Christ in Concrete*). The hero of Charles Brockden Brown's *Wieland; or, The Transformation* (1798) is transformed into a "Man of Sorrows" in America; Melville's Billy Budd dies as a Christ symbol; Uncle Tom suffers contumely and martyrdom with Christic dignity; and even Conrad Dryfoos in William Dean Howells's *A Hazard of New Fortunes* (1890) bears features of Christ. The forcefulness of the Christ type is so strong that it even affected the works of the most radical nonmainstream writers. Richard Wright's "Bright and Morning Star" (1938) refers both to the star of Bethlehem and to the red star of Communism; and in Wright's *Native Son* (1940), Bigger Thomas becomes a suffering Christ who ironically feels that through his actions the people's "shame was washed away." Claude McKay was attracted to the radical journalism of *The Masses* when he saw the artistic depiction of a lynching as a crucifixion on the cover of the August 1915 issue.

Martin Delany's *Blake, or the Huts* (1859–1861) was perhaps the most heretical African American novel of the nineteenth century, both in the creation of a black protagonist who is an aristocratic hero and a revolutionary superman and in a more or less continuous opposition to America's national symbolism. When Henry Blake sees the American flag on the slave prison in Washington, DC, he thinks of "stars as the pride of the white man, and stripes as the emblem of power over the blacks." Yet despite his emphasis on the earthly struggle against slavery through a universal slave revolution, Blake suggests: "Let us at once drop the religion of our oppressors, and take the Scriptures for our guide and Christ as our example." One of the most radical Jewish-American novels, Mike Gold's *Jews without Money* (1930) ends with the call for a new messiah who will raze the world of inequality: "O, workers' Revolution, you brought hope to me, a lonely suicidal boy, You are the true Messiah. You will destroy the East Side when you come, and build there a garden for the human spirit."

Gold's revolutionary messianism is not Christian, but Ezra Brudno's *The Fugitive* (1904) and Edward Steiner's *The Mediator* (1907) are Jewish immigrant novels that specifically embrace Christ as the mediator and unifier of Jews and Gentiles in America, where, in Steiner's words, "a new race might be born, which should know nothing of the ancient hate and the ancient wrongs." And for an even more astounding use of the Christian theme in American ethnic writing, Hisaye Yamamoto's story "Yoneko's Earthquake" (1951) provides the setting of a Japanese-American detention camp in World War II.

In American literature, the rebels and martyrs are likely to be Christlike. Henry David Thoreau's address to his readers in his "Plea for Captain John Brown" (1860) is typical: "You who pretend to care for Christ crucified, consider what you are about to do to him who offered himself to be the saviour of four millions of men." American ethnic writing is part of that same tradition, from the crucifixion-lynchings in African American literature to David Schearl's Christlike suffering in Henry Roth's *Call It Sleep* (1934) to Studs Lonigan's death in James T. Farrell's *Judgment Day* (1935); from Casimir Pijanowski's *Passion Play of Chicago* (1924) to Piri Thomas's *Savior, Savior, Hold My Hand* (1972). America is Christ in mission and in suffering; in the realm of popular culture, Paul Simon's "American Tune" deplored the failure of the American Dream to the tune of Paul Gerhardt's "O Haupt voll Blut und Wunden," and the "American Tune" merged with one of the most famous Protestant songs of Christ's contumely.

William Faulkner is perhaps the most important American writer who both apotheosized and transcended the typological inheritance. His novels are a comprehensive literary counterstatement to America as a promised land and to Christic ethnicity. In *Absalom, Absalom!* (1936), he created an Edenic myth and its critique; his *Light in August* (1932) is the most comprehensively Christic novel in America and, at the same time, subversive of the typological assumptions of American culture. In the former book, Faulkner made Thomas Sutpen an archetypal American "founding father" with an obsessive "design" and a sense of mission. Sutpen is the pioneer who wants to start a "house," "plant" a family; yet his progeny destroys him. Quentin Compson is the problematic heir who desperately tries to divest meaning from his Southern cultural heritage yet arrives at the defiantly self-destructive conclusion, "*I dont hate it! I dont hate it!*" In *Light in August*, Joe Christmas is the Christic man whose ambiguous racial identity sets different actions in motion, all of which hinge on the questionable assumption that he must be black. He is loved and hated, he kills and he is lynched for his metaphoric, yet doubtful, ethnic identity. Faulkner consciously played with all the traditional Christic devices in creating Joe Christmas, who shares more than his initials with Jesus Christ. He was found on Christmas, yet Faulkner makes sure to note that he was not born on that day; he is described as thirty-three years old when he moves to Jefferson, not when he is crucified-killed; and he is arrested on Good Friday, though not lynched that day. Faulkner realized that the Christic assumptions were so strong in American culture that his qualifiers would have to be misread. He therefore used the questionable Christic identity to buttress the theme of doubtful ethnic identity, and the novel becomes a modernist assault on preconceptions.

Red, Black, and White: Ethnicity and History

The rhetoric of American ethnicity was derived from religious terminology and strengthened through Puritan typology. As rhetoric, the concepts of America as the golden promised land, as melting pot, or as Christ's kingdom, belong to the realm of ideology, not to be confused with material reality. American literary ethnicity has to be read against the histories of the various ethnic groups. One is perhaps not necessarily part of an apocalyptic tradition if one follows Cora Daniels Tappan's sarcastic statement: "A government that has for nearly a century enslaved one race (African), that proscribes another (Chinese), proposes to exterminate another (Indians), and persistently refuses to recognize the rights of one-half of its citizens (women), cannot justly be called perfect" (1869). To say that much rhetoric of ethnicity simply covered up "reality," however, is not enough. There were positive and negative sides to the capacity of ethnicity to be substituted for history, for social class, and even for sexual polarization in American literature. Of those substitutions, the use of ethnicity as would-be history in America has been the most pervasive.

In G. W. F. Hegel's *Lectures on the Philosophy of History* (1837), the United States was not yet considered part of "history" in any traditional sense. In Hegel's view, "a real State and a real Government arise only after a distinction of classes has arisen" or when "a large portion of the people can no longer satisfy its necessities." America is hitherto exempt from this pressure" because of the safety valve of the frontier through which "multitudes are continually streaming into the plains of the Mississippi." Despite emigration, Europe is the place of history, America the land of the future. "Had the woods of Germany been in existence, the French Revolution would not have occurred." As a land without the pressures of history, America cannot be compared with the Old World. Louis Hartz questioned America's relationship to history in a similar way when he wondered about the possibilities of an American Enlightenment if there are no dark ages to precede it, and posed the related question concerning the lack of socialist tendencies except among recent migrants. Hartz concluded, in *The Founding of New Societies* (1964), that America was a "fragment culture" that had frozen at the historical point of its detachment from the Old World, the bourgeois point, and that was equally separated from the preceding Middle Ages as cut off from the socialist "future." America's problematic relationship to history is reflected in the literary uses of ethnicity.

The achievement of a Christian and American selfhood was always part of the struggle against a heathenish, ethnic "otherness." Here more of the etymological weight of the term "ethnicity" becomes significant. Indian and black ethnicity were perceived—by the colonists who after about 1680 began to refer to themselves as "whites"—as that otherness which became the most important part of defining selfhood. The confrontation and cooperation with Indians and blacks inevitably changed the white colonists' outlook and confirmed their newness in a new world. As they ate corn and potatoes and smoked sotweed, as Cotton Mather used African vaccination methods in the 1721 smallpox epidemic in Boston, as Virginian participants in Bacon's Rebellion (1675) first got high on the strange "Jamestown weed," as the General Court of Massachusetts ordered five hundred pairs of moccasins, and as Puritans accepted, with fascination and fear, the elements of folk superstition that the Salem slave woman Tituba and her half-Indian husband introduced to the witch hunts, the settlers were becoming more American. James Kirke Paulding's *Letters from the South* (1835) merely reiterated a popular theme when they explained the phenomenon of American mobility: "The people of the United States partake, in no small degree, of the habits of their predecessors, the aborigines, who, when they have exhausted one hunting-ground, pull up stakes, and incontinently march off to another, four or five hundred miles off, where game is plenty." At least the seventeenth-century Narragansetts believed that the English settlers were migrating to America because they "must have burned all the firewood in their previous country and come to live where there was more."

If the Europeans became culturally Americanized through their contacts with blacks and Indians, they also saw their own mission in the conversion, education, and "civilization" of the people whom they came to think of, in the course of the eighteenth century, as "races." Cotton Mather's "Life of John Eliot" is an early American immigrant biography that defines Eliot, not through his Old World roots, but through his New World mission. Mather calls the Atlantic a "River of Lethe" that "may easily cause us to forget many of the things that happened on the other side." If England enjoyed Eliot's first breath, "it is *New-England* that with most Right can call him *hers*; his *best Breath*, and afterwards his *last Breath* was here; and here 'twas, that God bestow'd upon him *Sons and Daughters*." The drama of the American future against the Old World past finds its symbolism in the transatlantic crossing, in the disruption of parental lineage, and in the emphasis on descendants instead of ancestors. But it is in his contact with the Indians that Eliot finds his typological identity as an American evangelist. Mather's description of these contacts is torn between contempt for the Indians' barbarous way of living and admiration for their hygienic sophistication and their "extraordinary Ease in Childbirth." Mather's Eliot is ethnologist and missionary when he realizes that the first step toward Christianization had to be to learn the Indian language. Eliot, "the Anagram of whose Name was TOILE," learned to master the Algonquian language and published a translation of the Bible, *Mamusse Wunneetupanatamwe Up-Biblum God* in 1663.

It is difficult to generalize the varieties of European contacts with the various Indian nations in America. But whether the Indian appeared in literature as a heathen who could be converted, as prelapsarian or postlapsarian Adamic being, or as a member of a lost tribe of Israel, a constellation emerged that increasingly associated Indians with heathendom and the past and white Americans with Christianity and the future.

Roger Williams reminded the colonists, in *Christening Make Not Christians; or, A Briefe Discourse Concerning that Name Heathen, Commonly Given to the Indians* (1645), that the Indians were no more "heathen" than most Europeans and wrote an interesting study of Indian culture, *A Key into the Language of America* (1643) that, ironically because of Williams's belief in typology, stayed clear of religious or cultural snobbery. Yet no easy cultural synthesis emerged. The promise of Harvard's charter of 1650 to provide education "of the English and Indian Youth of this Country" led to the establishment of the Harvard Indian College and President Dunster's hope "to make Harvard the Indian Oxford as well as the New-English Cambridge." But the results of the educational and missionary efforts and the attempts at transcultural understanding remained of less importance than the continuous appropriation of Indian land, which could be rationalized most easily if the Indian could be viewed as the "other." The Indian became important for the English-American mind, according to Roy Harvey Pearce, "not for what he was in and of himself, but rather for what he showed civilized men they were not and must not be." Cotton Mather could sometimes see the Indians as part of the adversary and speculate that "probably the devil decoyed those miserable salvages [*sic*] hither" or that the devil instigated the Pequot War. With the growth of historical imagination, however, the Indian in American literature came to stand for something else the white settlers "were not and must not be": he became the aristocrat.

American writers defined the past in European terms and were therefore looking for indigenous equivalents to Gothic castles and medieval ruins. In the course of the debate about a "native muse," Charles Brockden Brown wrote *Wieland; or, The Transformation* (1798), an early American immigration novel whose German protagonist brings sectarian Calvinist missionary zeal and Gothic horror to America. His attempts at Indian evangelization fail, and the horror elements move toward the psychological sphere. One year after *Wieland*, Brown suggested in the preface to *Arthur Mervyn* that "Gothic castles and chimeras" were unnecessary for the creation of effective literature: "The incidents of Indian hostility, and the perils of the western wilderness, are far more suitable." Brown's suggestion was the reformulation of a widely accepted view of the Indians as doomed kings, a dying class of feudal lords of the land, heroic victims of the progress of bourgeois civilization. The Indians became a would-be aristocracy in American literature, and thus ethnicity substituted itself for history.

Aristocratic Indians were commonplace after John Smith's story of Pocahontas (1608) and could be seen on American stages as *Ponteach* (1766) or John Augustus Stone's *Metamora; or, The Last of the Wampanoags* (1829). "Tammany," a familiar word in the political history of immigration, was the adoption of an Indian ancestry for political clubs that were at first more social and ceremonial in function. The first American opera, Ann Julia Hatton's *Tammany* (1794), was reputedly based on genuine Indian music and popularized the image of the Indian who became the mascot of Tammany Hall. The classic American writer who solidified the notion of the Indians as an American aristocracy was James Fenimore Cooper. Cooper disliked his popular epithet, "the American Scott," but he did, in fact, "Americanize" Walter Scott's patterns for historical romances. Cooper's figure of Chingachgook, the idealized Noble Indian, symbolizes the pervasive vision of American Indians as a doomed class as much as Magua and his tribe of "bad" Indians.

Mark Twain, the notorious notekeeper of Cooper's literary offenses, had one thing in common with his literary archenemy: the association of Indians with the European aristocracy. Counting the broken twigs in Cooper's novels, Mark Twain did not notice the literary branch that he transplanted into his own fiction, the myth of "the" Indian as an aristocrat. Of course, Mark Twain had fewer sympathies for the aristocracy than Cooper and not only created Indians who resemble Magua but also referred to French noblemen as "Comanches." There is thus a link between "Injun Joe" in *The Adventures of Tom Sawyer* (1876) and the French aristocrats in "The French and the Comanches" (1879), which points to Cooper as a prototype. In *A Connecticut Yankee in King Arthur's Court* (1889), Mark Twain's problems of identifying a European feudal past with American history recall Hawthorne's difficulties with the theme of ethnicity as ancestry.

Mark Twain's blindness toward his Indian characters is all the more surprising because he made very serious attempts at creating more subtly conceived black characters in *Adventures of Huckleberry Finn* (1884) and *Pudd'nhead Wilson* (1894). Though by 1700 the term "Christianity" had become linked with "complexion," and "red" and "black" were equally "heathen" and "nonwhite," the black man did not often serve as a substitute aristocrat in American literature. The tradition of the African king abducted into slavery who meets a tragic death in his quest for freedom, a story told in Sarah Wentworth Morton's poem "The African Chief" (1792) and in George Washington Cable's story of Bras-Coupé in *The Grandissimes* (1880) may perhaps live on in an aristocratic feeling about African American culture that Albert Murray described so well in *The Omni-Americans* (1970). (Are Nat "King" Cole, "Count" Basie, or "Duke" Ellington merely random names for entertainers?) In American literature, however, blacks often take the position of the working class, where their quality of "endurance" is idealized. At the same time, they may be soulful and knowing, dialectically related to the American soil and to history, as well as free, often comical spirits, who know how to laugh and dance.

In William Hill Brown's *The Power of Sympathy* (1789), which is considered the first American novel, the confused protagonist Harrington, who has fallen in love with a woman who turns out to be his own sister, takes a trip to Carolina, unrelated to the rest of the plot. He meets a slave woman with a scar on her shoulder and learns that she was whipped because her son broke a glass, and that she accepted the guilt and punishment joyfully because she could thus protect her son by her own suffering. The slave woman temporarily becomes the source of inspiration for Harrington who discovers his own "soul" and "sensibility" in this instance. Black slaves, servants, and workers have provided a similarly regenerating influence upon countless characters in

American literature, from *Uncle Tom's Cabin* to Sherwood Anderson's *Dark Laughter* (1925)—which Hemingway parodied by substituting an "Indian war-whoop" for the revelatory black laughter in *The Torrents of Spring* (1926)—and from Faulkner's *The Sound and the Fury* (1929) to Jack Kerouac's *On the Road* (1957).

Sometimes the figure of the Indian as a doomed nobleman and the African American as an inspiring working man merge, as perhaps in the half-Indian, half-black character Sam Fathers in Faulkner's "The Bear." The image of the nonwhite woman as a mother figure also appears in black and Indian guise. Philip Young has traced the origin of this notion to Pocahontas, "the Mother of Us All." Powhatan's daughter, who rescued John Smith and married John Rolfe, has been cast in such a way as to become identical with the land, as Hart Crane wanted her to be in "The Bridge": as "the natural body of American fertility," the land "like a woman, ripe, waiting to be taken."

The image of the Indian princess or queen as a national and, before that, continental symbol goes back to allegorical representations on sixteenth-century maps of America, although the name "America" was conferred to the continent in honor of Amerigo Vespucci, a man, by Martin Waldseemüller's 1507 world map. At times, the Indian princess was the barbarian opposite to the allegorical figure of Europe; at other times, she came close to the womb image of the melting-pot symbolism. Thus the 1787 edition of Crèvecœur's *Letters from an American Farmer* has a frontispiece that shows a deminude plumed Indian princess, on whose breasts the putti-like, reborn and rejuvenated immigrants are feeding as Romulus and Remus do on the Roman wolf. The subtitle, *Ubi panis et libertas, ibi patria*, taken from the immediate vicinity of the passage concerning the "melting" in the "lap" of the Alma Mater, strengthens the implications of the picture as that of an American Indian Ceres, as Mother Earth, as alchemical vessel, and as the womb symbol in which the rebirth of immigrants takes place. Vachel Lindsay's poem "Our Mother Pocahontas" (1918) gives full expression to the Indian mother as a melting pot.

The relation of immigration to Pocahontas-Ceres is also reflected in the burlesque theater of the nineteenth century, John Brougham's *Pocahontas, or The Gentle Savage* (1855) was a travesty of the noble Indian drama that blatantly punned itself through the plot; more interestingly, the play is an ethnic variety show with Irish brogue and black musical interludes, and even John Rolfe is transformed into a "Dutch" immigrant who speaks with a heavy accent.

The mother image of Pocahontas, of course, allows us to conceive of an American self-creation: through the leap into the earth-womb, immigrants become their own ancestors. Neither this use of the Pocahontas tale, nor the view of the noble Indian as an aristocratic ancestor, lends itself to a vision of the melting pot as an encouragement of sexual unions across ethnic boundaries. Paradoxically, the melting pot promised a "new man" psychologically rather than genetically. Actual unions between Indians and whites and between blacks and whites often appeared dangerous in American literature, and the offspring of such unions doomed. Thus Poe's half-Indian character Dirk Peters in *The Narrative of Arthur Gordon Pym* (1838) is as awesome as Hawthorne's Septimius Felton is morbid, and "mulattoes" have evoked a fairly persistent treatment as tragic figures. The cause for their tragic roles, however, is not usually assigned to social prejudice but to the original sin of miscegenation. Irish-born playwright Dion Boucicault in 1859 published *The Octoroon*, the most influential "tragic mulatto" melodrama. Interestingly, an English version of the play allowed a happy ending and a union between white lover George Peyton and "octoroon" slave girl Zoë, whereas the American version ends tragically with Zoë's suicide.

In the 1920s, Sherwood Anderson and William Faulkner supposedly debated the question of whether "mixed breeds"—like mules—were infertile. But the story most central to a nervous national self-consciousness is James Thompson Callender's apocryphal relation of Thomas Jefferson's slave progeny. Henry Adams quotes Irish poet Thomas Moore's allusion to the "weary statesman's" flight "From halls of council to his negro's shed; / Where, blest, he woos some black Aspasia's grace, / And dreams of freedom in his slave's embrace." William Wells Brown, the first black novelist, used Callender's story of Jefferson's reputed affair with the slave woman Sally Hemings (whom Brown baptizes "Currer") as the plot of his abolitionist novel *Clotel; or, The President's Daughter* (1853). Brown's Clotel is a national symbol of the injustice that slavery perpetrates upon womanhood; she dies with arms outstretched and eyes lifted up to heaven, pursued by slave catchers onto a bridge across the Potomac, "in full view of the capitol." She dies for the national sin of slavery, but also for the president's sin of the flesh.

A taboo on sexual arrangements between white and black or white and red brings back Cooper's world in relation to Scott's. Scott's novels often mediate the historical conflicts through marriage; Cooper's Indian romances leave the opposites unreconciled. Instead of a middle ground between warring Indians and Americans, a mediating home, Cooper chooses an interesting, and culturally significant, alternative. The relationship between white man and nonwhite woman is limited to a Pocahontas-mother myth and must apparently not be extended to a more traditional male-female opposition; the literary reflections of contacts between white women and nonwhite men are, perhaps, typically rendered by captivity narratives in the tradition of Hannah Duston, who plays the role of a leitmotif in much American literature from Hawthorne's "The Duston Family" (1836) to Thoreau's *Week on the Concord and Merrimack Rivers* (1849). Aware of the complications inherent in the relationships between white man and Indian woman or between white woman and Indian man, Cooper created an important character confrontation on ethnic rather than sexual grounds, and developed the white man-nonwhite man constellation from its tentative appearance in the narrative of Alexander Henry (1809) into a major theme of American literature.

Cooper's focus is so concentrated on the relationship between Hawkeye and Chingachgook (whose name means "big serpent" and thus led Leslie Fiedler back to the Edenic myth) that his female characters—white and Indian—become his weakest figures. The transethnic friendship of males cannot result in an offspring, but it assimilates Indian and white man to each other so that both become exceptional in their cultures. The Last of the Mohicans is as lonely as Natty Bumppo, the equally tragic pioneer for a civilization in which he will not be able to live. The mediation between white and nonwhite protagonists takes place in a middle ground of freedom that will soon be superseded by civilization. This pattern of freedom temporarily achieved through a transethnic friendship of males appears in some major works of American literature, notably in the comic wedding ritual of Ishmael and Queequeg in Melville's *Moby-Dick* (1851) and in Huck and Jim's experiences in Mark Twain's *Adventures of Huckleberry Finn* (1884). Leslie Fiedler has discussed the latent homosexual implications in these transethnic encounters and has delineated their recurrence in texts from Richard Dana's *Two Years Before the Mast* (1840) to Ken Kesey's *One Flew over the Cuckoo's Nest* (1962).

Red and black ethnicity are as pervasive in minority and immigrant writing as in mainstream literature. Mike Gold describes youth gangs on Manhattan's Lower East Side in Indian terms; when the narrator of *Jews without Money* is surrounded by Italian boys who are "whooping like Indians" and who call him "Christkiller," he views the territory of Hester and Mulberry streets as the Wild West and soon yearns for a "Messiah who would look like Buffalo Bill." In Rølvaag's *Giants in the Earth*, Norwegian settler Per Hansa has encounters with Indians that elevate his status as that of a white chieftain and patriarch. Abraham Cahan's *Yekl* interestingly depicts the protagonist's wife, Gitl, as a "squaw" when she arrives in America and is met by her Americanized husband, Jake; being a squaw makes her a mother figure and underlines her incompatibility with her spouse. In Willibald Winckler's *Die deutschen Kleinstädter in Amerika* (1871), the heroine is abducted by the Chippewas, and in the anonymous GermanAmerican play *Die Emigranten* (1882), a German-speaking black working woman tells a recently arrived immigrant that it only takes five years for immigrants to turn black.

Occasionally, even the rhetoric of black or Indian writers echoes these tendencies. In 1869, Frederick Douglass stated that "the negro is more like the white man than the Indian, in his tastes and tendencies, and disposition to accept civilization. [. . .] You do not see him wearing a blanket, but coats cut in the latest European fashion." James Weldon Johnson's *Autobiography of an Ex-Colored Man* (1912), which is full of observations on the national character of different Americans and Europeans, voices the assumption that the Negro's capacity for humor saved him from going the way of the red man. Vine Deloria's essay *Custer Died for Your Sins* (1969) welcomes Black Power and speaks analogously of "Red Power," but deplores the fact that former slaves have never been treated as a people, an entity white Americans would negotiate with, because black people never owned reservations. And Bobby Seale's autobiography *A Lonely Rage* (1978) reveals the deepseated adolescent dream of the later Black Panther to adopt an Indian name and escape to a Sioux reservation.

Perhaps the most profoundly satirical and iconoclastic cultural statement against such black and Indian stereotypes can be found in Mel Brooks's movie *Blazing Saddles* (1974). Brooks's black railroad workers are sophisticated urbanites who claim to know neither the song "Camptown Races" nor any Negro spirituals; when pressed by the white overseers to sing, they present a smooth version of Cole Porter's "I Get a Kick out of You." The Indian chieftain, played by Brooks himself, is quite unaristocratic, speaks Yiddish, and releases black captives with the nonchalance of a Brooklynite. By going back to the vaudeville mix of Indian, black, and immigrant lore, Brooks has inverted and exploded some important ingredients of an American ethnic myth.

The Divided Heart: Classic Ethnic Literature and Realism

The Indian-black-white triangle remained a powerful basis for literary ethnicity but became more complicated as America became more ethnically diverse. The flow of immigrants demanded recognition by imaginative writers, both among the earlier migrants and among the newcomers themselves. The responses sometimes reflected a continued substitution of ethnicity for history and expressed anxieties and fears of "otherness." The uncertainties of an American cultural identity—which was problematic within each ethnic tradition as disrupted ancestry—became even more pressing when different ancestries interacted with each other. As many studies of literary stereotypes have shown, American literature abounds with prejudices against newcomers of all backgrounds as well as animosities against older settlers and, of course, against Indians and blacks. But at times, the shared experience of Americans—having left an old identity and struggling for a new one—was understood by writers, artists who could create literary works without fear, prejudice, or ethnocentrism.

One response was to portray German and Irish immigrants in the tradition of Indians and blacks. Some buffo roles of Negroes and Irishmen could be exchanged with ease. Similarly, Germans often assumed the pseudo-aristocratic parts. In 1700, Cotton Mather delivered the sermon "A Pillar of Gratitude" in which he described as "formidable Attempts of Satan and his Sons" the proposal that "a Colony of Irish might be sent over to check the growth of this Countrey." Mather concluded with great satisfaction that "an overwhelming blast from Heaven has defeated all those attempts." Mather's fear of an Irish colony in America reflected the Protestant feeling that "Popery" held Catholics in bondage, as they had to answer to the ultimate Old World authority, the Vatican; and perhaps a similar fear of foreigners who adhere to Old World ways has been felt in American literature about Communists, German Fifth Columnists, or science-fiction androids who take orders from an Old World power center.

Mather's fear of the Irish resembles Benjamin Franklin's anxiety about the "swarthy" Germans; in 1751, Franklin asked, "Why should *Pennsylvania*, founded by the *English*, become a Colony of *Aliens*, who will shortly be so numerous as to Germanize us instead of our Anglifying them, and will never adopt our Language and Customs, any more than they can acquire our Complexion?"

Could everybody be converted to an American identity? Could a national unity be forged out of ethnic diversity? A pseudonymous "Celadon" answered these questions negatively in *The Golden Age; or, Future Glory of North-America* (1785) and mapped out the United States of the future as a confederation of ethnic nation states; "Nigrania" and "Savagenia" were black and Indian states in the Southwest, and Celadon anticipated the establishment of "a French, a Spanish, a Dutch, an Irish, &c. yea, a Jewish state." In Charles Jared Ingersoll's *Inchiquin, the Jesuit's Letters* (1810), a Frenchman suggests with outrageous irony that American unity could be achieved quite easily—by substituting the French language "for the German, Irish, English, and other dialects that prevail," and Roman Catholicism for "the deplorable deluge of creeds" in the United States!

Emerson's notebook entry on the "smelting pot"—written in 1845 in opposition to the Native American party—attempts to define the collective process to forge a unified American identity as an equivalent to the feudal past: "[A]s in the old burning of the Temple at Corinth, by the melting & intermixture of silver & gold & other metals, a new compound more precious than any, called the Corinthian Brass, was formed so in this Continent,—asylum of all nations, the energy of Irish, Germans, Swedes, Poles, & Cossacks, & all the European tribes,—of the Africans, & of the Polynesians, will construct a new race, a new religion, a new State, a new literature, which will be as vigorous as the new Europe which came out of the smelting pot of the Dark Ages, or that which earlier emerged from the Pelasgic & Etruscan barbarism. La Nature aime les croisements." Of course, the interplay of ethnics in American literature is generally less harmonious than in this aphorism.

Characters and themes in the literature of the nineteenth century reflect more ethnic concern than understanding or sympathy. Though Henry Wadsworth Longfellow's *Tales of a Wayside Inn* (1886), for example, deal sympathetically with a French, Spanish, and Jewish vantage point, ethnic characters by America's major writers are often no more than stereotypes. Howard Mumford Jones observed that American literature fails to treat the "alien" equally "unless he is good and dead"; a living alien "is reduced to a subordinate role and expected to furnish comic relief." Even Washington Irving's famous Dutch characters are portrayed positively only because they are part of the past. The roles of a tragically extinct aristocratic ancestry and of an inspiring and amusing buffo underclass remained fixed points in American literature. Cooper, who helped to create the Indian aristocrat, also imagined many comic-relief ethnics, such as Caesar Thompson, a faithful black servant, in *The Spy* (1821), and Elizabeth Flanagan, a stage Irishwoman who supplies liquor for the troops, speaks with a heavy accent, and is the source of much comic relief in the same novel.

One of Cooper's foreign admirers ironically contributed to the gradual growth of more "realism" in the picturing of ethnic characters when his works became popular in America. Eugène Sue in *Les Mystères de Paris* (1843) promised the French readers merely an urban and local sequel to the *Leatherstocking Tales*; instead of Cooper's Indians, Sue presented "other barbarians, also outside of civilization." Sue was referring to the Parisian underworld of crime and poverty, where his French "Apaches" "have customs of their own, women of their own," and even "a language of their own [. . .] full of dark images and of bloody and disgusting metaphors." Sue's works, which became increasingly concerned with pressing social questions, were immensely popular as they satisfied both the needs for romance—the Cooper legacy—and for realism—the socialist leader Daniel De Leon was among Sue's American translators. Sue was not merely translated; he was widely copied and adapted to American urban settings by George Lippard and Dion Boucicault as well as by minor immigrant writers. Lippard's *The Quaker City; or, Monks of Monk Hall* (1844) transposed the picturesque argot of Sue's Parisians into vaudeville ethnic accents of Philadelphia, including not only Negro speech but also, perhaps for the first time in American fiction, the Jewish idiom of a character named Gabriel Van Gelt. Ethnic otherness is rendered no more subtly here than by Cooper, but the attention paid to urban types and to social reformism heralds the concerns of realistic writers. An anonymous German-American novel, *Die Geheimnisse von Philadelphia* (1850), similarly transposed Sue's Paris to America; and Emil Klauprecht's *Cincinnati oder Geheimnisse des Westens* (1854–1855) did not merely adapt plot elements of the city *Mysteries*; but also of those popular novels that formed the basis of *The Octoroon*, resulting in a wide spread of ethnic types: the heroine Isabelle of French descent; Habakkuk Maleachi, the mysterious Indian herb doctor; Zenobia, the passionate octoroon girl; as well as Herrnhuter, Italian Jesuits, and German immigrants. Klauprecht's novel is perhaps the first immigrant novel that juxtaposes a visionary newcomer, artist Wilhelm Steigerwald who remembers his heritage, with a practical man, his thoroughly Americanized brother Carl, who has made a successful career as a businessman and is eager to forget or conceal his background. The tendency toward a more realistic differentiation of ethnic characters is palpable. Dion Boucicault moved in the same direction. He derived his play *The Poor of New York* (1857) from a French drama of the Sue school and adapted it, with a change of title, to the tenement setting of many different cities. Boucicault also departed from the stage-Irish tradition in 1860 and created more realistic renditions of Irish life in *The Colleen Bawn*, whose Old World Irish gentlefolk and villagers exhibit neither burlesque nor sentimentality.

In the second half of the nineteenth century, the rise of serious ethnic literature was linked with an opposition to stereotypes and with the claims for realism and authenticity against malicious, sentimental, or careless distortion. American writers have traditionally tried to present their imaginative products as truth in order to avoid religious, moral, or pragmatic censure. But in the case of ethnic writing, the claim that literature represented truth meant more than that. It stood for the demand for an inside view of ethnicity and for a growing concern with social reform. The alliance of ethnic realism, spokesmanship, and social criticism has remained powerful for more than a century.

The point of departure of classic ethnic literature, and especially of writings in English, often was to blur ethnic stereotypes by presenting an inside view of ethnicity that could make otherness understandable to general American readers. Consciously or unconsciously, ethnic writers often assumed the roles of pleaders, mediators, or translators who explained ethnic traits, annotated ethnic jokes and phrases, or provided glossaries for the benefit of the reader. African American writer Charles Chesnutt, realizing that the bastion of racial prejudice could not be taken by assault, decided to undermine it by creating a Yankee narrator who often misunderstands the Southern blacks he encounters and describes. Explaining to the imagined descendants of Puritans and Pilgrims the uprooting, migrations, miseries, and achievements of more recent immigrants or of former slaves, writers instinctively chose a language and symbology derived from the first English migrants to America; and this is perhaps one decisive factor in accounting for the pervasiveness of typological elements in ethnic literature. Thus the ethnic writer as "mediator" set out to break down the partition walls between ethnic group and larger culture.

The mediating process is not necessarily harmonious. Daniel Aaron delineated three typical stages in the development of "hyphenate writers," in the process from marginal to mainstream literature. In the first phase, the writer as "a kind of local colorist" exploits the strangeness of his human material to win the sympathies of the unhyphenated, "but also in the hope of humanizing the stereotyped minority and dissipating prejudice." In the second, less conciliatory stage, the author lashes out at political, social, and economic restrictions and the consequences of discrimination and exploitation, risking criticism both from the larger society and from his ethnic group. In the third stage, the writer acquires F. Scott Fitzgerald's "double vision," moves from marginality to the mainstream center, and loses the sense of hyphenation while retaining a critical relationship to society. Since Aaron's essay appeared, a fourth stage has emerged among some writers of the "new ethnicity," which we might call a phase of renewed ethnic spokesmanship, social criticism, and retrospective romanticization. In all phases, ethnic writers have worked with similar themes.

There are two significant clusters of classic ethnic themes and an interesting area where both clusters converge. The first group of themes concerns ethnicity as ancestry, and in the treatment of these themes, minority and mainstream writing are close to each other. The second cluster consists of themes resulting from ethnicity as diversity. The motif of the divided self marks the area of convergence of the two main clusters. The themes of genealogy, relationship of Old World and New World, and struggle for an American identity were discussed earlier; another theme related to ethnicity as ancestry is that of generational progression and conflict. Generations often represent the Old World and the New World to each other, and generational conflicts with ethnic significance are ubiquitous in American literature, from Theodore Dreiser's *Jennie Gerhardt* (1911) to Martha Ostenso's *Wild Geese* (1925) and *O River, Remember* (1943), Joseph Pagano's *The Paesanos* (1940), Charles Driscoll's *Kansas Irish* (1943), and the classic Freudian formulation of the tensions in an immigrant family in Henry Roth's *Call It Sleep* (1934). Ethnic family sagas provide many illustrations of and variations on the return of the third generation. In such books, the first generation is non-American in origin, migrates and gets into conflicts in the New Land. The second generation wholeheartedly absorbs the new and discards the old, repeating the antiparental and profilial gesture of its own parents. The third generation, while also future-oriented and perhaps even more intensely "American" than the second, opposes the second generation by embracing some elements of its grandparents' ethnicity that its parents repressed. There are elements of this pattern in Rølvaag's *Giants in the Earth* (1927), *Peder Victorious* (1929), and *Their Father's God* (1931); in Daniel Fuchs's *Williamsburg Trilogy* (1934–1937); in Harry Mark Petrakis's *The Odyssey of Kostas Volakis* (1963); and in Ferris Takahashi's "The Widower."

In ethnic literature, as in American literature as a whole, many protagonists are orphaned. This is, of course, especially true for the first generation, which sometimes associates the departure for the New World with the symbolic or literal death of its Old World parents. Upon the death of his mother, Abraham Cahan's David Levinsky first contemplates going to America (1917). Yet even second-generation heroes may be orphaned or become orphans, as Paul does in Pietro di Donato's *Christ in Concrete* (1939). When the orphan theme interferes with the theme of generational progression and conflict, the result is often a mediation of generational conflicts through the uncle-nephew constellation.

Because ethnic realism sets out to overcome prejudices against the ethnic group spoken for, not to combat prejudice as such, one finds the same array of stereotypes in the literature by ethnics as in mainstream writing. It would be easy to collect, for example, anti-Semitic caricatures in minority literature, from Lars A. Stenholt's *Chicago anarkisterne* (1888) to African American poetry of the 1960s. The German trickster Till Eulenspiegel became, in Pennsylvania Dutch folklore, an "Irish pickle," and Irish buffos are as much at home in Cooper's world as they are in Charles Sealsfield's frontier novels.

The cultural conflict with the dominant society in America is the most important theme in ethnic writing and can be found in literature of childhood and adolescence, in stories of education and of ethnic politics, or in the context of religion and work. The conflicts of cultural opposition are especially exciting when they are associated with the theme of love and marriage. In Hjalmar Hjorth Boyesen's story "A Good-for-Nothing" (1875), Norwegian-born Ralph Grim, a gentleman, falls in love with the peasant girl Bertha, who tells Ralph that he must do "one manly deed" to prove his independence from the "life of idleness and vanity" the Old World class structure provided for him. A student prankster, Ralph propositions six ladies, all of whom accept him; in the ensuing scandal, Ralph emigrates to America, convinced that the New World will provide the opportunity for the manly deed that will prove him worthy of Bertha. In America, however, he associates with "high-minded and refined women"; and when he returns to marry Bertha, they discover that they have grown too far apart and that "the gulf which separates the New World from the Old [. . .] cannot be bridged." Interestingly, it is Bertha's complexion that signals to Ralph his alienation from the narrow past: while her face reminds him of "those pale, sweet-faced saints of Fra Angelico," "her forefinger was rough from sewing, and [. . .] the whiteness of her arm [. . .] contrasted strongly with the browned and sun-burned complexion of her hands."

A black and a Jewish writer continued Boyesen's theme by developing more full-fledged alternative figures to the values Bertha embodies. Charles Chesnutt's "The Wife of His Youth" (1898) and Abraham Cahan's *Yekl: A Tale of the New York Ghetto* (1896) show the dilemma of modernized protagonists who have to choose between two women who represent "ethnicity" and "America." Negro migrant and Jewish immigrant have changed their names (from Sam Taylor to Mr. Ryder and from Yekl to Jake) and try to be successful on the terms of their new environments. In the Blue Vein Society, Mr. Ryder has made the acquaintance of a widow, Mrs. Molly Dixon, who is much younger, lighter complexioned, and better educated than Ryder and comes from the nation's capital. In the dancing academy, Jake makes friends with Mamie Fein, a woman with a shrewd sense of business and a strong character, who speaks better English than Jake. Suddenly, both Jake and Ryder are confronted with their past, represented in both cases by an ethnic wife. Both marriages were Old World arrangements: Ryder's slave marriage was not legalized after emancipation, and Jake's wedding was a parentally arranged affair lacking any consideration of love or free choice.

The wife of Mr. Ryder's youth "seemed quite old; for her face was crossed and re-crossed with a hundred wrinkles, and around the edges of her bonnet could be seen protruding here and there a tuft of short grey wool. [. . .] And she was very black,—so black that her toothless gums, revealed when she opened her mouth to speak, were not red, but blue." Jake's wife, Gitl, is "un-American" in appearance and conceals her hair under "a voluminous wig of pitch-black hue," which also makes her seem stouter, shorter, and older. "She was naturally dark of complexion, and the nine or ten days spent at sea had covered her face with a deep bronze, which combined with her prominent cheek bones, inky little eyes, and, above all, the smooth black wig, to lend her resemblance to a squaw." The ethnic wives are dark mother figures, represent ethnicity as ancestry (even as pseudo-Indian Pocahontas ancestry), but are antithetical to all the values of their husbands' New World.

The conclusions to these tales refer us back to the growth of urban and ethnic realism out of Cooper's and Sue's romances. Chesnutt chooses an idealized ending and lets Mr. Ryder renounce mobility, Blue Vein status, and the attractive Molly Dixon by accepting Liza Jane, the "wife of his youth" (cf. *Proverbs* 5:18–20). *Yekl*, on the other hand, concludes with the breakup of Jake's marriage and his imminent alliance with Mamie Fein.

The tension between an idealized acceptance of the past and a realistic account of plausible behavior in new environments informed much ethnic literature in the period of realism. As literature, ethnic realism made more sense against the backdrop of romance, which it replaced. Boyesen, Chesnutt, and Cahan—as well as many other ethnic writers—wrote in close literary contact with William Dean Howells. If Boyesen's statement, "Howells Americanized me," is typical of his generation of ethnic writers in America, it is interesting to note that Boyesen often associated the Old World with romance and the New World with realism.

The focal point of ethnicity as ancestry and ethnicity as diversity, and perhaps one of the most fascinating themes of ethnic literature, is the experience of ethnicity by a divided self. W.E.B. Du Bois's famous formulation of a "double consciousness" as "an American, a Negro" is applicable to writers who are visibly ethnic—who not only feel the tensions of "the divided heart" inwardly but whose ethnicity is easily recognizable to others. Yet American writers have expressed anxiety concerning their identity generations and centuries after their ancestors left Old Worlds. In the quest for identity, a narcissistic tendency could ally itself with ethnicity as the literature developed a concern with that individual under the accidental skin or language, mask or veil. Self-division, self-pity, and self-love may be close to each other in acts of literary revelation or unmasking.

In Johan G.R. Banér's *Barr* (1926), the hyphenate makes an asset out of ethnic dualism that makes it superior to any single national identity: "You are ONE, but—I am TWO!" This attitude implies a degree of imperviousness to traditional sex roles; the human being with a double identity in literature is related to Christ and Superman rather than to average mortals and he is both yin and yang in himself. Characters with a divided self are less likely to find love for another person than they are to be attracted to mirrors, reflecting windows, or smooth-surfaced ponds. Confronted for the first time in his life with the ultimate slur, "Nigger, nigger, never die, / Black face and shiny eye," the narrator-hero of James Weldon Johnson's *Autobiography of an Ex-Colored Man* (1912) rushes to the mirror and discovers his own beauty in black-white ambiguity: "I noticed the ivory whiteness of my skin, the beauty of my mouth, the size and liquid darkness of my eyes, and how the long, black lashes that fringed and shaded them produced an effect that was strangely fascinating even to me." And Cahan's David Levinsky feels attracted by his own new image—without sidelocks and in American clothes—that he sees reflected in mirrors and shop windows.

The novels of both Johnson and Cahan can be read as exegeses of the theme of the divided self. *The Autobiography of an Ex-Colored Man* and *The Rise of David Levinsky* (1917; first serialized in 1913 as "The Autobiography of an American Jew") are told by omnipresent first-person narrators. Though each purports to be telling his own true story, confiding his innermost secrets, the reader is aware in both narratives of an ironic voice that is closer to the author's than the narrator's point of view. Both heroes are outwardly successful at the expense of losing their inner identity, their birthright, and their loyalty to kin; they are ethnic renegades. But neither Cahan nor Johnson sees ethnicity as a static factor that Americanized men should return or withdraw to; they advocate neither Jewish nor black ethnocentrism. In their works, ethnicity stands for those facets of self-realization that the retrospective mind of practical men perceives as the lost potential of childhood or as the sacrifice made to America: it is the visionary quality that these characters (though not their creators) have surrendered. The ideal remained in the fusion of the legacy of childhood, folk, parish, and poverty with the experience of manhood, America, secular world, and success in the individual self's creative mind.

Cahan and Johnson describe the tensions of ethnic dualism as a tremendous artistic force yet create their businessmen protagonists as traitors to that force, as artists manqués. In their moments of introspective remorse and self-pity, Levinsky and the ex-colored man wish that they had created the new American music as a synthesis of folk tradition and New World. Not persistent enough, they remain divided selves. The musical imagery, which has been part of the literature of ethnicity from melting-pot propagators like Zangwill to opponents like Horace Kallen, is here extended to the notion of the right artistic response, the truly multiethnic form, that might solve the dilemma of ethnic dualism.

Ethnicity and Literary Form

It is customary to ascribe the origins of America's most characteristic art forms—jazz, musicals, and movies—to the influences of ethnic diversity. Yet attempts to relate ethnicity with literary forms are usually limited to classic ethnic realism; and in this context, "authentic" and documentary qualities are more highly valued than formal intricacies and innovations. The tendency to exclude writers with great formal accomplishments from the category of ethnic writing—Nathanael West, Eugene O'Neill, John Dos Passos, F. Scott Fitzgerald—is indicative of an enforced limitation of the scope of what we define as ethnic literature.

The development of American literature is viewed as growth, as a process of increasing formal complexity from travelogues and letters (starting with John Smith's *True Relation* (1608), which is, perhaps, the first America letter), sermons, essays, and biographies, to the increasingly successful mastering of poetry, prose fiction, and drama. Analogously, we may view the development of ethnic writing as a process of growth; and again, the beginning is with immigrant and migrant letters—those collected, for example, by Everett Emerson and Charlotte Erickson for British emigrants, Alan Conway for the Welsh, Karl Larsen for the Danes, Abraham Cahan for the Jews, Thomas and Znaniecki for the Poles, and by the *Journal of Negro History* for black migrants. The literature then "grows" from nonfictional to fictional forms or from an autobiography to an autobiographic novel; from folk and popular forms to high forms, as from Uncle Remus tales to Charles Chesnutt's *The Conjure Woman*; from Indian folklore to N. Scott Momaday's *House Made of Dawn* or Hyemeyohsts Storm's *Seven Arrows* or from MexicanAmerican popular culture to Luis Valdez's dramatic *Actos*. It grows from lower to higher degrees of literary complexity, from Dion Boucicault to Eugene O'Neill, from Abraham Cahan to Saul Bellow, or from James Weldon Johnson to Ralph Ellison. It grows finally from "parochial" marginality to "universal" significance: the American literary mainstream now consists predominantly of writers with identifiable "ethnic" backgrounds.

In many instances, this model of growth yields an accurate picture of literary developments against the background of an opposition between parochial ethnicity and modern movements in art and literature. In other cases, however, ethnicity and modernity do not necessarily contradict each other. Writers may adhere to Old World languages and yet be more modern than their Americanized counterparts. Ethnic writers may feel the need for "new" forms more intensely than mainstream authors. Furthermore, the rhetoric of ethnicity—as problematic ancestry and as diversity—has militated toward the new and thus supported the drive toward formal innovation.

Because of their close connections to another culture, American ethnic writers sometimes participated in literary innovations of other national literatures before such innovations became more widespread in America. At the beginning of the twentieth century, for example, the Scandinavian, German, and especially the Yiddish stages were more "modern" than the average American theater. Similarly, ethnic poets who used languages other than English were often more willing to work with the new forms of Whitman and the French symbolists than poets who wrote in Whitman's native tongue. The rebellious and aggressive Yiddish poets who, in 1907, formed Die Yunge (The Young Ones) and published their initial anthology, *Yugend* (Youth) by "self press," shared a common ground with the modernist rebels in Europe and America, despite the language barrier. At a time when Jewish-American writing in English showed few traces of modernist influences—only Henry Roth's *Call It Sleep* marks the breakthrough of high modernism in 1934—Die Yunge and Insichisten (Introspectivists) created a Yiddish avant-gardism in America.

When ethnic writing in languages other than English is more innovative and modern than its English-language counterpart the reason for this phenomenon lies in the problem of the audience. James Weldon Johnson, who realized that African Americans do not have the option to create for exclusively black audiences, described the "Dilemma of the Negro Author" (1928) as the "problem of the double audience." Ethnic writers who use English confront a double audience of readers who are familiar with their ethnic groups and readers who are not. Imperceptibly, and sometimes involuntarily, an author may become a translator of ethnicity to ignorant, and sometimes hostile, outsiders. Such a writer may feel compelled to avoid anything that might give fuel to antiethnic sentiment among the majority audiences, and this attitude of caution and explanation may be an obstacle to the freedom of innovation. In stories written for an ethnic group and rewritten for an "American" audience—such as Abraham Cahan's "Mottke Arbel" (1891–1892), redone in English as "A Providential Match" (1895)—a distinctive and characteristic formal element of much immigrant literature appears: an omniscient narrator who explains to the reader, whose values he seems to share, aspects of the immigrant culture. This narrative voice inhibits literary experimentation and absolute freedom in the language.

The tenuous situation of writers caught between two cultures, as mediators who are alienated from both camps, however, also lends itself to a transcending "leap ahead" in literary form. Seen this way, even James Joyce's modernism was related to his Irish ethnicity, and Franz Kafka's "minor literature" (Gilles Deleuze and Félix Guattari) was written by a German-speaking Jew in Czechoslovakia in a situation of exaggerated ethnic alienation. The American ethnic writer could leave the weight of cultural dualism behind by taking a position of extreme individualism, by denying the adequacy of any existing language for his vision, and by pushing himself into linguistic innovation as an assault on those conventions, patterns, and habits that also form one basis of nativism and ethnocentrism.

Among the most interesting ethnic modernists between the wars are Jean Toomer and Jose Garcia Villa. Toomer, a light-skinned African American whose family had been living on both sides of the color line for generations, viewed racial categories with a great sense of ironical distance. In his collection of aphorisms, *Essentials* (1931), he opposed ethnicity and all other accidental and divisive categories while advocating a Whitmanesque sense of panethnic and pansexual wholeness: "I am of no particular race. I am of the human race, a man at large in the human world, preparing a new race. I am of no specific region. I am of earth. I am of no particular class. I am of the human class, preparing a new class. I am neither male nor female nor in-between. I am of sex, with male differentiations. I am of no special field. I am of the field of being." Toomer's *Cane* (1923), a book that significantly defies genre categorization, is an experimental search for reality beyond labels, and for mankind above race and nationality. The section entitled "Bona and Paul" opposes imaginative vision to the ethnic blindness of a priori assumptions, and as Robert Bone has shown, "Toomer's central metaphor [. . .] is drawn from St. Paul's first epistle to the Corinthians: 'For now we see through a glass darkly, but then face to face: now I know in part, but then shall I know even as I am known.'"

If Toomer's creative thrust is directed at restoring the noumenal unity beyond the phenomenal diversity of, for example, ethnic categories, Jose Garcia Villa's poetry similarly attempts to create its own formal rules and its own area of freedom and true vision. In *Have Come, Am Here* (1942), Villa—who was born in the Philippines—proudly used "a new method of rhyming, a method which has never been used in the history of English poetry, nor in any poetry," the principle of reversed consonance: "Nobody yet knows who I am, / Nor myself may, / Nor yet what I deal, / Nor yet where I lead." While ethnic literature abounds in musical imagery so that the notion of a multiethnic "harmony"—as in Horace Kallen's definition of American civilization as an "orchestration of mankind"—has become a trite cliché, unusable for the subtle poet. Villa finds an adequate formal prototype in painting. He translates Georges Seurat's pointillism into punctuation that blurs the sequence of lines and forces the reader to take a total view from a certain distance. Villa concludes a poem about "Christ, Oppositor, /

Christ, Foeman" with the lines: "After, pure, eyes, have peeled, / Off, skin, who, can, gaze, unburned? Who, / Can, stand, unbowed? Well, be, perceived, / And, well, perceive. Receive, be, received." Villa's comma poems may be, as Renato Poggioli claimed, an "extreme and absurd extravagance," but they indicate a radical formal response to the ethnic writer's need for a new poetic language.

Ethnicity has also been a factor in the choice of less extreme formal patterns. The belief that a new national or ethnic consciousness has to be rendered in new forms is a significant element in the criticism of works that express American themes in English forms or ethnic themes in mainstream forms. Claude McKay's work in the sonnet form has often been read as a contradiction to his themes of black pride and self-defense, as in "If We Must Die" (1919). In 1788, Nicholas Pike, the author of a mathematical textbook, was hopeful that "American arithmetic" would emerge, and in 1969, Nathan Hare similarly predicted "Black math."

One persistent literary expression in America has been the epic, which seemed suited to render the grandeur and dimensions of the new experiences and historically related to the rise of empires. The image of an American "Odyssey" is almost as popular as that of a New World exodus; and the Vergilian epic has influenced a great many American writers. Among the earliest colonial writings in America is Gaspar Pérez de Villagrá's ambitious and consciously Vergilian epic *Historia de la Nueva Mexico* (1610). Cotton Mather's famous introduction to the *Magnalia Christi Americana* (1702) begins with the Vergilian formula: "I WRITE the *Wonders* of the CHRISTIAN RELIGION flying from the Depravations of *Europe* to the *American Strand*." Epic epithets are further elements that seemed especially appropriate to American subject matter.

The perception of the multiethnic character of America has often encouraged the creation of exuberant multilingual forms in which ethnic contradictions may be absorbed as in a sponge, or organized in an encyclopedic and panoramic fashion. A manuscript by "the Pennsylvania Pilgrim" and founder of Germantown, Francis Daniel Pastorius, entitled "Bee-Hive or Bee-Stock" (1897; first printed in 1697), is a conglomerate of proverbs and folk wisdom, personal observations and messages for the second generation. One commentator has called it "the first American encyclopedia." Pastorius, who describes modern English as "a Minglemangle of Latin, Dutch & French" uses seven languages in his book but mostly German, English, and Latin. The focus and central image of the book is the "bee-hive" in its literal, metaphoric, and cultural implications. The comprehensiveness of Pastorius's method makes his work a minor precursor of Melville's encyclopedic view of whales in *Moby-Dick*. Pastorius's learned and multilingual exuberance is reminiscent of Nathaniel Ward's *Simple Cobble of Aggawam* (1647) and much of Cotton Mather's work. The culmination of this rhetorical tendency (which originated perhaps merely as a baroque joy in language but persisted in American writing) was reached in Walt Whitman's poetry; and Whitman's all-absorbing, panethnic, and future-oriented poetic consciousness has often been interpreted as peculiarly American.

Tocqueville's reflections on the question "Why American Writers and Orators Often Use an Inflated Style" (in the second volume of *Democracy in America*, 1840) have been related to an American style ranging from Whitman's poetry to Faulkner's prose; yet the opposing tendency toward a "plain style" has also been associated with American writing from William Bradford to Ernest Hemingway. Whereas the inflated style may reflect the desire to incorporate multiethnicity into literary form, the plain style may advocate linguistic simplicity in order to reach all those new men who are in the process of forging their American identity.

Another formal tendency in American literature that can be related to ethnicity is a sense of humor or irony, which is often derived from the disparity between "sivilized" and natural behavior in the sense of Mark Twain's *Huckleberry Finn*, or from the difference between outside assumptions and inside awareness in the sense of Langston Hughes's Jesse B. Semple or Finley Peter Dunne's Mr. Dooley. Sometimes the irony goes so deep that any connection between assumptions about ethnic background and a literary character becomes tenuous. Basil Ransom in Henry James's *The Bostonians* (1886) is a cardboard Southerner perhaps because the author hesitated to use regional or ethnic characteristics as the center of character motivation. Grace Paley's "The Immigrant Story" (1975) shows even greater ironic detachment from ethnicity as a motivating force by separating a long conversation about the difficulty and dubiousness of remembering from a consciously trite ethnic memoir which begins with the classic formula: "My mother and father came from a small town in Poland. They had three sons. My father decided to go to America, to 1. Stay out of the army, 2. Stay out of jail, 3. Save his children from everyday wars and ordinary pogroms." The reasons for migration ultimately say nothing about the narrator's ethnic background.

In Gertrude Stein's *The Making of Americans* (1934) the rhetoric of the New World and of ethnicity is churningly regurgitated and spewed out as a critique of the realistic and semiautobiographic novels one might expect from such a title. What could illustrate the new consciousness of earlier ethnic writers better than Mary Antin's awareness that she was "nobly related: "Undoubtedly I was a Fellow Citizen, and George Washington was another." Susannah Rowson, author of the first American best-selling novel, *Charlotte* (1791), considered American authors more fortunate than Homer who had only "barbarous chieftains" to write about, while they had "matchless Washington." The relationship to Washington is crucial to Cooper's *Spy*; in *MobyDick*, Melville refers to Queequeg as "George Washington cannibalistically developed." Stein's *The Making of Americans* ironically reflects the Washington rhetoric and, at the same time, responds to the epithet "dirty" that is so often hurled against minorities. Stein writes of the immigrant boy George, who "was not named after his grandfather," that he was "strong in sport and washing. He was not foreign in his washing. Oh, no, he was really an american." Stein continues: "It's a great question this question of washing. One never can find any one who can be satisfied with anybody else's washing. I knew a man once who never as far as any one could see ever did any washing, and yet he described another with contempt, why he is a dirty hog sir, he never does any washing. The French tell me it's the Italians who never do any washing, the French and the Italians both find the Spanish a little short in their washing, the English find all the world lax in this business of washing, and the East finds all the West a pig, which never is clean with just the little cold water washing. And so it goes." In Stein's writing—as in Toomer's or Henry Roth's—the "new style" is related to ethnicity; in the mode of "ethnic modernism" ethnicity remains palpable while the writing transcends it. "Yes, George Dehning was not at all foreign in his washing but for him, too, the old world was not altogether lost behind him."

Ironically, some American modernists who defied ethnic categories and were associated with transethnic art movements developed a pseudoethnic identity as Bohemians. Andrew Greeley once suggested that intellectuals form an "ethnic group," and Waldo Frank saw artists, in the familiar terms of ethnicity and typology, as a new "chosen people." Modernists might denounce "Puritanism," by which they often meant Victorian moralism and nativist arrogance rather than the historical culture of seventeenth-century New England, but defined even their "trans-nationalism" in the rhetoric of ethnicity. Van Wyck Brooks, for example, described the "nationalism of the poets, novelists and thinkers" as "a golden world in which one finds neither Roman, Jew, Barbarian nor Greek, for the prejudices of the brazen world are left behind there." Brooks cites Frank Lloyd Wright's "open plan" in architecture as an appropriate example of melting-pot art forms because it "abolishes all the partitions that have divided room from room" in the same way the "human laboratory" of America "abolishes the barriers between man and man in the interest of a wide sociality and all-human freedom. Wright has translated Walt Whitman into architecture." And Whitman is, as Waldo Frank noted, the formal prototype of ethnic modernists, the Moses of the new chosen people, the Bohemians.

Ethnicity in American Literature: Rosebud or MacGuffin?

Can American literature help define the meaning of ethnicity? Read as simple "information," not as validation of social interpretations, ethnic literature often reveals more through its cultural allusions, language, imagery, and forms than through motifs and themes. Writers have been criticized for using an assimilationist melting-pot perspective when they were creating rebirth experiences as Paul's "new man" that were somewhat more complex than much melting-pot sociology. If we look for motifs in literature we may, for example, find several occurrences of ghetto rooftop settings in Jewish-American writing; however, we miss the point if we simply read such passages as evidence that tenement houses had flat roofs on which immigrants spent time. In Cahan's *Yekl,* for example, the "housetop idyl" is more than an incidental "realistic" setting for immigrant Jake's incipient alliance with the more Americanized Mamie Fein; as Jules Chametzky has pointed out, this scene is a symbolic battle between the Old World past and the New World future, and the sheets on the clothesline are consciously metamorphosed into the shrouds of Jake's father and the covers of Mamie's bed. In Zangwill's *Melting Pot* the final scene takes place on the tenement rooftop to allow the cosmic dimensions of the American symphony full play against the red skies of the Fourth of July and with a full view of the Statue of Liberty. David Quixano, about to marry Vera, whose father was the Russian baron responsible for the pogrom in which David's parents died, becomes the prophet of the promised melting pot; the rooftop functions as Mount Sinai. Even in Gold's *Jews without Money* the rooftop is the place of metaphoric closeness to the Old World, where the narrator's father tells Romanian folk tales. And in Roth's *Call It Sleep* the rooftop is the locus of a Joycean epiphany, a revelation of great complexity.

Few readers attempt to read ethnic literature as evidence for the existence of rooftops; but the example of what even "realistic" or "socially oriented" writers do with as simple a motif serves as a warning against reading imaginative literature as social evidence. This caution is especially necessary because reading ethnic literature is sometimes motivated by an interest to find out what it is like to be "other" and to discover the true meaning of the mysteries of "ethnicity." In a situation where ethnicity is no longer merely feared as dangerous otherness but is almost worshiped as a form of inspiration, writers have been able to combine demands for authenticity and spokesmanship as they symbolically claimed to represent whole ethnic groups in addressing general American audiences. When ethnic writers maintain that they are "Speaking for Ourselves," the reader has to decide whether to interpret the pronoun "ourselves" in the sense of "ethnic groups" (as Lillian Faderman does) or in the sense of "writers" (as Herbert Gans argues), for despite all claims of ethnic representation, writers are more usually alienated from "ethnicity" than part of it. Writers may, in fact, be once de-ethnicized and later re-ethnicized intellectuals whose relationship to the group they supposedly represent may be quite romantic—or, in any event, more problematic than they sometimes care to admit.

In "The Custom-House," Hawthorne ironically defies filiopietism as he describes himself, from the point of view of "the old trunk of the family tree, with so much venerable moss upon it" as "its topmost bough, an idler." "A writer of story books!" Hawthorne hears the gray shadow of a forefather murmur disapprovingly about his descendant's choice of a profession. "Why, the degenerate fellow might as well have been a fiddler!" The gulf that separates most writers from "their" groups and alienates them from their backgrounds is as important a factor as the cultural socialization that shaped them. The tendency to become an "ethnic" writer is offset by the literary consciousness that transcends ethnicity. When Howells tried to encourage the development of an American literature independent of British influences, he suggested the Spanish picaresque mode as a prototype, and when today's ethnic writers sometimes turn away from the American tradition, they often opt for equally American literary alternatives.

Despite ethnocentrism and filiopietism on the one side, and outside ethnic prejudice on the other, there has been an amazing amount of cross-cultural, transethnic literature in America. The curiosity about *How the Other Half Lives* was not limited to muckraking photojournalists. There were slummers like Carl Van Vechten and Hutchins Hapgood, who used black and Jewish ethnicity as an inspiration and as a validation for their own desires to innovate American literature; there were authors who, like Henry Harland—"Sidney Luska"—changed their names in order to write "ethnic," and there were Americans like Waldo Frank, John Howard Griffin, and even Superman's Lois Lane ("I am curious black"), who become "ethnic transvestites" for a time. Since the turn of the century, many American Bohemian art movements have emerged that are essentially transethnic; ironically, some writers would consider themselves merely as writers, whereas some of their colleagues might look upon them as representatives of ethnic groups. If Philip Yordan's play *Anna Lucasta* (1944) is really a Polish immigrant play, which became successful only after it was rewritten as a black play, then this example of literary transethnicity is another indication of the structural nature of literary ethnicity: the literary interest lies less in the specific cultural emanation of one ethnic group than in the relationship of a minority to a majority—which often makes it ethnically interchangeable.

What then is "ethnicity," this new word? In literature, it may appear as a bloody footprint or as an adaptation of biblical lore, as wife of youth, as otherness, or as divided self. A word, a gesture, a gut reaction, a double entendre may be at the heart of ethnic consciousness. Sometimes characters in ethnic literature act like opera singers who are suddenly placed on a drama stage and have to thematize and defend their traditional form in a different medium. At other times, they appear displaced in time, like Rip Van Winkle who once said: "I am not myself—I'm somebody else [. . .] everything's changed, and I'm changed, and I can't tell what's my name, or who I am!"

The specific nature and meaning of ethnicity often remain less clear than its literary function. Alfred Hitchcock called the secret that spies are pursuing the "MacGuffin" and explained that "the logicians are wrong in trying to figure out the truth of a MacGuffin, since it's beside the point. The only thing that really matters is that [. . .] the plans, documents, or secrets must seem to be of vital importance to the characters. To me, the narrator, they're of no importance whatever." It may be heartless to view literary ethnicity as such a MacGuffin; yet the sum total of an experience, the pride and suffering of a specific ethnicity must be functionalized for the sake of a story—and thus ethnicity becomes a literary vehicle that may mean everything for a character, but remain general or cryptic to the reader. "Old World," "mother," "romance," "complexion," or "melting pot" are words that may be very specifically charged for different ethnic characters; yet the literary forms that have developed from such bases use the center of emotionality structurally and make felt and experienced ethnicity a MacGuffin. Perhaps the most successful literature of ethnicity, then, does not attempt a full and truthful initiation into the mysteries of ethnicity but stops with partial revelations and a sense of secrecy and mystery. The word may temporarily be attached to scenic revelations—as in the confrontation with those dark mysterious mothers who pass as ethnic wives in Chesnutt and Cahan. But after such moments a sense of wonder needs to be restored. If Charles Foster Kane's last word is seen as a version of ethnicity, then it becomes apparent how "Rosebud" in *Citizen Kane* (1941) succeeds in arousing curiosity and concern because of the mystery that remains attached to the word. "Maybe Rosebud was something Kane couldn't get or something he lost, but it wouldn't have explained anything!" Thompson says in the film, and adds a remark that is as appropriate for "Rosebud" as it is for "ethnicity": "I don't think any word can explain a man's life."

If "Rosebud" cannot explain one man's life, then how could "ethnicity" account for the shape of a whole nation's literature? Despite the astonishing connections that the concept of ethnicity allows us to perceive within American culture, we must remember that "ethnicity" is an abstraction, too. When Karl Marx and Friedrich Engels first developed their principles of literary realism—interestingly, in the context of a debate about Eugène Sue's *Mystères de Paris*—they reminded German Hegelians that the word "fruit," for example, was merely an abstraction, which only "the mystery of speculative construction" could place on a level superior to that of apples, pears, almonds, or raisins. This procedure allows Hegelians to maintain that "the essential qualities of these things are not to be found in their real, palpable existence, but in their essence as 'fruit'—which I first abstracted and assigned to them in my imagination" (*The Holy Family*, 1844). It may be useful to remember that the situation of the abstraction "ethnicity" is analogous to that of Marx's "fruit." No matter to what extent different literary renditions of "ethnicity" may resemble each other and be part of American patterns, "ethnicity as such" only exists as an abstraction in need of continuous concretization.[1]

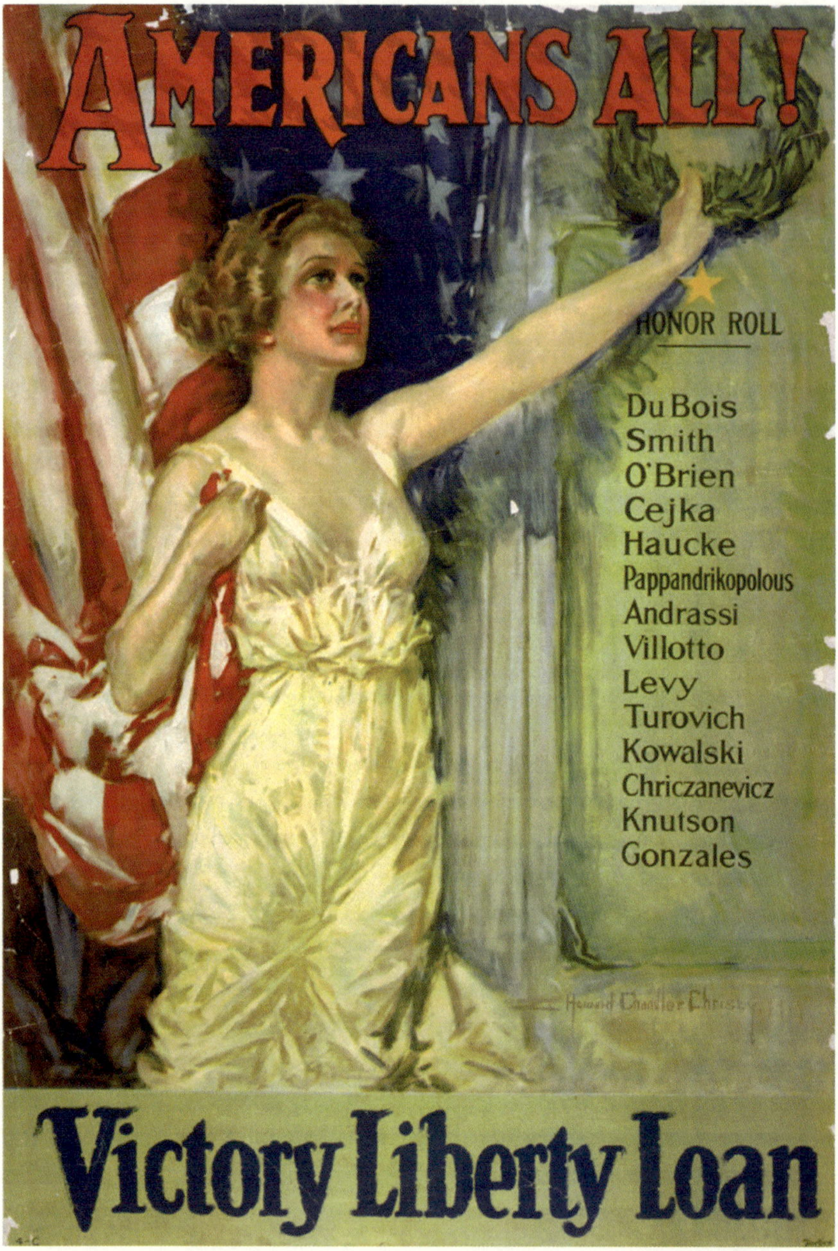

FIGURE 2 Howard Chandler Christy. *Americans All!* 1917. Poster. Private collection.

2

National Identity and Ethnic Diversity

Modern geographers named the New World "America" in honor of the Italian explorer Amerigo Vespucci. Martin Waldseemüller's map of 1507 is considered the first instance of the word; the mapmaker argued that because Asia and Europe had received their names from women, no one could object to the naming of the new continent after a man.[1] The term "American" referred to the original inhabitants, or Indians; in Puritan New England, however, it was increasingly adopted to refer to the *British* colonists, as when Nathaniel Ward in 1647 spoke of an "American Creed"—and meant the beliefs of the English settlers in North America. In the American Revolution, the term was used to emphasize less the British origin than the new makeup of the settler population of the United States. In Crèvecœur's famous answer to the question "What is an American?" in the third of his *Letters from an American Farmer* (1782), he singled out "that strange mixture of blood, which you will find in no other country."[2] For

SOURCE *Immigrants in Two Democracies: French and American Experience*, ed. Donald Horowitz and Gérard Noiriel. New York: New York University Press, 1992, 205–244. By permission of New York University Press.

Crèvecœur, the term "American" referred to the ethnic diversity of at least the white colonists in the New World.

Anchoring national identity in mixing goes back at least to Daniel Defoe's English model that he advanced in *The True-Born Englishman* of 1701: "I would examine all Nations of Europe and prove, that those Nations which are most mix'd, are the best, and have least of Barbarism and Brutality among them."[3] The hyphenated Anglo-Saxons thus provided a prototype for Crèvecœur's supposedly uniquely mixed Americans and for the melting-pot metaphor.

Initially applied to the Indians, then taken on by the British and applied generally to white settlers, by 1900 the term "American" had undoubtedly become problematic. In 1907, Henry James asked: "Who and what is an alien [. . .] in a country peopled from the first under the jealous eye of history?—peopled, that is, by migrations at once extremely recent, perfectly traceable and urgently required. [. . .] Which is the American [. . .]—which is *not* the alien, over a large part of the country at least, and where does one put a finger on the dividing line?"[4] "American" could mean all sorts of things; the ethnic dividing line could be drawn on linguistic or religious grounds, making the English language and a certain form of Protestantism touchstones of America. Even the Americanness of the first group of people called "Americans" could now become questionable. Thus the sociologist Robert Park told the story of an old lady who visited the Indian village at the World's Fair and, "moved to speak a friendly word to one of these aborigines," actually asked: "How do you like our country?"[5] The hero of Maxine Hong Kingston's novel *Tripmaster Monkey: His Fake Book*, the Chinese-American beatnik tellingly named Wittman Ah Sing, mentions the same question as one that white Americans should never ask him.[6]

At the center of the debates about the nature and future of America was the problem of ethnic heterogeneity: How inclusive and how exclusive could "America" be? An extreme position was taken by the political journalist David Goodman Croly, who had coined the word "miscegenation" in 1863, was a Democratic campaign biographer and also the father of *New Republic* founder Herbert Croly. In 1888, David Croly published *Glimpses of the Future, Suggestions as to the Drift of Things*. Contemplating the future American, Croly's mouthpiece "Sir Oracle" makes the following prophecy:

> We can absorb the Dominion [. . .] for the Canadians are of our own race [. . .] but Mexico, Central America, the Sandwich Islands, and the West India

> Islands will involve governments which cannot be democratic. We will never confer the right of suffrage upon the blacks, the mongrels of Mexico or Central America, or the Hawaiians. [. . .] I presume the race of mulattoes is dying out. [. . .] The white race is dominant and will keep their position, no matter how numerous the negroes may become.[7]

For Croly "American" meant "white"—hence nonwhite and mixed races were not considered "absorbable" or eligible for full citizenship rights. Not even Central America counted as "American." Croly himself was an Irish immigrant but did not wish to extend Americanness to nonwhites; and his use of the term "mongrel" makes clear his aversion to racial mixing. Of all the fault lines, "race" (or more precisely, the decision whether a person was white and thereby a potential American or nonwhite, hence not absorbable) has perhaps remained the deepest ethnic boundary.

Liberal reformers could have a different sense of "America." The old-stock newspaper editor Hamilton Holt, for example, ran a series of first-person singular accounts by people of many racial and ethnic backgrounds in the *Independent*. When he published sixteen of those "lifelets" in book form in 1906, he chose the programmatic title *The Life Stories of Undistinguished Americans: As Told by Themselves*, using the elastic term "American" to refer to a very broad spectrum of the populace: Rocco Corresca, an Italian bootblack; Sadie Frowne, a Jewish sweatshop worker from Poland; Amelia des Moulins, a French dressmaker; Ann, an Irish maid; Agnes M., a German nurse girl; Axel Jarlson, a Swedish farmer; L.J.A., a Syrian journalist,; Antanas Kaztauskis, a Lithuanian butcher; an anonymous Negro peon, a Japanese manservant, a Greek peddler, a midwestern farmer's wife, and a handicapped Southern Methodist minister; Lee Chew, a Chinese laundryman and businessman; Fomoaley Ponci, a foreign nonimmigrant Igorrote chief from the recently conquered Philippines who was on display at Coney Island; and Ah-nen-la-de-ni, an Indian.[8] Holt includes everyone in his notion of the "American": black, white, Indian, Asian, native born, immigrant, refugee, temporary migrant, sojourner, men, women—people from all walks of life. The book is one of the most inclusive "American" texts early in the century, as the collection virtually transformed the inhabitants of the whole world into potential Americans. The contrast between Croly's exclusive and Holt's inclusive "America" was dramatic. On such a contested terrain, attempts at symbolizing the country had to yield contradictory results.

Americans All!

"AMERICANS ALL!" was the title of a poster designed by Howard Chandler Christy in 1917, used to promote Victory Liberty Loans, employment opportunities for soldiers, and other war efforts. (See Figure 2.) It depicts a scantily clad young blond woman in front of an American flag, holding a laurel wreath under which an "honor roll" of ethnic names appears: Du Bois, Smith, O'Brien, Cejka, Haucke, Pappandrikopolous, Andrassi, Villotto, Levy, Turovich, Kowalski, Chriczanevicz, Knutson, and Gonzales; they were all to be Americans at a time when World War I made undivided loyalties mandatory. At first glance this may have seemed to constitute an invitation to foreigners who were thus honored to become eligible as Americans—in the vein of Holt's *Undistinguished Americans*. Yet the allegorical figure who accompanies this incorporation of various ethnic groups into "America" is not a mulatto Madonna with an Indian headdress (which is actually the way the new, oxidized bronze Statue of Liberty on top of the Washington Capitol appeared to Croly in his *Miscegenation* pamphlet of 1863 "as a symbol of the future American of this continent," "not white, symbolizing but one race, nor black typifying another, but a statue representing the composite race, whose sway will extend from the Atlantic to the Pacific ocean, from the Equator to the North Pole—the Miscegens of the Future.")[9] No, the national allegory on this poster is "the American girl," an English-looking white woman, not sturdy like the Statue of Liberty—for which the Alsatian sculptor Frédéric Auguste Bartholdi's mother had posed[10]—but with a glitzy Christy-style look. As Martha Banta suggested, the poster did not simply honor ethnic diversity. Christy's image contains a double message as ethnics are asked to assimilate to an Anglo-Saxon norm (its origin in mixing forgotten) that is constituted precisely in opposition to them. They are told to be "Mr. American" by conforming to something that they might never become physically.[11] The representative American body of 1917 does not include their features, and their names sound like those of many Hollywood actors and actresses before they changed them into more palatable ones: from Betty Joan Perske to Lauren Bacall, from Dino Crocetti to Dean Martin, from Margarita Cansino to Rita Hayworth, from Doris von Kappelhoff to Doris Day, or from Bernard Schwarz to Tony Curtis. Incidentally, most Hollywood performers have stopped camouflaging their ethnic names behind anglicized ones, and an anglicized name may now be an ironic comment on the old status quo—as when a transgender star in Andy Warhol's Factory appears under the name "Holly Woodlawn." And the French author Sanche de Gramont consulted a specialist in anagrams who offered him many options for scrambling the letters of his surname, among them Tod German, Red Montag, Mort Degan, Tom Danger, O.D. Garment, Monte Drag, Madge Torn, Margo Dent, Demo Grant, Gert Monad, Mart Ogden, Gen. Montard, Rod Magnet, Mo Dragnet, Dr. Montage, Mr. de Tango, R. D. Megaton, and Grand Tome. As he writes in his book *On Becoming American* (1978), he chose "Ted Morgan."

Christy's World War I poster could be read both inclusively (as in Holt's *Life Stories*) and exclusively (as in Croly's *Glimpses*); and it is interesting to consider how important the manipulation of such symbols can be for the establishment of a national identity as well as for various ethnic identities.

The Statue of Liberty

A famous example is the Statue of Liberty. The dedication of the statue on October 28, 1886, inspired the aging political poet John Greenleaf Whittier, whose career had climaxed before the Civil War with his widely cited antislavery verse, to compose the poem "The Bartholdi Statue" (1886). Whittier stresses Franco-American liberty as an enlightening force, singing: "O France, the beautiful!" and concluding with the lines:

Shine far, shine free, a guiding light
    To Reason's ways and Virtue's aim,
A lightning-flash the wretch to smite
    Who shields his license with thy name!

Whittier thus presents the official "Franco-American" interpretation of the statue as advanced during the dedication ceremony, which included only very brief references to immigrants. Yet the poet also celebrates the abolition of slavery as the realization of the dream of American liberty:

Unlike the shapes on Egypt's sands
    Uplifted by the toil-worn slave,
On Freedom's soil with freemen's hands
    We rear the symbol free hands gave.[12]

Whittier's national and official reading thus also contained his own cause, the memory of the abolition of slavery. This element did not remain in the foreground of later interpretations of the statue, despite the inviting presence of the broken shackles of tyranny on the monument.

The poet Emma Lazarus saw a different statue in her sonnet "The New Colossus" which constituted an inofficial recasting of the statue's officially intended meaning. Lazarus's statue, a "Mother of Exiles," speaks:

> "Keep, ancient lands, your storied pomp!" cries she
> With silent lips. "Give me your tired, your poor,
> Your huddled masses yearning to breathe free,
> The wretched refuse of your teeming shore.
> Send these, the homeless, tempest-tost to me,
> I lift my lamp beside the golden door!"[13]

Whittier's apostrophe "shine far" contrasts markedly with Lazarus' well-known motto "send these to me." The New England poet James Russell Lowell seems to have been among the first to recognize the significance of Lazarus's poem. When he was the United States ambassador to England, he reportedly wrote her that he liked her poem better than Bartholdi's statue: "But your sonnet gives its subject a *raison d'être* which it wanted before quite as much as it wanted a pedestal."[14] A plaque with Lazarus's sonnet was affixed to the Statue of Liberty in 1903; and though this was noted in the *Baedeker* of 1909[15] and in immigrant writing, it remained, according to John Higham's book, significantly entitled *Send These to Me*, relatively unnoticed until the mid-1920s, when the immigration restrictions were legislated.[16] While the overt message of Lazarus's poem seemed to be foremost an invitation to immigrants ("From her beacon-hand / Glows world-wide welcome") and thus offered a reinterpretation of the Statue of Liberty that was offbeat enough to remain ignored or at least of secondary importance for some time, the reference to the newcomers as "wretched refuse" also permitted a reading that the immigration historian James P. Shenton convincingly paraphrased in a lecture as "welcome, garbage!"[17] In any event, the nativist James H. Patten applied Lazarus's phrase "Wretched refuse!" in 1906 to "the beaten people of beaten races" who come to America in order "to desecrate / Thy Sabbath and despoil thy rich heritage / Purchased with so much Anglo-Saxon blood and treasure."[18] The adaptation of Lazarus's poem that was used at John F. Kennedy Airport simply omitted the lines with the phrase "wretched refuse."[19]

No matter how multivalent Lazarus's imagery was, ethnic writers often adopted her reinterpretation of the Statue of Liberty as the symbolic space where "foreign" and "American" identities meet. In this fashion, the Swedish-American journal *Valkyrian*, published from 1897 to 1909, had as its permanent cover illustration the image of a big Valkyrie, whereas a small Statue of Liberty in New York Harbor was recognizable in the background,[20] thus connecting a Norse and an American goddess—proportionate to their meaning, perhaps; and in Maxine Hong Kingston's *China Men* (1980), Ed buys a postcard of the Statue of Liberty with his first spending money and first pastes the card and only then personal photographs into his picture album.[21]

The anarchist Emma Goldman gave a curiously ironic testimony to the power of the statue as the dominant symbol of immigrant arrivals. She remembers in her autobiography *Living My Life* (1931) how when she first came to America, she was "enraptured by the sight of the harbour and the Statue of Liberty, suddenly emerging from the mist": "Ah, there she was, the symbol of hope, of freedom, of opportunity! She held her torch high to light the way to the free country, the asylum for the oppressed of all lands. [. . .] Our spirits were high, our eyes filled with tears."[22] Yet, as immigration historians have noticed, Emma Goldman could not have seen the statue because she arrived in New York on December 29, 1885, months before the pedestal was completed and over half a year before the statue was assembled.[23] In retrospect, even a radical like Goldman subjugated her own specific memory to the meaning of the statue that the other Emma had helped to propagate and that had found triumphant expressions in such images as Adolph Treidler's war bonds poster of 1917, "Remember Your First Thrill of American Liberty."[24]

Lazarus's voice opposed not only the sentiments that Whittier was to express but also opinions like those of Croly that were often represented in anti-immigrant cartoons and put into poetry by the New Englander Thomas Bailey Aldrich in his once famous "Unguarded Gates" (1892), another version of "Liberty."

> Wide open and unguarded stand our gates,
> And through them presses a wild motley throng—
> Men from the Volga and the Tartar steppes,
> Featureless figures of the Hoang-Ho,
> Malayan, Scythian, Teuton, Kelt, and Slav,
> Flying the Old World's poverty and scorn;

These bringing with them unknown gods and rites,
Those, tiger passions, here to stretch their claws.
In street and alley what strange tongues are these,
Accents of menace alien to our air,
Voices that once the Tower of Babel knew!
O Liberty, white Goddess! is it well
To leave the gates unguarded?[25]

Aldrich's liberty is not imagined as a "Mother of Exiles" but, in exactly opposite terms, as a "white Goddess" who should guard freedom *against* the menace of beastly invaders. It is clear that Aldrich did not believe in the message "send these to me," but he also had little faith in liberty's ability to "shine far." Aldrich polemicized against immigration by arguing that America's true emblem was no longer the eagle but "some sort of unnaturalized mongrel."[26] It is a measure of the transformation of public memory that by the time of the statue's centennial celebrations in 1986 Lazarus's voice had clearly won out over Whittier's and Aldrich's.

At the peak of the new immigration, however, some "old-stock" American intellectuals believed in "race suicide."[27] Lothrop Stoddard, an opponent to immigration, thought that "the lower a class is in the scale of intelligence, the greater is its reproductive contribution." Invoking the eugenicist Charles Davenport, he calculated that "at present rates of reproduction, 1,000 Harvard graduates of to-day would have only fifty descendants two centuries hence, whereas 1,000 Rumanians to-day in Boston, at their present rate of breeding, would have 100,000 descendants in the same space of time."[28] Some Americans perceived themselves to be outnumbered by the "invasion" of "strangers" in the country their ancestors, real or adopted, had founded. I say "real or adopted" even in thinking of the group that was dubbed the "Brahmin Caste of New England" in Oliver Wendell Holmes's novel *Elsie Venner* in order to describe a collegiate "race of scholars" different from the type of the common country boy.[29]

Arrival Points as Myths of Origin: Jamestown, Plymouth, Ellis Island

Many of the intellectuals who adopted the term Brahmin were, as William Taylor pointed out, *not* old-stock descendants but upwardly mobile young men, several of whom had married into old families.[30] Such intellectuals adopted and increasingly stressed the symbols of the *Mayflower* and Plymouth Rock as mythic points of origin. At the end of the nineteenth and the beginning of the twentieth centuries, the invention of Plymouth (and especially Plymouth Rock) as an exclusivist ethnic symbol replaced earlier ideological readings in revolutionary, religious, or abolitionist contexts.

The Pilgrims had landed in 1620 at the Pamet Sound near Truro (Cape Cod), and leaving the *Mayflower* at Provincetown, they sailed on to Plymouth a month later. The rock that commemorates this second landing is of dubious authenticity and, geologically considered, of African origin.[31] In 1741, Elder Faunce, then ninety-five years old, had identified a boulder as the "place where the forefathers landed," a phrasing that was probably misunderstood as referring to the "first landing";[32] this led to the increasing sacralization of the rock—as well as of fragments that were supposedly chipped off from it—in the nineteenth and twentieth centuries. Like relics, exhibits, or souvenirs, pieces of the rock have been taken to Immingham, Lincolnshire (the point of the Pilgrims' departure for Holland) and the Plymouth Congregational Church in Brooklyn; other pieces were sold in the 1920s as paperweights by the Antiquarian Society of Plymouth, and one piece was sent to President Eisenhower by a citizen.[33] In a footnote to *Democracy in America*, Tocqueville observed:

> This rock has become an object of veneration in the United States. I have seen bits of it carefully preserved in several towns of the Union. Does not this sufficiently show how all human power and greatness are entirely in the soul? Here is a stone which the feet of a few poor fugitives pressed for an instant, and this stone becomes famous; it is treasured by a great nation, a fragment is prized as a relic. But what has become of the doorsteps of a thousand palaces? Who troubles himself about them?[34]

In 1852, Lydia Hunt Sigourney viewed Plymouth Rock as a sacred stone, similar to the Muslim Kaaba:

> And give him praise, whose Hand
> Sustained them with His grace,
> Making this Rock, whereon ye stand,
> The Mecca of their race.[35]

James Kirke Paulding wrote an "Ode to Jamestown" (1836), in which he celebrated John Smith and Pocahontas; he also cast America as the peaceful synthesis of Plymouth and Jamestown, North and South:

Jamestown, and Plymouth's hallowed rock
    To me shall ever sacred be,—.
I care not who my themes may mock,
    Or sneer at them and me.

And in the couplet ending the next and last stanza he proclaimed:

He is a bastard, if he dare to mock,
Old Jamestown's shrine or Plymouth's famous rock.[36]

This was apparently the special interest of a Northerner with strong sympathies for the South and for slavery who wanted to reconcile Puritans and Cavaliers and defy abolitionist readings of the rock in the wake of Daniel Webster's address of 1820.

In the world of widely shared national public memorialization Plymouth Rock played an increasingly important role after the Civil War.[37] The Society of *Mayflower* Descendants, for example, was founded in 1894.[38] The 1920 tercentenary inspired the National Society of the Colonial Dames (a women's association constituted in 1891, incorporated in 1899, and dedicated to preserve shrines of Anglo-American history under the motto "Not Ancestry but Heredity") to erect the present memorial by the famous architects McKim, Mead, and White, completed only in 1921.[39]

Turn-of-the-century *Mayflower* legends pursued the unanswerable question whose foot had first touched Plymouth Rock. One claimant to this honor was John Alden, another the maiden Mary Chilton. A 1906 version of the legend concluded as follows:

> A youth in the full vigor of manhood, whose posterity should inherit the virgin land, sets his nervous foot upon the cornerstone of a nation, and makes it an historic spot. A young girl in the first bloom of womanhood, the type of a coming maternity, boldly crosses the threshold of a wilderness which her children's children shall possess and inhabit, and transforms it into an Eden. Surely John Alden should have married Mary Chilton on the spot.[40]

This story makes the supposed "cornerstone of a nation" nicely vivid in the dream of a founding couple, here imagined of pure English and *Mayflower* origin.

It seems likely that the new immigrants and their reinterpretation of the Statue of Liberty helped to strengthen the Brahmins' countervailing consciousness of Plymouth. At least the granite-sculpted, toga-clad allegorical figure representing Faith that crowns the National Monument to the Forefathers in Plymouth, was dedicated on August 1, 1889, three years after the Statue of Liberty, and does resemble her much larger sister in New York harbor. Faith's left "foot rests upon Forefather's Rock (supposedly an actual piece of Plymouth Rock); in her left hand she holds a Bible, not the Declaration of Independence; and with the right uplifted she points to heaven" rather than clasping a torch.[41]

In his famous essay of 1915, "Democracy Versus the Melting-Pot," Horace Kallen argued that it was the new presence of vast non-English populations, the feared "barbarian hordes," in the United States that had the effect of throwing back "the Brito-American upon his ancestry and ancestral ideals," a development that manifested itself in the heightened public emphasis upon "the unity of the 'Anglo-Saxon' nations" and in the founding of societies such as the Sons and Daughters of the American Revolution that, Kallen argues, "have arisen with the great migrations."[42]

The more heterogeneous the country was perceived to be, the more Plymouth origins came to be stressed as a mark of distinction. This tension erupted in the controversy about the Russian-Jewish immigrant Mary Antin, the author of the autobiography *The Promised Land* (1912). Antin suggested the compatibility of Jewish and American identity, viewing the transatlantic crossing as a new *Exodus* (as the Puritans had done), and she expanded Lazarus's reinterpretation of the Statue of Liberty as a symbol of welcome to immigrants:

> Let it [. . .] be repeated that the Liberty at our gates is the handiwork of a Frenchman; that the mountain-weight of copper in her sides and the granite mass beneath her feet were bought with the pennies of the poor; that the verses graven on a tablet within the base are the inspiration of a poetess descended from Portuguese Jews; and all these things shall be interpreted to mean that the love of liberty unites all races and all classes of men into one close brotherhood, and that we Americans, therefore, who have the utmost of liberty that has yet been attained, owe the alien a brother's share.[43]

Though the word was not yet in use, this was indeed a "multicultural" reading.

What Antin did for the Statue of Liberty, she boldly extended to the core symbols of Brahmin descent: "The ghost of the Mayflower pilots every immigrant ship, and Ellis Island is another name for Plymouth Rock."[44] Antin courageously equated the Pilgrim Fathers' increasingly enshrined American beginnings with the modern clearing center (opened January 1, 1892, and closed November 3, 1954) in which approximately twelve million immigrants and remigrants were processed from 1892 to 1924 alone—and about three thousand committed suicide.[45] Thereby Antin attempted to subvert the point of view from which a Plymouth Rock and *Mayflower* ancestry gave a speaker the right to reject an Ellis Island immigrant as a potential citizen. For Antin, *any* arrival in America after a transatlantic voyage was thus comparable; and her view of Ellis Island as a synonym for Plymouth Rock as well as her self-inclusion as an "American" were to become central to the expansion of the term "American" that supported the integration of minorities. In developing her elaborate analogy between Puritans and immigrants, she invokes the Brahmin James Russell Lowell and finds that he is a writer who chips "away the crust of historic sentiment and show[s] us our forefathers in the flesh. Lowell would agree with me that the Pilgrims were a picked troop in the sense that there was an immense preponderance of virtue among them. And that is exactly what we must say of our modern immigrants."[46]

Our Forefathers

Antin's position illustrates the complications of national integration in a polyethnic country: nations often need founding myths and stories of origins, beginnings in the past that authenticate the present. Those who do not share such pasts, or at least their myths, can then be excluded from the concept of the nation: if they mean "foreigners" when they say "our forefathers," then they may define themselves "out" as aliens—as did those Swedish-American intellectuals in 1890 who wished to celebrate "Our Forefathers' Day" or those Norwegian Americans who rallied around the association *For fædrearven* after World War I;[47] if they mean the Puritan and Revolutionary heroes, as the Russian Antin did, they "forget who they are" or they seem to be sounding a false note, as did the immigrant poet Agnes

Wergeland who in 1912 chose the *Mayflower* rather than the Norwegian *Restaurationen* for her poem "America Magna."[48]

By contrast, a myth of origin in a mésalliance may stimulate polyethnic integration as ever newly combining mixed marriages (and not just ethnically endogamous unions à la Mary Chilton and John Alden) can then be regarded as the fulfillment of a prophecy in the national past, and not as a new and threatening penetration by foreigners; the children of such unions may combine memories of different, even antithetical pasts. By such myths of origins, immigrants and ethnic minorities can become directly related and affiliated with a shared national past. Such "foundational fictions"—the term is Doris Sommer's—were common in Latin American literature but somewhat more problematic north of the border.[49]

In 1918, the New York trial of the Russian-Jewish anarchist immigrant Jacob Abrams, who had arrived at Ellis Island in 1908, illuminated the problem involving forefathers. At the point in the trial when Abrams was about to defend himself for having distributed English and Yiddish leaflets against Wilson's war policies by invoking American revolutionary beginnings, declaiming, "When our forefathers of the American Revolution—" the federal judge Henry DeLamar Clayton Jr. (from Alabama) interrupted, "Your what?" When Abrams repeated, "My forefathers," the judge asked in disbelief, "Do you mean to refer to the fathers of this nation as your forefathers?" In the course of the trial Abrams was asked twice "Why don't you go back to Russia?" Later, the judge recalled responding to Abrams's phrase, "our forefathers": "What? You were born in Russia and came here four or five years ago and not a citizen, an anarchist, who can never become a citizen. Our forefathers . . . why, just look at it." Abrams received a twenty-year sentence.[50] Like the Abrams case, Antin's literary reception shows how difficult the process of becoming "American," of adopting another country's past could be. The New Englander Barrett Wendell, for example, who was among the first professors of English to teach American literature at Harvard University, wrote in a letter of 1917 that Antin "has developed an irritating habit of describing herself and her people as Americans, in distinction from such folks as Edith [Wendell's wife] and me, who have been here for three hundred years."[51] Wendell's genealogical consciousness rests on the male line of descent. He says little about his mother's ancestors, and her middle name, Bertodi, is mentioned but not explained in a most detailed genealogical account.[52] His wife Edith Greenough Wendell served, incidentally, as president of the Colonial Dames' Plymouth Executive Committee in 1920.[53] Wendell at least conceded that Antin's grandchildren might "perhaps come to be American in the sense in which I feel myself so—for better or worse, belonging only here. And that is the kind of miracle which America, for all its faults and its vulgarities, has wrought."[54] Americanness was thus imaginatively placed in the future.

In 1916, the conservative *Atlantic Monthly* journalist Agnes Repplier was also troubled by Mary Antin's presumptuousness in calling the Pilgrim fathers "our forefathers" as well as by her critical attitude. "[W]hy should the recipient of so much attention be the one to scold us harshly, to rail at conditions she imperfectly understands, to reproach us for [. . .] our slackness in duty, our failure to observe the precepts and fulfill the intentions of those pioneers whom she kindly, but confusedly, calls '*our* forefathers.'"[55] Repplier failed to see any parallels between Plymouth Rock and Ellis Island:

> Had the Pilgrim Fathers been met on Plymouth Rock by immigration officials; had their children been placed immediately in good free schools, and given the care of doctors, dentists, and nurses; had they found themselves in infinitely better circumstances than they had ever enjoyed in England, indulging in undreamed-of luxuries, and taught by kind-hearted philanthropists,—what pioneer virtues would they have developed [. . .] ?[56]

Reviewing some evidence of the new ethnic heterogeneity, Repplier concluded with the question that gives away her restrictive sense of a national identity "It is all very lively and interesting, but where does the American come in?"[57] Repplier (incidentally, not of Brahmin New English but of Franco-German background) resented Antin's use of Lowell as a misquoting of the dead[58] and, in turn, invoked the antiassimilationist Horace Kallen in order to support her dislike of "Mrs. Amadeus Grabau," alluding publicly to the fact that Antin had married an "American"—that is, a non-Jewish German-American Barnard professor. Kallen had criticized Antin as "intermarried, 'assimilated' even in religion, and more excessively, self-consciously flatteringly American than the Americans";[59] yet Kallen had also partly adopted Antin's argument and, for example, compared Polish immigrants with the Pilgrims when he wrote: "[T]he urge that carries [the Poles] in such numbers to America is not so unlike that which carried the pilgrim fathers."[60]

Repplier recognized the danger with Antin's position: assimilation, full American identity, even if adopted unilaterally by declaration of will rather than by birth or acceptance from old-stock Americans, and the notion of equal merit of Plymouth Rock and Ellis Island origins entitled Antin to criticize her adopted "promised land" quite openly.

Some Americans were so resentful of the erosion of the word "American" that alternative terms were launched such as "native Americans," "100% Americans," "only Americans," or "real Americans"—as a white neighbor stylizes himself in order to distinguish himself from Chinese immigrants in Sui Sin Far's book *Mrs. Spring Fragrance* (1912). The Chinese-American characters, however, also silently accept the identification of "American" and "white," and Mrs. Spring Fragrance quotes "a beautiful American poem written by a noble American named Tennyson."[61] Both Nicholas Roosevelt and Brander Matthews called themselves "American-Americans" (a term coined by Langdon Mitchell) when they reviewed Horace Kallen's manifesto for cultural pluralism, *Culture and Democracy*, in 1924, Matthews under the worried headline, "Making America a Racial Crazy-Quilt."[62]

Immigrant intellectuals sharply recognized the unfairness of the situation. Waldemar Ager, for example, wrote in his essay "The Melting Pot" in 1916: "There are no definite rules for what is truly 'American.' [. . .] We encounter a culture which is regarded as being American, but on closer examination we find that it is 'English' and that it has no more valid claim to be native here than the Norwegians' *norskdom* or the Germans' Germanness."[63]

Transnational America

Young radical intellectuals among old-stock Americans also could find non-English ethnicity useful for their political purposes as invoking it helped them to attack representatives of the genteel tradition on ethnic grounds—casting it as "Anglo-Saxon" and the result of a British colonial mentality.[64] The most outstanding representative of this tendency was Randolph Bourne who was acutely aware of the political implications of the New Englanders' reaction to Mary Antin. "We have had to watch," Bourne wrote in the famous essay of 1916, programmatically entitled "Trans-National America," "hard-hearted old Brahmins virtuously indignant at the spectacle of the immigrant refusing to be melted, while they jeer at patriots like Mary Antin who write about 'our forefathers.'"[65] Ellery Sedgwick, then the editor of the *Atlantic Monthly* (in which Antin's autobiography had been serialized and Repplier's critique had appeared) and a long-standing admirer of Bourne, wrote him, "I profoundly disagree with your paper." Sedgwick sounded the voice of an older gentility when he insisted that the United States was "created by English instinct and dedicated to the Anglo-Saxon ideal"—exactly the tenets Bourne tried to undermine. Sedgwick criticized Bourne by saying, "you speak [. . .] as though the last immigrant should have as great an effect upon the determination of our history as the first band of Englishmen." For Sedgwick, Bourne's essay was simply a "radical and 'unpatriotic' paper"—though he did publish it in the *Atlantic Monthly*.[66]

In the course of Bourne's essay, the "American" core definitions were revised: "Mary Antin is right when she looks upon our foreign-born as the people who missed the Mayflower and came over on the first boat they could find. But she forgets that when they did come it was not upon other Mayflowers, but upon a 'Maiblume,' a 'Fleur du mai,' a 'Fior di Maggio,' a 'Majblomst.'"[67] While implying in this example that various ethnic histories could be understood as "translations" of an original *Mayflower* voyage, Bourne did perceive the tremendous cultural opportunity of creating a cosmopolitan civilization that thrives upon the linguistic and cultural richness that ethnic variety brings to what he envisioned as a truly "Trans-National America" in which each American citizen could also remain connected with another culture.[68] Bourne envisioned a cosmopolitan intelligentsia that could struggle free from an English orientation in American culture and from the requirement that newcomers shed their cultural, religious, or linguistic pasts upon becoming Americans.[69] This was compatible with Ager's view that the function of Americanization was "to denationalize those who are not of English descent."[70] Bourne also did not think that immigrants could remain fixed to their pasts. Instead Bourne advocated the new ideal of "dual citizenship," both for immigrants who came to the United States and for the increasing number of internationally oriented individuals who, like American expatriates in France, were born in one country but live in another. In Bourne's hands, the contemplation of Americanness in the face of diversity led to a reconsideration of the nationalist premises of citizenship, and Bourne's nationalism was, in fact, anchored in diversity: "Only the American—and in this category I include the migratory alien who has lived with us and caught the pioneer spirit and a sense of new social vistas—has the chance to become that citizen of the world."[71]

In order to strengthen his argument, Bourne also recapitulated the substance of Antin's plea to regard the new immigrants as latter-day Puritans, and with a touch of Henry James's perception of the difficulty of putting one's finger on the dividing line between the "alien" and the "American." Thus Bourne argued memorably: "We are all foreign-born or the descendants of foreign-born, and if distinctions are to be made between us they should rightly be on some other grounds than indigenousness."[72] It is this proposal, clearly a minority voice in 1916, that became the semiofficial core of the redefinition of "America" during the World War II and Cold War years, and finally, the official line for celebrations from the Bicentennial in 1976 to the centennial of the Statue of Liberty in 1986 and the dedication of Ellis Island as a museum in 1990. Immigrants had slowly become accepted as prototypical Americans after being considered among the problematic exceptions.[73]

However, those redefiners of "America" who wanted to make it more "ethnic" and "pluralistic," such as Kallen, Antin, and even Bourne, paid little or no attention to nonwhite Americans in their attempts at broadening American cultural categories. As Higham writes, their theses were "from the outset [. . .] encapsulated in white ethnocentrism."[74] As Higham also stresses, however, the victory of pluralism may have been bought at a terrible price: the battle (Higham calls it another *Kulturkampf*) with its political attacks in the name of ethnicity pushed the conservatives toward racism, anti-Semitism, nativism, and anti-intellectualism, and it alienated radical young intellectuals "from the rank and file of the American working people—that is, from all the people except the culturally distinctive minorities."[75]

Nowhere is Bourne's blind spot more apparent than in his disdain for assimilation. He writes: "It is not the Jew who sticks proudly to the faith of his fathers and boasts of that venerable culture of his who is dangerous to America, but the Jew who has lost the Jewish fire and become a mere elementary, grasping animal."[76] It is telling that Bourne, too, used a sinister animal image as well as the nativist term "hordes"—in order to deplore the assimilated "men and women without a spiritual country, cultural outlaws without taste, without standards but those of the mob."[77] Bourne surrendered to a strikingly paradoxical argument for ethnic purity in the service of cosmopolitan diversity. In order to construct a dynamic pluralistic trans-nationalism, Bourne needed monistic stable ethnic identities based on fixed national origins (that he questioned elsewhere); there was no room for "dangerous" marginal men and women and little sympathy for intermarriage, which threatens the neat system of closed-off subcultures. This is the dilemma of many pluralistic models of American culture, and it may be an inherent problem in "multiculturalism," too.

We have come to expect from the racial right, from Croly, Aldrich, or Repplier, a contempt for assimilation, often used as a code word for that widespread American practice and great cultural anathema of "mixing blood," which the right called "mongrelization." Yet Bourne proposed it from the left and helped to create a legacy of liberal faith in ethnic purity as a necessary foundation of pluralism. Bourne's reliance on a romantic model of ethnic identity also made him loathe much of what made actual ethnic culture tick, "the cheap newspaper [. . .], the popular song, the ubiquitous automobile, our vapid moving pictures, our popular novels." As in Kallen's "Democracy Versus the Melting-Pot," resistance to messy syncretism is what models of America as Plymouth Rock or as Ellis Island could share.

Nation of Immigrants?

After the battles of the 1910s and the 1920s, which resulted in the enactment of immigration restrictions, pluralistic thinking gained ground in the period from the 1930s to the 1950s. In the late 1930s and early 1940s, the Slovenian immigrant Louis Adamic helped to further superimpose the American origins at Plymouth Rock and those at Ellis Island, in the section "Ellis Island and Plymouth Rock" in a book entitled, in the Antin tradition, *My America* (1938), and in lectures to hundreds of audiences, with due homage to Emma Lazarus.[78] Adamic wrote that he wanted to

> work toward an intellectual-emotional synthesis of old and new America; of the Mayflower and the steerage; of the New England wilderness and the social-economic jungle of the city slums and the factory system; of the Liberty Bell and the Statue of Liberty. The old American Dream needs to be interlaced with the immigrants' emotions as they saw the Statue of Liberty. The two must be made into one story.[79]

Adamic reiterated the parallels between "old" and "new" American symbols, exclaimed "Americans All!" (now with more varieties of body features), and invoked Walt Whitman's revived poetic formulation from the preface to *Leaves of Grass* (1855): "Here is not merely a nation but a teeming nation of nations,"[80] stressing a phrase that has since become associated with Ellis Island. President John F. Kennedy made this view of America official in *A Nation of Immigrants* (1964). One must remember, however, that as late as 1956—two years after the Immigration and Naturalization Service had abandoned Ellis Island—the Eisenhower government tried unsuccessfully to sell the island and its buildings, which suggests that its symbolic role had then hardly been officially recognized.[81]

Comparisons and parallels between Plymouth Rock and Ellis Island became more and more widespread up to the point at which the two alternatively conceived symbols seem, indeed, to have merged. No satirists seemed to comment on the strange fact that America's former First Lady, Barbara Bush, paid one hundred dollars to commemorate her Puritan ancestor Thomas Thayer, who emigrated from England in 1630, by having his name put on a copper plaque on the Wall of Honor now surrounding the Ellis Island immigrant museum,[82] a wall that displays nearly two hundred thousand other names, among them that of the prototypical Plymouth character Myles Standish and John Alden, though not of Mary Chilton. It is also perfectly fitting that Pamela Berger's 1989 film *The Imported Bridegroom*, based on a story by Abraham Cahan, represents the Old World Jewish shtetl by what looks very much like the living-history museum of Plymouth Colony. Plymouth Rock and Ellis Island seem to have become interchangeable in contemporary American culture. And this is where accounts of an "Americans All! Ethnics All!" success story sometimes end.

Yet the old-stock/new immigrant distinction did not, of course, apply to all ethnic groups. Unless forced into the somewhat misleading notion that they constituted "America's first immigrants," American Indians may have had an equally problematic relationship to Plymouth Rock and Ellis Island, though attempts have been made to connect them with both symbols. At Plymouth, Native Americans have been celebrated as the coinventors of Thanksgiving; and when during the restoration work of Ellis Island skeletal fragments were found, they were blessed in a public ceremony performed by Willy Snake of the Delaware Indians at Ellis Island.[83]

Those Mexican Americans whose ancestors became Americans by annexation and conquest are also likely to have a somewhat ironic relationship to the "nation of immigrants" and its symbols of arrival as well as to the narrowing of the meaning of "America" to stand for the United States rather than for the whole continent, as Croly had used the word.

Among immigrant groups proper, American citizens of Japanese descent were, at the very time that Adamic popularized the reinterpretation of the immigrants as new Puritans, stripped of their rights as citizens and property owners and interned in detention camps—as a *race* (unlike German- or Italian-Americans, who were generally detained only on the grounds of individual affiliations or political acts).

And other transpacific immigrants? Maxine Hong Kingston ends a long story about her father's possible arrival in the United States being smuggled into New York harbor—where he notices a "gray and green giantess" and is told that she is not a goddess but "the symbol of an idea"—only to continue: "Of course, my father could not have come that way," followed by a long scene in Angel Island that contrasts sharply with his imagined happy observation that "Americans saw the idea of Liberty so real that they made a statue of it."[84] The 17,500 Chinese immigrants who, from 1910 to 1940, were processed through the detention center at Angel Island in San Francisco bay, may have gone through a clearing house modeled on Ellis Island; yet Angel Island, called Devil's Pass by the Chinese migrants, undoubtedly treated immigrants much worse than its model. Several of the Chinese poems that were written of the walls of Angel Island comment explicitly on the immigration procedure. For example:

> Alas, yellow souls suffer under the brute force of the white race!
> Like a homeless dog being cursed, we are forced into jail.
> Like a pig chased into a basket, we are sternly locked in.
>   Our souls languish in a snowy vault; we are not even the equal of cattle and horses.
>   Our tears shower the icy day; we are not even equal to bird or fowl.[85]

One also wonders what significance any of the old threshold symbols could have for the recent immigrants for whom the borderlands around the Rio Grande, Kennedy Airport, or the green card might be more suitable alternatives.

National Myths and Racial Integration

I shall here, however, in conclusion, concentrate on the problematic situation of black Americans, one of the "oldest" and most "indigenous" yet most persistently excluded groups that consists mostly of descendants of people who *did* cross the Atlantic, though involuntarily and as slaves. Is Ellis Island a more appropriate myth than Plymouth Rock for African Americans? How would the American story have to change in order to accommodate black history? In his last writings, the historian Nathan Huggins took American historians to task for dealing with African American history only too rarely, and then usually as an "exception" and "anomaly" in their generalizations about America,[86] and I would like to continue his questioning with a few literary texts.

Identifying himself in the *Atlantic Monthly* merely as "a peaceable man," an astute observer wrote during the Civil War that there was a special affinity between Puritans and Southern blacks:

> There is an historical circumstance, known to few, that connects the children of the Puritans with these Africans of Virginia, in a very singular way. They are our brethren, as being lineal descendants from the Mayflower, the fated womb of which, in her first voyage, sent forth a brood of Pilgrims upon Plymouth Rock, and, in a subsequent one, spawned slaves upon the Southern soil,—a monstrous birth, but with which we have an instinctive sense of kindred, and so are stirred by an irresistible impulse to attempt their rescue, even at the cost of blood and ruin. The character of our sacred ship, I fear, may suffer a little by this revelation; but we must let her white progeny offset her dark one,—and two such portents never sprang from an identical source before.[87]

The observer was Nathaniel Hawthorne, and his appears to have been a lonely voice. The relationship between Plymouth Rock and American slavery has more typically been drawn as a contrast rather than as an affinity. Malcolm X, for example, who said at Harvard, "I'm not a Democrat. I'm not a Republican. I don't even consider myself an American," put it most vividly: "We didn't land on Plymouth Rock, my brothers and sisters—Plymouth Rock landed on *us!*"[88] This may be a statement with a "separatist" thrust; yet Malcolm X may also have been thinking of Cole Porter's song "Anything Goes" (1934), which opens with the claim that if the Puritans were to arrive today "'Stead of landing on Plymouth Rock, / Plymouth Rock would land on them."

In "Plymouth Rock and the Pilgrims," an 1881 dinner address at a New England Society, Mark Twain said that "those Pilgrims were a hard lot. They took good care of themselves, but they abolished everybody else's ancestors."[89] Then he offered his own imagined genealogy:

> My first American ancestor, gentlem[e]n, was an Indian—an early Indian. Your ancestors skinned him alive, and I am an orphan. [. . .] The first slave brought into New England out of Africa by your progenitors was an ancestor of mine—for I am of a mixed breed, an infinitely shaded and exquisite mongrel. I'm not one of your sham meerschaums that you can color in a week. No, my complexion is the patient art of eight generations.[90]

His joyful acceptance of the derogatory term "mongrel" led Mark Twain to a full-fledged attack on the genealogical associations:

> O my friends, hear me and reform! [. . .] Oh, stop, stop, while you are still temperate in your appreciation of your ancestors! Hear me, I beseech you; get up an auction and sell Plymouth Rock! [. . .] Disband these New England societies, renounce these soul-blistering saturnalia, cease from varnishing the rusty reputations of your long-vanished ancestors—the super-high-moral old ironclads of Cape Cod, the pious buccaneers of Plymouth Rock—go home, and try to learn to behave![91]

Extending Shelley Fisher Fishkin's question about Huck Finn one could also ask, "Was Mark Twain black?"

For a long time, African American writers have questioned American national symbols by confronting them with the history of slavery, miscegenation, and segregation. In the first novel published by an American Negro, William Wells Brown's *Clotel, or the President's Daughter* (1853), the author dedicated a whole page to the contrast between the two American beginnings of the "May-flower" and of Jamestown, of freedom and of slavery.[92] At the end of the novel, the titular heroine and slave woman dies, pursued by slave catchers, in the Potomac, "within plain sight of the President's house and the capitol of the Union."[93] Her father, Thomas Jefferson, was the "author" not only of the Declaration of Independence but also of unacknowledged slave children; whether or not this was literally the case is not important, Huggins continued, because it is "*symbolically* true."[94]

In *The Souls of Black Folk* (1903) W.E.B. Du Bois also specifically mentioned the slave ship that "first saw the square tower of Jamestown" as an American beginning point and asked, "Your country? How came it yours? Before the Pilgrims landed we were there."[95] Richard Wright in his *12 Million Black Voices* (1941) came close to Hawthorne's critique when he wrote: "The *Mayflower*'s nameless sister ship, presumably a Dutch vessel, which stole into the harbor of Jamestown in 1619 and unloaded her human cargo of 20 of us, was but the first ship to touch the shores of this New World, and her arrival signalized what was to be our trial for centuries to come."[96]

For a black perspective, "Jamestown" memorializes—not 1607, John Smith, and Pocahontas—but *1619*, the first arrival of Africans in the English colonies that were to become the United States. This is, incidentally, an event that until somewhat recently has not been remembered much even in Jamestown itself. It has hardly played a part in the 1907 and 1957 anniversaries of the founding of Jamestown,[97] though on August 20, 1994, the 375th year of the African arrival was celebrated at the Jamestown Settlement.[98]

African American artists, however, did react to Jamestown of 1619. Meta Vaux Warrick Fuller contributed a commissioned series of sculptures on the "advancement of the Negro since he landed" to the Jamestown tercentennial in 1907; in less than two months, she modeled "fifteen groups with one hundred and fifty figures" that were "in the nature of models, to be dressed in historic costume."[99] Duke Ellington in 1944 publicly claimed Jamestown descent.[100] James Edwin Campbell's poem "The Pariah" makes an explicit case for the merger of Plymouth Rock and Jamestown through the union of the black-white couple that follows the formula: "She the Brahmin, I the Pariah." Speaking about the woman's father, the poem explicates:

> Traced he back his proud ancestry
>   To the Rock on Plymouth's shore,
> Traced I mine to Dutch ship landing
>   At Jamestown, one year before.[101]

Whereas Paulding wanted to see a Northern-Southern merger of Puritans and Cavaliers, and immigrant enthusiasts such as Antin and Adamic thought that the whole American synthesis was embodied in the fusion of Ellis Island and Plymouth Rock (leaving out the legacy of slavery that way), the black poet Campbell viewed the matrimony of the black Pariah and the white Brahmin as the hope for a casteless country of Jamestown *and* Plymouth Rock (as in Paulding's "Ode to Jamestown," with echoes of the Pocahontas story, with a focus on an intermarriage, and ignoring the arrival point of later immigrants). Both the "Jamestown" of black Americans and the "Ellis Island" of European immigrants were, in different fashions, symbolic alternatives to the narrow interpretation of America as *Mayflower* descended, yet alternatives that—even though they were both "thresholds"—could also exclude each other.

In 1942, the black modernist poet Melvin B. Tolson contributed to Louis Adamic's journal *Common Ground* the poem "Rendezvous with America," in which he seems to have desired to represent America as the merger of *all* points of arrival. The poem opens with the lines:

> Time unhinged the gates
> Of Plymouth Rock and Jamestown and Ellis Island,
> And worlds of men with hungers of body and soul
> Hazarded the wilderness of waters,
> Cadenced their destinies
> With the potters'-wheeling miracles
> Of mountain and valley, prairie and river.[102]

Tolson's critique of American symbols is directed against their exclusiveness that he tries to break (unhinging Aldrich's "gates") by the listing of many points of entry. The Whitmanian conflation of old and new national symbols reaches a higher pitch when Tolson explicitly makes a special place for those groups (such as Indians) not included by the "Plymouth Rock and Ellis Island" formula, when blind bigots are rebuked for their prejudices, or when the question "America?" is answered in the following way:

> America is the Black Man's country,
> The Red Man's, the Yellow Man's,
> The Brown Man's, the White Man's.
> America?
> An international river with a thousand tributaries!
> A magnificent cosmorama with myriad patterns and colors!
> A giant forest with loin-roots in a hundred lands!
> A mighty orchestra with a thousand instruments playing
> *America!*[103]

Tolson worries about inadequacies in the image of the Statue of Liberty; yet his poem, written upon the occasion of Pearl Harbor, sees this inadequacy in a tranquilized Uncle Sam's lack of watchfulness: he "Pillows his head on the Statue of Liberty."[104] In his harmonic vision of a polyethnic America the shadow of one enemy—Japan—remains (though Tolson does mention "Patriots from Yokosuka and Stralsund" in one of his melting-pot catalogues).[105] In a similar vein, the post–Pearl Harbor *Life* magazine carried the American flag on the cover, while the issue was full of anti-Japanese materials. Perhaps the Japanese enemy image may even have helped with the project of integrating red, black, and white.

The incorporating mood of the depression and war years affected even politically radical writers such as Richard Wright. He did not only publish radical American paeans such as "Transcontinental,"[106] but he also let his character Boris Max, the communist lawyer, defend the black murderer Bigger Thomas in the novel *Native Son* with the plea: "In him and men like him is what was in our forefathers when they first came to these strange shores hundreds of years ago. We were lucky. They are not."[107] When Wright was invited to go to France shortly after World War II and repeatedly denied a passport, however, he sounded a different note. His friends, among them the painter Marc Chagall, appealed to the French cultural attaché Claude Lévi-Strauss, and Wright received an official invitation by the French government and, finally, after much more maneuvering, a US passport, too. In an allusion to the classic Ellis Island scene, Wright described his emotions in the essay "I Choose Exile": "I felt relieved when my ship sailed past the Statue of Liberty!"[108] The feeling is familiar, except that Wright was *leaving* the United States, for France! A few years later Wright described the American Negro as "an American who is not accepted as an American, hence a kind of negative American."[109]

Exclusion of any group from national symbolism may generate not only the insistent argument for the group's compatibility with those symbols but also a rejection of such symbols. This rejection may also be undertaken with the intention of facilitating an ultimate integration on equal footing. Wright's ironic reversal of interpreting the Statue of Liberty was not a unique occurrence. Thus, Du Bois—whose analysis of double-consciousness as "an American, a Negro" is often cited—described in his *Autobiography* how, upon returning from Europe in 1894 on an immigrant ship, he saw the Statue of Liberty: "I know not what multitude of emotions surged in the others, but I had to recall [a] mischievous little French girl whose eyes twinkled as she said: 'Oh yes the Statue of Liberty! With its back toward America, and its face toward France!'"[110] Though both Du Bois and Wright tilted the interpretation of the statue from the "immigrant" toward the "Franco-American" reading—that they, however, slanted toward French liberty—neither of them drew on Whittier's connection between the Statue of Liberty and slavery.

The strategy of paradoxically associating the Statue of Liberty with political tyranny is, of course, a politically radical as much as an ethnic device. Thus, Emma Goldman may have misremembered her happy arrival in American *with* the Statue of Liberty precisely in order to build up a more dramatic contrast between what "the generous heart of America" meant to her when she arrived and her political imprisonment—she highlights a Fourth of July in prison—before she was ultimately deported from Ellis Island in 1919.[111] Seeing the "revolutionary martyrs being driven into exile" she asks whether this was Russia, only to answer: "But no, it was New York, it was America, the land of liberty! Through the port-hole I could see the great city receding into the distance, its sky-line of buildings traceable by their rearing heads. It was my beloved city, the metropolis of the New World. It was America, indeed, America repeating the terrible scenes of tsarist Russia! I glanced up—the Statue of Liberty!"[112] And Ellis Island could be used explicitly to incorporate African Americans, too. Thus, the black former congresswoman Barbara Jordan, together with Frank Sinatra, was awarded the Ellis Island Medal of Honor by the Statue of Liberty-Ellis Island Foundation;[113] Alex Haley was posthumously honored with the same medal, along with a most amazing lineup of winners: Natalie Cole, Norman Schwarzkopf, Connie Chung, Elie Wiesel, Strom Thurmond, and Arnold Schwarzenegger.[114]

It was during World War II and in the Supreme Court decisions and Civil Rights bills of the 1950s and 1960s that the term "American" actually became intertwined with ethnicity and flexible enough to include—in widely accepted public and official usage—such groups as immigrants, African Americans, and American Indians. Minorities have moved into the center of the cultural industry, and the metaphor of the "invading hordes" seems to have fallen into disfavor. The growth of a more flexible term for an American national identity thus *seems* to be a success story. Yet it is not only that, and the hymnic synthesis invoked by some poets has hardly become an American reality. After all, the successful expansion of the term "America" came about only in the heated debates about national loyalty generated by two world wars and after immigration had been severely limited along racial categories. The broad notion of "America" has never really included everybody, all the arguments for compatibility notwithstanding; and the inclusive use of "American" remains ambiguous even today. Xenophilic cosmopolitanism may have helped to alienate some liberal intellectuals from people other than those in distinct ethnic groups and encouraged some conservatives to embrace racism and anti-intellectualism with less restraint. The educational system confronts tough debates over *which* American culture should be taught to children and adolescents. The battle for "America" continues, and there are today more contradictory notions and definitions of what is or ought to be "American" than there are views of the Statue of Liberty.

FIGURE 3 Two-dollar bill. 1995. Design taken from John Trumbull's 1819 painting *Declaration of Independence, July 4, 1776*.

3

Dedicated to a Proposition

What an admirable place for a Declaration of something! What could one here—what *couldn't* one really declare? [. . .] I say, why not our Independence?—capital thing always to declare, and before any one gets in with anything tactless. You'll see that the fortune of the place will be made.
—Henry James at Independence Hall, *The American Scene* (1907)[1]

In 1970, the American-born Frederic Rzewski created a startling composition for piano and voice. Recorded at Cologne's radio station WDR, it is entitled *Jefferson*, and the whole piece is set to the text of the Declaration of Independence from "When in the course of human events" to "guards for their future security," rendered as a soprano solo performed by Carol

SOURCE *America in the Course of Human Events*, ed. Josef Jařab, Marcel Arbeit, and Jenel Virden. Amsterdam: VU Press, 2006, 13–38.

Plantamura, that makes the most familiar phrases from the Declaration sound fresh and startling. The somewhat radical Rzewski, whose political œuvre also includes music set to Bertolt Brecht's *Antigone-Legend* as well as the thirty-six piano variations on the theme of the Chilean chant "El pueblo unido jamás será vencido" (A people united will never be defeated), studied in the United States and Italy and has been associated with John Cage and the MEV (Musica Elettronica Viva) group; since 1977, he has been professor of composition at the Conservatoire Royal de Musique in Liège, and he has also taught at numerous institutions in the United States as well as in Holland and Germany.

The Declaration of Independence

> The course of human events [. . .] separate and equal station. [. . .] We hold these truths to be self-evident [. . .] all men are created equal [. . .] certain inalienable rights [. . .] life, liberty, and the pursuit of happiness [. . .] the consent of the governed [. . .] the right of the people to alter or abolish [. . .] duty to throw off such government.

The short opening invoking the principles of the Declaration of Independence may be the best-known piece of American prose. Phrases from it have been recited, echoed, varied upon, used as social criticism, and have themselves been criticized throughout the past two and a quarter centuries. Fourth-of-July speeches have quoted from it and the key phrases are known to every school child in the United States of America.

Though the declaration emerged in a draft from a committee, it was Thomas Jefferson who left his decisive rhetorical imprint on the text. As Pauline Maier has written, Jefferson drew on much popular philosophy apparently from memory, and he used the musical *style périodique*, in which the meaning of longer sentences becomes apparent only at the very end. Though Jefferson was not a good orator and had to mark up the text heavily for oral delivery, it was an excellent piece of rhetorical writing. A good playwright need not be an actor, too, Maier comments.

Jefferson described the writing of the Declaration in a letter of 1825 as an attempt:

> Not to find out new principles, or new arguments never before thought of, not merely to say things which had never been said before; but to place before

> mankind the common sense of the subject, in terms so plain and firm as to command their assent. [. . .] Neither aiming at originality of principle or sentiment, nor yet copied from any particular and previous writing. It was intended to be an expression of the American mind.[2]

The single-sentence opening the Declaration, Maier says, "immediately conveyed a sense of epic importance. It suggested, without saying so directly, that the emergence of the American people to a 'separate and equal' station among 'the powers of the earth' was an event of note 'in the course of human events' on which, of course, mankind would have an opinion."[3] Maier points out that this view of history from up high "must have offered some consolation to soldiers [who] [. . .] were caught in a rather grubby, hand-to-mouth defense effort, with insufficient guns, ammunition, or food, and would soon be thrown against the most impressive army and fleet they'd ever laid their eyes upon."[4]

Jefferson changed and shortened the drafting committee's proposed document. "When in the course of human events" was already the opening of the draft, but what followed was the clumsy phrasing, "it becomes necessary for a people to advance from that subordination in which they have hitherto remained, and to assume." The passage "certain inherent natural rights, of which they cannot, by any compact, deprive or divest their posterity" became simply "inherent & inalienable rights" (the printer turning "inalienable" into the then apparently more popular form "unalienable"). Also, "the enjoyment of life and liberty, with the means of acquiring and possessing property, and pursuing and obtaining happiness and safety" turned into the more resonant and memorable phrase, "life, liberty & the pursuit of happiness."[5]

Jefferson also agreed to a number of cuts, the longest one of which concerned a passage about slavery in the long list of grievance against abuses of the present king of England:

> [H]e has waged cruel war against human nature itself, violating it's most sacred rights of life & liberty in the persons of a distant people, who never offended him, captivating & carrying them into slavery in another hemisphere, or to incur miserable death in their transportation thither. This piratical warfare, the opprobrium of *infidel* powers, is the warfare of the *Christian* king of Great Britain. Determined to keep open a market where MEN should be bought & sold, he has prostituted his negative for suppressing

> every legislative attempt to prohibit or to restrain this execrable commerce: and that this assemblage of horrors might want no fact of distinguished die, he now is now exciting those very people to rise in arms amongst us, and to purchase that liberty of which *he* has deprived them, by murdering the people upon whom *he* also obtruded them: thus paying off former crimes committed against the *liberties* of one people, with crimes he urges them to commit against the *lives* of another.[6]

Writing in his autobiography almost fifty years later, Jefferson remembered the debate that led to the omission of this passage:

> The clause [. . .] reprobating the enslaving the inhabitants of Africa, was struck out in complaisance to South Carolina and Georgia, who had never attempted to restrain the importation of slaves, and who on the contrary still wished to continue it. Our northern brethren also I believe felt a little tender under those censures; for tho' their people have very few slaves themselves yet they had been pretty considerable carriers of them to others.[7]

The signing of the Declaration in the Pennsylvania State House on July 4, 1776, was celebrated as an important historical act; and John Trumbull's gigantic (12' x 18') painting of 1819 memorializes this ritual moment for posterity. (There are several versions of it, including a smaller rendition that is now in the Yale University Art Museum.). The official interpretation on the Office of the Architect of the Capitol website reads in part: "The painting features the committee that drafted the Declaration of Independence—John Adams, Robert Sherman, [Robert Livingston,] Thomas Jefferson (presenting the document), and Benjamin Franklin—standing before John Hancock [seated], the President of the Continental Congress. The painting includes portraits of 42 of the 56 signers and 5 other patriots. The artist sketched the individuals and the room from life."[8] The painting was reproduced numerous times: the Post Office, for example, put it, in color, on four consecutive thirteen-cent stamps for the Bicentennial in 1776; and the Mint placed Trumbull's image, in engraved shades of green, on the back of the rarely used 1995 two-dollar bill. (See Figure 3; it is a bill that shows Jefferson on the front.)

What did it mean that this Declaration presented as a "self-evident truth" that "all men are created equal" and that, at the same time, the critique of slavery—that institution most clearly aimed at perpetuating inequality—was omitted in the final version? What did the Declaration mean for American slaves?

In the wonderfully sharp and pointed essay "A Little Revenge from the Periphery" (1998), Jamaica Kincaid contemplated the Declaration and Trumbull's painting of the signing in the following way:

> America begins with the Declaration of Independence, the most important clue to the character of Americans as a people. It is true what everybody says: it is a remarkable document, seeming to be divinely inspired, and no one who reads it can fail to be moved by it. But who really needs this document, the Declaration of Independence?
>
> There is a painting [. . .] of the men who signed it. These men are relaxed; they are enjoying the activity of thinking, the luxury of it. They have the time to examine this thing called their conscience and to act on it. They need to feel compromised because they do not need to compromise. They are wonderful to look at. Some keep their hair in an unkempt style (Jefferson, Washington), and others keep their hair well groomed (Franklin). Their clothes are pressed, their shoes polished; nothing about their appearance is shameful. Can they buy as much land as they like? Can they cross the street in a manner that they would like? Can their children cleave to their breast until death, or until the children simply grow up and leave home? The answer is yes. They can do whatever they want. The fact is, there isn't anything we can do today that they could not do then, and we consider ourselves a free people. We consider ourselves such an example of free people-ness that we kill other people in the world if we find that they can't agree to our present idea of free-people-ness. So who needs this document [. . .] ?[9]

Jamaica Kincaid quotes from the declaration, reiterates her question, and moves toward her answer:

> Who needs this document? The people sitting around the table, with their nice hair, their well-pressed suits, their nice warm homes, their supine wives, their even more supine concubines, their ability to cause suffering and to alleviate suffering, or the people who made the physical, material existence of the people sitting around the table possible? The people outside the picture could not decide on the style of their hair, they could not buy clothes that fit some idea they had of their own personality. [. . .] The solemnity of this occasion, the signing of this missive to the Toy Tyrant George III, must have seemed

> humorous to the person who had just styled Ben's and George's hair. He or she might have broken into sidesplitting laughter at the thought of these people being regarded as the Founding Fathers, for surely these people (the ones in the picture, the ones whose signatures follow the missive to the Toy Tyrant) would have seemed as nothing so much as ventriloquists, the Founding Father Ventriloquists, for their powerful feelings about their situation bore no resemblance to reality. The Declaration of Independence was not about them; it was about the people who were in their midst, it was about the people they held in bondage, it was about the existence of their slaves.[10]

After quoting Jefferson's omitted paragraph about slavery, she comments

> I can so well imagine the situation: his fellow ventriloquists, when coming upon this paragraph, took him into a room, a room in which they could not hear their own consciences, and said to him, "Tom, Tom, are you nuts? The one good thing King George has done—made the seas safe for the slave trade, which makes our high-minded insights into the subjugation of others and our feelings of goodwill toward each other possible—you are calling a crime." And this: "Tom, you can't be left alone in a room with words. You get so carried away."[11]

Jamaica Kincaid's hovering over the scene of the signing, her emphasis on the omitted passage about slavery and her persistent questioning of who needed this declaration comes after two centuries of reflections upon and creations in response to Jefferson's Declaration, some examples of which I shall be presenting here. There was, as Jamaica Kincaid suggests, a disjunction between the text's self-evident truth and the country's continued practice of racial slavery.

Freedom Suits and the American Paradox

Some Massachusetts slaves seem to have acted on the cognitive dissonance that their status meant in the light of the fact that the Declaration did say that "all men are created equal" (a phrasing that was adopted in the Massachusetts constitution). The result was the filing of a number of freedom suits, legal cases in which slaves, their lawyers, or a judge invoked the egalitarian language of the Declaration in order to achieve a legitimation of the status of free people.

In a series of cases involving Quok Walker, the Massachusetts courts had to decide on Walker's status. Walker was a slave who had run away from his master, Nathaniel Jennison of Barre, and was working for John and Seth Caldwell. When Jennison saw and recognized Walker, he beat him, took him home, and locked him up. The Worcester Court of Common Pleas ruled in Walker's favor: he was not a slave, and Jennison had no right to hold him against his will. When Jennison appealed, the Supreme Judicial Court dismissed it, ruling that Quok Walker was free and could work for the Caldwells. In a later criminal case concerning only Jennison's assault, one of the five judges, Chief Justice Washington Cushing "in his charge to the jury, stated that in his opinion the clause of the constitution which declared all men to be free and equal clearly abolished slavery."[12] As Arthur Zilversmit has shown, it remains somewhat unclear whether this decision constituted a ruling on the constitutionality of slavery.

Other Massachusetts freedom suits followed. In Berkshire County, Elizabeth Freeman, also known as Mumbet, sued her owner, John Ashley, for freedom. The novelist Catherine Sedgwick later wrote about the background of that suit: Elizabeth Freeman

> chanced at the village "meeting house," in Sheffield, to hear the Declaration of Independence read. She went the next day to the office of Mr. Theodore Sedgewick, then in the beginning of his honourable political and legal career. "Sir," said she, "I heard that paper read yesterday, that says, "all men are born equal, and that every man has a right to freedom. I am not a dumb critter; won't the law give me my freedom?" I can imagine her upright form, as she stood dilating with her fresh hope based on the declaration of an intrinsic, inalienable right. Such a resolve as hers is like God's messengers—wind, snow and hail—irresistible.
>
> Her application was made to one who had generosity as well as intelligence to meet it. Mr. Sedgewick immediately instituted a suit in behalf of the extraordinary plaintiff; a decree was obtained in her favour. It was the first practical construction in Massachusetts of the declaration which had been to the black race a constitutional abstraction, and on this decision was based the freedom of the few slaves remaining in Massachusetts.[13]

The Court of Common Pleas ruled in favor of Freeman but without giving a basis for the decision; and as Zilversmit concludes, there is "no evidence that any of the freedom suits established that slavery *per se* was illegal."[14]

The Declaration did matter a great deal for the most radical African American pre-Civil War writer, the North Carolina-born David Walker who had come to Boston and whose *Appeal, in Four Articles; Together with a Preamble, to the Coloured Citizens of the World, but in Particular, and Very Expressly, to Those of the United States of America* (1829, republished 1848) explicitly invoked and cited at length the Declaration of Independence and chastised white Americans in no uncertain terms for their hypocrisy.

> See your Declaration Americans!! Do you understand your own language? Hear your language, proclaimed to the world, July 4th, 1776—"We hold these truths to be self evident—that ALL MEN ARE CREATED EQUAL! *that they are endowed by their Creator with certain unalienable rights; that among these are life, liberty, and the pursuit of happiness!!*" Compare your own language above, extracted from your Declaration of Independence, with your cruelties and murders inflicted by your cruel and unmerciful fathers and yourselves on our fathers and on us—men who have never given your fathers or you the least provocation! ! !
>
> Hear your language further! "But when a long train of abuses and usurpations, pursuing invariably the same object, evinces a design to reduce them under absolute despotism, it is their *right*, it is their *duty*, to throw off such government, and to provide new guards for their future security."
>
> Now, Americans! I ask you candidly, was your sufferings under Great Britain, one hundredth part as cruel and tyrannical as you have rendered ours under you? Some of you, no doubt, believe that we will never throw off your murderous government and "provide new guards for our future security." If Satan has made you believe it, will he not deceive you?[15]

Frederick Douglass sounded by far more conciliatory when he turned the disparity between the words of the Declaration of Independence and the continued existence of slavery—nearly twenty years after England had abolished it—into a political ritual. Invited to speak in the chichi Corinthian Hall in Rochester on July 4, 1852, Douglass refused to appear on the national holiday itself and chose, instead, the fifth of July, on which he shamed his audience of mostly female antislavery activists and Douglass fans and sympathizers (the Rochester Ladies' Anti-Slavery Society) to wish for Douglass's inclusion in the promise made by the Declaration: "WHAT TO THE SLAVE IS THE FOURTH OF JULY?" he asked right in the title of his address when he reprinted it in the second edition of his *Autobiography*.

> Fellow-Citizens—Pardon me, and allow me to ask, why am I called upon to speak here to-day? What have I, or those I represent, to do with your national independence? Are the great principles of political freedom and of natural justice, embodied in that Declaration of Independence, extended to us? and am I, therefore, called upon to bring our humble offering to the national altar, and to confess the benefits, and express devout gratitude for the blessings, resulting from your independence to us?[16]

And following the exordium in which Douglass briefly goes through the topos of modesty, he comes right to the point.

> I am not included within the pale of this glorious anniversary! Your high independence only reveals the immeasurable distance between us. The blessings in which you this day rejoice, are not enjoyed in common. The rich inheritance of justice, liberty, prosperity, and independence, bequeathed by your fathers, is shared by you, not by me. The sunlight that brought life and healing to you, has brought stripes and death to me. This Fourth of July is *yours*, not mine. You may rejoice, I must mourn. To drag a man in fetters into the grand illuminated temple of liberty, and call upon him to join you in joyous anthems, were inhuman mockery and sacrilegious irony. Do you mean, citizens, to mock me, by asking me to speak to-day? [. . .]
>
> Fellow-citizens, above your national, tumultuous joy, I hear the mournful wail of millions, whose chains, heavy and grievous yesterday, are to-day rendered more intolerable by the jubilant shouts that reach them. If I do forget, if I do not faithfully remember those bleeding children of sorrow this day, "may my right hand forget her cunning, and may my tongue cleave to the roof of my mouth!" To forget them, to pass lightly over their wrongs, and to chime in with the popular theme, would be treason most scandalous and shocking, and would make me a reproach before God and the world. My subject, then, fellow-citizens, is AMERICAN SLAVERY. I shall see this day and its popular characteristics from the slave's point of view. Standing there, identified with the American bondman, making his wrongs mine, I do not hesitate to declare, with all my soul, that the character and conduct of this nation never looked blacker to me than on this Fourth of July. Whether we turn to the declarations of the past, or to the professions of the present, the conduct of the nation seems equally hideous and revolting. America is false to the past, false to the present, and solemnly binds herself to be false to the future. Standing with God and the crushed and bleeding slave on this occasion, I will, in the name

> of humanity which is outraged, in the name of liberty which is fettered, in the name of the constitution and the bible, which are disregarded and trampled upon, dare to call in question and to denounce, with all the emphasis I can command, everything that serves to perpetuate slavery—the great sin and shame of America![17]

Yet Douglass does not end on a fire-and-brimstone note. Instead he looks forward to progress in the technological advances of the nineteenth century. "Thoughts expressed on one side of the Atlantic are, distinctly heard on the other," he told his audience, which was probably receptive for the Rochester bourgeoisie was heavily invested in such new fields as telegraph development. Most especially, he returned to the Declaration:

> Allow me to say, in conclusion, notwithstanding the dark picture I have this day presented of the state of the nation, I do not despair of this country. There are forces in operation, which must inevitably work the downfall of slavery. "The arm of the Lord is not shortened," and the doom of slavery is certain. I, therefore, leave off where I began, with hope. While drawing encouragement from the Declaration of Independence, the great principles it contains, and the genius of American Institutions, my spirit is also cheered by the obvious tendencies of the age.[18]

More than one reader has referred to this speech as a jeremiad in which Douglass made the very document that had excluded the indictment of slavery the groundwork of a hope for a future that would live up to the letter of the Declaration.

Douglass also included in his newspaper *Frederick Douglass's Paper* a sarcastic comment from the *Oneida Telegraph*, which once again went for the disparity between the Declaration and American racism and mocked a racist opponent to the very idea that Douglass, a "partly black" man, could be editing a newspaper:

> We can give no sort of countenance to the idea of a *nigger* endeavoring to assume an equal position with the rest of us. "We hold these truths to be self-evident; that all men are created equal," (except niggers;) "that they are endowed by their Creator with certain unalienable rights; that to secure these rights governments are instituted among men, deriving their just powers from *the consent of the governed*," (except the niggers aforesaid).[19]

Type scenes of a slave auction that contrast with symbols of American egalitarian ideals became common in abolitionist writing, among them the first African American novel, *Clotel; or, The President's Daughter* (1853), written by runaway slave William Wells Brown who uses the central passage of the Declaration as the book's general motto, right on the title page.

Clotel also drew on a long tradition of taking Jefferson to task specifically, not only for being a slaveholding egalitarian in the abstract, but also as the author of the Declaration of Independence who reputedly fathered slave children. The story of Jefferson's relationship with Sally Hemings was in the headlines again in connection with the DNA analysis of Jefferson's "black" descendants. In Brown's *Clotel*, Jefferson leaves his beloved slave woman (here called Currer) in order "to fill a government appointment"[20] and fails to provide legal recognition for her or for their children, exposing them to the extraordinary cruelties of slavery. The narrator exclaims pointedly that "two daughters of Thomas Jefferson, the writer of the Declaration of American Independence, and one of the presidents of the great republic, were disposed to the highest bidder!"[21] This Founding Father's double family story was, for antislavery activists and readers, a representative national allegory, an embodiment of the American paradox that an egalitarian republic could also be a slave-holding state.

This story had its origins in the Scotch adventurer James Thompson Callender's slander that was widely disseminated and cast into poetic form as early as 1807 by Thomas Moore, who wrote the lines:

> 'Tis evening now; beneath the western star
> Soft sighs the lover through his sweet cigar,
> And fills the ears of some consenting she
> With puffs and vows, with smoke and constancy.
> The patriot, fresh from Freedom's councils come,
> Now pleased retires to lash his slaves at home;
> Or woo, perhaps, some black Aspasia's charms,
> And dream of freedom in his bondsmaid's arms.[22]

Moore added a note that the "The 'black Aspasia' of the present --------- of the United States, inter Avernales haud ignotissima nymphas,[23] has given rise to much pleasantry among the anti-democrat wits in America."[24] It was easy to fill in the word "president." Henry Adams commented: "[T]o leave no doubt of his meaning, he [Moore] explained in a footnote that his allusion was to the President of the United States."[25]

Captain Frederick Marryat's *Diary in America* (1839) drew attention to Jefferson in a general critique of white slaveholders' failure to recognize their slave children when he wrote:

> I suspect that I have read more of Mr. Jefferson and other American authors than ever the Reviewer has; and I consider the writings of this Father of Democracy, opposed to his private life, to be a remarkable type of democracy in theory and in practice. To borrow a term from the Reviewer, those writings are "brave words" to proceed from an infidel, who proved his ardent love of liberty by allowing his own children to be put up to auction at his death, and wear away their existence in misery and bondage.[26]

The poem was authenticated by the following comment: "It is asserted, on the authority of an American newspaper, that the daughter of Thomas Jefferson, late President of the United States, was sold at New Orleans *for 1000 dollars*."[27]

What was the truth of all these stories? The historian Nathan Huggins argued some years ago: "The evidence is circumstantial; we will never get at a truth everyone will accept. Custodians of the Jefferson legacy seek to protect his historical reputation and demand substantial and irrefutable evidence." Yet Huggins continued boldly: "I venture to say that most black people *know* the rumors are essentially true despite gaps and problems with the evidence." Whether or not Callender's assertion was "*actually* true," the story was "*symbolically* true," and for a good reason: "Like other legitimizing myths, the Sally Hemings story ties a people to the founding of the nation, reinforcing birthright claims."[28] These claims—and their continued denial—have permeated the discussions about Jefferson and about presidents, sex, and race. Huggins saw in the "desire to merge national and racial identity into a single myth" the reason for the "compelling persistence of the story of Sally Hemings."[29]

Slavery was the central paradox in the country devoted to equality, numerous writers and activists harped upon it, and it remained such until Lincoln signed the Emancipation Proclamation in 1863—an act that prompted Frederick Douglass to think of January 1 as the new national holiday for blacks (even though emancipation was effective only in those areas of the United States that the Union troops did not control).

Students of today, however, are more easily struck by the emphasis on "men" in "all men are created equal"—even though that did not apparently deter Elizabeth Freeman from seeking her freedom on the basis of that phrase. Yet the exclusion of women from the text of the Declaration was as glaring as was the slavery paradox, and this disparity did not escape women in the first century of the republic. In fact, some readers have probably already been thinking about the Declaration of Sentiments in which the women's movement articulated its dissent—in the very language of the Declaration, sentence by sentence. Elizabeth Cady Stanton wrote the text and the Women's Rights Convention in Seneca Falls ratified it in July 1848. It opens in the familiar way:

> When, in the course of human events, it becomes necessary for one portion of the family of man to assume among the people of the earth a position different from that which they have hitherto occupied, but one to which the laws of nature and of nature's God entitle them, a decent respect to the opinions of mankind requires that they should declare the causes that impel them to such a course.
>
> We hold these truths to be self-evident: that all men and women are created equal.[30]

The list of grievances is prefaced by the general statement: "The history of mankind is a history of repeated injuries and usurpations on the part of man toward woman, having in direct object the establishment of an absolute tyranny over her."[31] Grievance # 1 is "He has never permitted her to exercise her inalienable right to the elective franchise."[32] This demand for suffrage passed only after Frederick Douglass had expressed his support.[33] Family law and education are also important aspects of the document. For example: "In the covenant of marriage, she is compelled to promise obedience to her husband, he becoming, to all intents and purposes, her master—the law giving him power to deprive her of her liberty, and to administer chastisement." And: "He has denied her the facilities for obtaining a thorough education, all colleges being closed against her."[34]

Were slaves, were women better off because of the original Declaration to which they could appeal? After all, it took eighty-seven years from the Declaration to emancipation from slavery and seventy-two years from the Declaration of Sentiments to women's suffrage in the United States. Sacvan Bercovitch argued that feminists of 1848 may have "believed that they were merely *using* patriotism, manipulating the rhetoric of the republic for ulterior radical ends." He continues: "But if so, they were miscalculating the relation of ends and means. In effect [. . .] they were conforming to a ritual of consensus that defused all issues in debate by restricting the debate itself, symbolically *and substantially*, to the meaning of America."[35]

Bercovitch sees feminists in a similar light as abolitionists and points to Douglass's fifth of July oration with its invocation of "America's 'destiny,' the 'sacred meaning' of July Fourth, and 'the genius of American institutions,' which would one day [. . .] transform the world [. . .] in 'all-pervading light'" [36]

Does the existence of a written declaration of basic human rights serve as a consensus-enforcing smokescreen, or does the disparity between text and practice create openings for activism, reform, and meaningful change? This may simply be a rephrasing of Jamaica Kincaid's question, "So who needs this document [. . .] ?"[37]

The Gettysburg Address

Perhaps the best-known political speech that the Declaration inspired was Abraham Lincoln's Gettysburg Address of November 19, 1863. Honoring the dead of the bloody Pennsylvania battlefield, Lincoln avoided such touchy issues as the still fresh Emancipation Proclamation and went straight to the Declaration of Independence instead.

What Rzewski did for Jefferson's Declaration, the contemporary composer David Diamond did for Lincoln's Address. In the finale of *This Sacred Ground* (1962), first performed at the centennial of the Gettysburg Address, Diamond set Lincoln's speech to a mixed and children's chorus, baritone solo, and orchestra. As does Rzewski, Diamond has had a bicontinental career in Europe and the United States. Born in the United States of Polish Galician immigrants, Diamond studied in Paris with Nadia Boulanger and later became friends with Aaron Copland. Diamond also lived in Italy for nearly fifteen years (and that is where he composed *This Sacred Ground*). He later served as Professor of composition at the Juilliard School.

> Four score and seven years ago [. . .] conceived in liberty [. . .] dedicated to the proposition [. . .] for us the living [. . .] a new birth of freedom [. . .]

> government of the people, by the people, for the people, shall not perish from the earth.

Like the wording of the Declaration, Lincoln's speech is full of well-known phrases, some of which have served as titles of novels. He uses the biblical (and popular nineteenth-century poetic "four score" rather than the prosaic "eighty") and speaks of a proposition, which is a hypothesis rather than the self-evident truth of the Declaration. Carolyn Porter stressed the extraordinary way Lincoln "adhered to a republican ideology rooted in the eighteenth century," defining the Civil War "simply, as a test of the initial claim of the Declaration of Independence."[38] Porter also notes that Lincoln's "one reference to God was added as he spoke: 'under God' does not appear in the original drafts."[39] The beauty and rhythm of the speech, its "simplicity and cleanness"[40] continue to impress readers.

Lincoln's speech, given at a somber moment in the deepest national crisis of the nineteenth century, was part of a rhetorical tradition in which the Declaration served many other writers, intellectuals, and activists as grounding.

Thus Herman Melville invoked the Declaration in order to remind the readers of *White-Jacket* (1850) that some of the most tyrannical English laws had been kept;[41] and Lydia Maria Child saw at the ending of *A Romance of the Republic* (1863) the fulfillment of the spirit of the Declaration with the end of slavery.[42] Whitman asked in the "Poem of Many in One" in the 1856 edition of *Leaves of Grass*: "Have you considered the organic compact of the first day of the first year of the independence of The States?"[43] and tried valiantly in the sermon-like "Respondez, Respondez" section of *Chants Democratic and Native American* (1860–1861) to give the word "inalienable" a poetic ring, as his prophecy "Let freedom prove no man's inalienable right! Every one who can tyrannize, let him tyrannize to his satisfaction!" is meant to challenge the reader to respond as one would to "Let murderers, thieves, bigots, fools, unclean persons, offer new propositions!"[44]

In the post–Civil War period, the American labor movement followed the abolitionists and the feminists in using the text of the Declaration as the model for manifestos. Philip Foner has collected an impressive number of such documents. In 1895, for example, Daniel De Leon published a "Declaration of Interdependence" of the Socialist Labor Party in the New York paper *The People*, which opens in the familiar vein: "When in the course of human progression, the despoiled class of wealth producers becomes fully conscious of its rights and determined to take them, a decent respect to the judgment of posterity requires that it should declare the causes which impel it to change the social order."[45] The "Declaration of Interdependence" speaks of "plutocracy" in analogy to the British crown, reminds readers that the "foundation of the Union was co-eval with the birth of the modern system of production by machinery" and that "the spirit of capitalism" soon manifested "its absorbing tendency and corrupting influence." The document deplores the "destruction of the middle class at an accelerating rate," resulting in growing unemployment, or "displacement, partly temporary, chiefly permanent, of the labor previously employed by the bankrupted firms."[46] Among the grievances cited was the charge that "even such a public calamity as war was turned by that selfish and unpatriotic class to its own enrichment"[47] and that the revolutionary promise of "liberty" meant only that "free scope was given to an economic system replete with injustice, pregnant with the seeds of domestic strife, destructive of every true element of happiness, and fatally tending toward class tyranny."[48] The "Declaration of Interdependence" is in part a meditation on the meaning of "property" (a word that had disappeared from precursor documents and become "the pursuit of happiness" in the Declaration): "From the fact that the instruments of production were the private property of individuals, the product itself was also the property of those individuals."[49] The frame of the source document is ultimately left behind, as the Socialist Labor declaration calls for an international socialist movement and ends with the exhortation: "Americans, fall into line! Onward to the Co-operative Commonwealth! To the industries the tools of industry; to the laborers the fruits of his labor; to mankind the earth!"[50] Many of the readers of the paper in which this manifesto appeared would have been immigrants; and we find another line of responses to the Declaration specifically articulated by immigrants who would often see the promise of the Declaration as a living reality, in sharp contrast to the hierarchical worlds they began to understand their countries of origin to be, and part of the lure of America.

Representative is "The Life Story of a Lithuanian" by Antanas Kaztauskis that was recorded by Ernest Poole and which opens the collection *The Life Stories of Undistinguished Americans As Told by Themselves* (1906). Before emigrating and finding work in the "in the cattle killing room"[51] of the Chicago stockyards, this Lithuanian listens to an old shoemaker who tells young men "to go where they can choose their own kind of God—where they can learn to read and write, and talk, and think like men—and have good things."[52] "Some day," he said, opening a newspaper banned by the Russian government, "I will be caught and sent to jail, but I don't care."

> Then he bent over the paper a long time and his lips moved. At last he looked into the fire and fixed his hair, and then his voice was shaking and very low:
>
> "We know these are true things—that all men are born free and equal—that God gives them rights which no man can take away—that among these rights are life, liberty, and the getting of happiness."[53]

The scene—there is a certain similarity here with the Elizabeth Freeman story as told by Catherine Sedgwick—has the feeling of a ritual; someone who is excluded from the American realm of "liberty" or still knows how to appreciate freedom of the press because he didn't have it in Lithuania reaffirms the principles of the Declaration that are all the more movingly endorsed, as the English-language reader encounters them in their retranslation from Lithuanian.

The effect of such story lines is a revitalization of what became known as the American Dream, as newcomers seemed so contagiously eager to live by the lofty principles that old-line Americans, who may have taken their liberties for granted, considered them unimportant, or simply ignored them, could not help but cheer the outsider or the newcomer on in rekindling the fire of enthusiasm for democracy.

The classic version of this immigrant vision is captured in the scene of a 1935 film by Leo McCary, *Ruggles of Red Gap* (1935), in which Charles Laughton plays the stone-faced and deferentially well-mannered English butler Marmaduke Ruggles. In a poker game in Paris, Lord Burnstead, his British employer, loses Ruggles to Egbert Floud, an uncultured Western cowboy from the state of Washington, whose snobbish wife, Effie, hopes that the presence of a formal British butler in their provincial home will raise their status. In the town of Red Gap, Ruggles is taken for a British colonel, however, and he does not mention to Prunella Judson, a woman whom he courts played by Zasu Pitts, what his real status is. This broad and often very funny comedy takes a serious and lofty turn when Ruggles is given a train ticket by a hypocritical villain figure who orders Ruggles to go back to England. Ruggles goes to the rowdy Silver Dollar Saloon where he meets his Egbert with the sympathetic "Ma" Pettingill and is soon joined by Prunella in a scene in which the English butler is the only one who knows "what Lincoln said," recites the entire Gettysburg Address, and then acts upon it by staying in America and starting his own business. This is the key scene of the movie, absent though it was from Harry Leon Wilson's 1908 novel by the same title, and it is followed by the American success story of "Bill" Ruggles's own restaurant, in which his former employer Lord Burnstead is one the first customers. The butler is not tempted to go back; he has learned to appreciate independence and free enterprise. It is hard to forget the serious undertone of the scene: Ruggles alone knows "what Lincoln said"—and the film leaves the *Blazing Saddles* atmosphere for a Depression-era (perhaps mildly anti-Fascist) democratic scene that is more in the manner of *It's a Wonderful Life*.

The totalitarian threat of the 1930s and 1940s seems to have provoked more responses to the Declaration and the Gettysburg Address, and the World War II years seem to have been particularly rich. A gouache and pen and ink on paper by William H. Johnson, entitled *Lincoln at Gettysburg II*, was created circa 1939–1942, and Johnson also drew in tempera and pen and ink with pencil on paper *George Washington Signing the Declaration of Independence* around 1942–1943 (both at the Smithsonian American Art Museum).

In 1943, Randall Thompson composed *Testament of Freedom* to words by Thomas Jefferson, and in the same year, Aaron Copland set *A Lincoln Portrait* to words by Carl Sandburg, spoken in a famous recording by Henry Fonda of *Young Mr. Lincoln* fame.

And also in 1943, Langston Hughes, still then in his radical leftist phase, published the longish poem "Freedom's Plow" that invoked the Declaration, Lincoln, and Frederick Douglass in order to make the case for more racial equality and social sharing. Hughes invokes America as the shared dream of freedom held by a long catalogue of workers of the land:

> Some were free hands
> Seeking a greater freedom,
> Some were indentured hands
> Hoping to find their freedom,
> Some were slave hands
> Guarding in their hearts the seed of freedom.
> But the word was there always:
> FREEDOM.[54]

These workers of the land and of the towns created America and the dream of freedom:

Out of labor—white hands and black hands—
Came the dream, the strength, the will,
And the way to build America.
[. . .]
A long time ago, but not too long ago, a man said:
ALL MEN ARE CREATED EQUAL [. . .]
ENDOWED BY THEIR CREATOR
WITH CERTAIN UNALIENABLE
RIGHTS [. . .]
AMONG THESE LIFE, LIBERTY
AND THE PURSUIT OF HAPPINESS.

His name was Jefferson. There were slaves then,
But in their hearts the slaves believed him, too,
And silently took for granted
That what he said was also meant for them.[55]

The poem, which repeatedly addresses the people, ends in an apotheosis of America:

Keep Your Hand On The Plow! Hold On!
That plow plowed a new furrow
Across the field of history.
Into that furrow the freedom seed was dropped.
From that seed a tree grew, is growing, will ever grow.
That tree is for everybody,
For all America, for all the world.
May its branches spread and shelter grow
Until all races and all peoples know its shade.
KEEP YOUR HAND ON THE PLOW!
HOLD ON![56]

As in the struggle against slavery, the critique of racial segregation was often phrased in terms of the Declaration, and Lincoln and the Lincoln Monument in Washington became important symbols in this struggle. At the dedication ceremony of the Monument in 1922, for example, Booker T. Washington's successor, Tuskegee president Robert Russa Moton gave a speech in front of a segregated audience in which he said (his original, much stronger text having been rejected by the Lincoln Memorial Commission) that in the South there are "found black men and white men who are working together in the spirit of Abraham Lincoln to establish in fact, what his death established in principle—that a nation conceived in liberty and dedicated to the proposition that all men are created equal, *can* endure."[57] And in one of his sarcastic chronicles of race relations, W. E. B. Du Bois wrote in *Phylon* in 1941 that a Georgia courthouse, "erected with taxpayers' money and dedicated to the proposition of meting impartial justice to all," had four elevators, one of which had a sign "For Colored Only" but was often "crowded with passengers, who do not believe in signs," whereas "Negroes who seek to ride the three other elevators are loudly rebuffed and embarrassed by the plainly hostile white operators."[58]

The single most influential study of American race relations of the 1940s, Gunnar Myrdal's *An American Dilemma* (1944), produced with the support of the Carnegie Foundation, "did not merely echo the view of American scholars" but offered, as the historian Walter A. Jackson has argued in his analysis of Myrdal's massive "study to end all studies," "an essentially new interpretation rooted in [Myrdal's] own experiences as a Swedish social scientist and policymaker."[59] Thus, "his critique of the denial of civil rights to blacks in the South was informed by his awareness of Hitler's destruction of constitutional government in Germany and the threat to the Swedish *rättstat* posed by the wartime emergency."[60] Myrdal, a foreign nonimmigrant economist and one of the "architects of the Swedish welfare state,"[61] was fascinated by what he called the "American Creed"—the ideological cement that seemed capable of holding together all the heterogeneity and dissimilarity and of forging a "strong unity in this nation" grounded in a "basic homogeneity and stability in its valuations."[62] "Americans of all national origins, classes, regions, creeds, and colors," Myrdal writes, "have something in common: a social *ethos*, a political creed."[63] This creed, a basic belief in liberty and equality, was shared across ethnic groups; the "Negro people in America are no exception to the national pattern."[64] It was deeply anchored in the Enlightenment roots of American history.[65] Myrdal found it "remarkable that a vast democracy with so many cultural disparities has been able to reach this unanimity of ideals and to elevate them supremely over the threshold of popular perception. Totalitarian Fascism and Nazism have not in their own countries—at least not in the short range of their present rule—succeeded in accomplishing a similar result, in spite of the fact that those governments, after having subdued the principal precepts most akin to the American Creed, have attempted to coerce the minds of their people by means of a centrally controlled, ruthless, and scientifically contrived apparatus of propaganda and violence."[66]

Myrdal succeeded in portraying the Creed as so universally shared that it could serve as the basis for changing the status quo of race relations because American racial "etiquette" was so obviously at variance with that Creed. Citing the "humanitarian idealism" of the Declaration of Independence, Myrdal agrees with Vernon L. Parrington that it "cannot be long ignored or repudiated, for sooner or later it returns to plague the council of practical politics. [...] Without its freshening influence our political history would have been much more sordid and materialistic."[67] This point raises an interesting possibility for a different line of research: What would America have been like without the Declaration of Independence? What might it be like if there were no more shared faith in the American Creed?

Myrdal was, one could say, a consensus activist who wanted to mobilize the ideological disparity he focused on in order to bring about social change for the better. As Jackson puts it, Myrdal "erroneously associated the birth of the United States with racial egalitarianism and portrayed the ideology of white supremacy as a nineteenth-century aberration from a national tradition that was fundamentally democratic."[68] This would help him, however, in opposing fatalist and do-nothing intellectuals and to "present racial liberalism as an attempt to recover the nation's democratic heritage."[69]

An American Dilemma can be said to embody both the war-time moment at which invoking national unity could be allied with a liberal call for fairly radical change and a sense of urgency that only grew in the 1950s when, as Roy Wilkins predicted, Myrdal's books "served as a bible for Americans concerned about racial injustice."[70] Myrdal's plea for the full inclusion of blacks into the American social system placed an emphasis on the damage that racial prejudice and discrimination did to blacks—and it is precisely for this emphasis, chosen to "shock white Americans into an awareness of the consequences of prejudice and discrimination," that Myrdal's approach would ultimately be faulted.[71]

Yet it was also this theory of the damage caused by racism (and particularly the demonstrable *black* damage) that inspired social scientists to attempt to change public policy, and that had the most palpable practical consequences. When Kenneth B. Clark testified in the 1951 *Briggs v. Elliott* case that the tested fact that black children preferred to play with white dolls showed that "segregation damaged the mental and emotional development of black children," and the "state of South Carolina was unable to find a prominent social scientist who would testify in favor of segregation."[72] And in the 1954 *Brown v. Board of Education* decision, Chief Justice Earl Warren famously cited Myrdal, Clark, E. Franklin Frazier, and other social scientists in support of the Court's ruling.

Undoubtedly, the culminating moment of the Civil Rights movement came on August 28, 1963, with the March on Washington, in which 200,000 participants rallied around the Lincoln Memorial, in the symbolic centennial year of Lincoln's Emancipation Proclamation, and urged the Kennedy administration to take a more active role in passing a general Civil Rights Act. The high point of the rally was Martin Luther King's "I Have a Dream" speech with its Gettysburg Address–inspired opening ("Fivescore years ago") and its explicit invocation of the Declaration of Independence, which King described as "a promissory note to which every American was to fall heir." King continued that this "note was the promise that all men [. . .] would be guaranteed the unalienable rights of life, liberty, and the pursuit of happiness. It is obvious today that America has defaulted on this promissory note in so far as her citizens of color are concerned." He spoke of the "marvelous new militancy" of the Negro community. And he very much argued along the lines of Myrdal's *American Dilemma*: "I still have a dream [. . .] that one day this nation will rise up and live out the true meaning of its creed—we hold these truths to be self-evident, that all men are created equal." He ended on a hopeful note: "When we allow freedom to ring, when we let it ring from every village and every hamlet, from every state and every city, we will be able to speed up that day when all of God's children—black men and white men, Jews and Gentiles, Catholics and Protestants—will be able to join hands and to sing in the words of the old Negro spiritual, 'Free at last, free at last; thank God Almighty, we are free at last.'"[73]

The Course of Human Events

This small sketch toward a tradition of reading and reenacting the language of the Declaration must remain open-ended, for there have undoubtedly been myriads of other poetic and artistic, political and polemical uses of Jefferson's words and of Lincoln's reiteration of them. Clarence Major's prose piece "TV" (1984), for example, contains snippets from both. Gregory Corso's poem "The American Way" (1970) proclaims: "Do I say the Declaration of Independence is old? / Yes I say what was good for 1789 is not good for 1960."[74] Lee Lozano produced a photolithograph in 1968 entitled "Thesis (All Men Are Hardly Created Equal)." Max Roach and Abby Lincoln's *Freedom Now Suite* ("We Insist!") reduces words to raw screams. Lawrence Ferlinghetti's poem "ONE THOUSAND FEARFUL WORDS FOR FIDEL CASTRO" (1967) uses "in the course of human events" as a refrain that recurs six times and informs the reader that "Honest Abe" was one of Fidel Castro's "boyhood heroes."[75] Joseph Schwantner composed, for speaker and orchestra, *New Morning for the World: "Daybreak of Freedom"* with Vernon Jordan reading from the words of Martin Luther King Jr. The line of Declaration-inspired manifestos continued, among other examples, with Henry Steele Commager's "A Declaration of Interdependence" (1975), an antiunilateralist summons with the opening, "When in the course of history the threat of extinction confronts mankind, it is necessary for the people of The United States to declare their interdependence with the people of all nations and to embrace those principles and build those institutions which will enable mankind to survive and civilization to flourish."[76] And Martin Espada wrote a witty poem "Thomas Jefferson and the Declaration of Food Stamps" that includes such lines as "I opened my booklet of food stamps / to see Thomas Jefferson / and the Founding Fathers / signing the Declaration of Independence / on every one dollar coupon" as well as the question to Thomas Jefferson: "Were you the inventor of the food stamp? / Did you give food stamps to Sally Hemmings [*sic*] [. . .]?"[77]

This is not to mention the mad world of websites where one can find, for example, a training manual for a cappella jazz groups that includes the following lesson:

> Each person in your a cappella jazz group should choose a phrase [. . .]; e.g., fourscore and seven years ago. [. . .] For your phrase, identify what syllables would be accented in normal speech, e.g., FOUR-score and SE-ven YEARS a-GO. Then practice repeating your phrase with the stress on syllables that are usually unaccented, e.g., four-SCORE and se-VEN years A-go. When all group members can say their phrases fluently, you are ready to make music.[78]

The most famous parodies of the two foundational texts are not only funny; by posing as "translations," they also drive home, even in their apparent irreverence, the rhetorical power of the originals. H. L. Mencken transposed the Declaration into "American": "When things get so balled up that the people of a country have to cut loose from some other country, and go it on their own hook, without asking no permission from nobody, excepting maybe God Almighty, then they ought to let everybody know why they done it, so that everybody can see they are on the level, and not trying to put nothing over on nobody. All we got to say on this proposition is this: first, you and me is as good as anybody else, and maybe a damn sight better; second, nobody ain't got no right to take away none of our rights; third, every man has got a right to live, to come and go as he pleases, and to have a good time however he likes, so long as he don't interfere with nobody else."[79]

The editor of *American Heritage* Oliver Jensen circulated a version of Lincoln's speech in "Eisenhowerese" that was perhaps written by the journalist Doris Fleeson:

> I haven't checked these figures but 87 years ago, I think it was, a number of individuals organized a governmental set-up here in this country, I believe it covered certain Eastern areas, with this idea they were following up based on a sort of national independence arrangement and the program that every individual is just as good as every other individual. Well, now, of course, we are dealing with this big difference of opinion, civil disturbance you might say, although I don't like to appear to take sides or name any individuals, and the point is naturally to check up, by actual experience in the field, to see whether any governmental set-up with a basis like the one I was mentioning has any validity and find out whether that dedication by those early individuals will pay off in lasting values and things of that kind.[80]

And Lord Buckley translated the Gettysburg Address into hip lingo: "Four big hits and seven licks ago, / our before-daddies swung forth upon this sweet groovey land / a jumpin', wailin', stompin', swingin' new nation, / hip to the cool sweet groove of liberty / and solid sent upon the Ace lick dat all cats and kiddies, / red, white, or blue, is created level in front."[81]

Instead of offering a conclusion, let me simply quote from the number "Abie Baby" from the 1968 production of the musical *Hair* (it is unfortunately not included in the movie version) that, written at the peak of the countercultural 1960s, suggests the long road that the self-evident truth and the proposition have traveled. Performed by Lorrie Davis, Donnie Burks, Lamont Washington and Ronnie Dyson, the broad, minstrel-parody opening with such lines as "I's free now, thanks to yo', Massa Lincoln, / Emancipator of the slave," gives way to an irreverent interruption of the word "emancipator": "Emanci, motherfuckin', pator of the slave, yeah yeah yeah."[82]

But what follows is another radical reenactment of the key phrases (wittily, the Shirelles' pop song "Dedicated to the one I love" interferes musically with the phrase "dedicated to the proposition"), and a radical rededication with the birthday wishes to Abie Baby:

> Fourscore . . . I said fourscore and seven years ago . . . oh, sock it to 'em, baby, you're soundin' better all the time! Our forefathers . . . I mean ALL our forefathers brought forth upon this here continent a newwwwwwww nation! Oh, come on, it's true! Rope me, Stokely! . . . Conceived . . . conceived, like we all was, in liberty and dedicated to the one I love. I mean dedicated to the proposition that alllllll men, honey, I tell you ALL men are created equal!
>
> Happy birthday, Abie, Baby, happy birthday to you. Yeah!
> Happy birthday, Abie, Baby, happy birthday to you.
> Bang!
> "Bang"?! Ha ha! "Bang"?! Shiiiiit, I'm not dyin' for no white man!
> Tell it like it is, baby!
> You tell 'im![83]

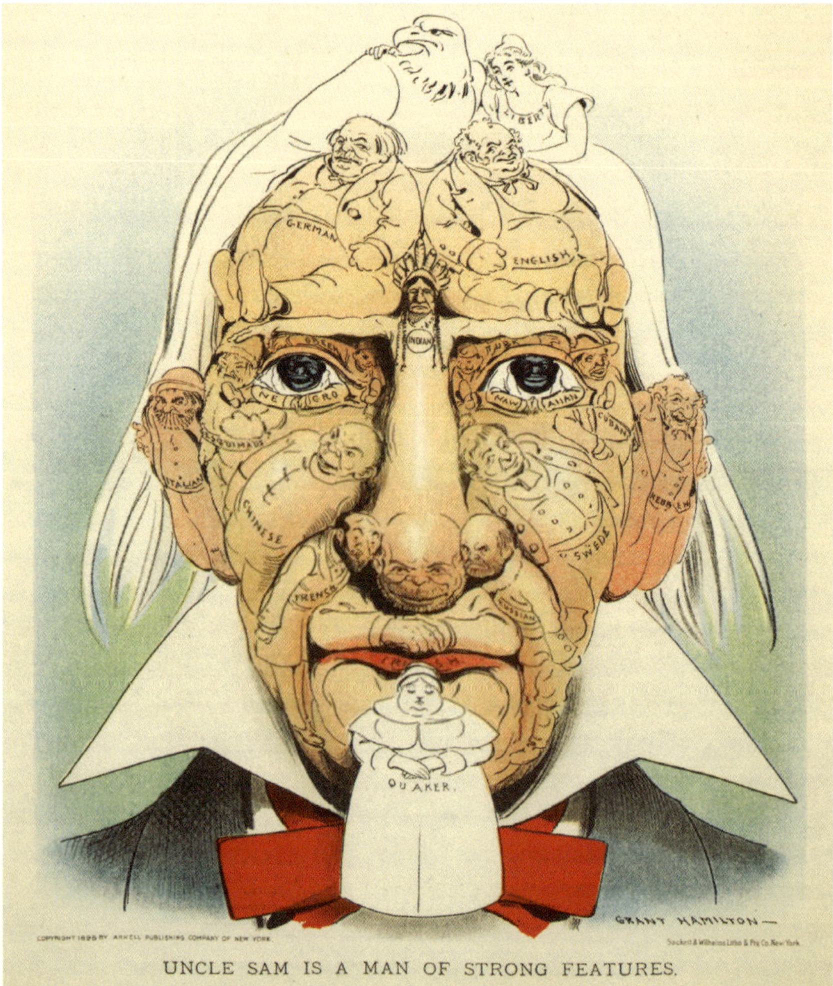

FIGURE 4 Grant E. Hamilton. *Uncle Sam Is a Man of Strong Features*. Cover of *Judge*, November 26, 1898. Billy Ireland Cartoon Library & Museum, Ohio State University.

4

A Critique of Pure Pluralism

> Men may change their clothes, their politics, their wives, their religions, their philosophies, to a greater or lesser extent: they cannot change their grandfathers.
> —Horace M. Kallen, "Democracy Versus the Melting-Pot" (1915)[1]

Reviewing the fifth edition of the *Oxford Companion to American Literature*, Joe Weixlmann praised the editor's effort to expand the coverage of black authors yet finds the volume's treatment of black, ethnic, female, and modern writers ultimately insufficient and wanting. Weixlmann concludes that "the old, venerable *Oxford Companion to American Literature*, despite its partial facelift, remains in its current incarnation, a product of such staid American and academic values as racism, sexism, traditionalism, and elitism."[2]

This identification of deplorable omissions with a scholar's bias is quite common in the current debates. Frequently an opposition is constructed between close-minded narrowness (sexism, racism, elitism) and the alternative of inclusive openness associated with what is often called "cultural pluralism." In his essay "Minority Literature in the Service of Cultural Pluralism," included in one of the several Modern Language Association readers on American ethnic literature that were published in the 1970s and 1980s, David Dorsey writes:

> Only from the diverse literatures can youth *feel* the meaning of the past. [. . .] At present diversity is everywhere tolerated in theory, punished in practice, and nowhere justified or justifiable beyond an appeal to solipsism. But America has no choice. Only a genuinely pluralistic society can henceforth prosper here. It must be nurtured in our diverse hearts. And for that we need literature, which is the language of the heart.[3]

In this scholarly drama of diversity and pluralism versus traditionalism and prejudice, there is emotion and prophecy just as there are heroes and villains. The editors of another MLA reader, *Ethnic Perspectives in American Literature* (1983), write:

> Ethnic pluralism, once the anathema to those who espoused the melting-pot theory, has become a positive, stimulating force for many in our country. [. . .] Transforming the national metaphors from "melting pot" to "mosaic" is not easy. Indeed, the pieces of that national mosaic have been cemented in place with much congealed blood and sweat. We must all continue to work at making the beauty of our multiethnicity shine through the dullness of racism that threatens to cloud it.[4]

Perhaps only surpassed by the "melting pot," the "literary canon" may hold a record as a contemporary scapegoat. Sometimes angrily described as the typical fiction of a rather malicious white male imagination, the canon has been seen as a central source of evil in literary scholarship, in ways not so different from the manner in which nineteenth-century nativists condemned "popery." Attacks on exclusionary canons of the past and their presumably bigoted institutionalizers have often been accompanied by arguments in favor of the assumed democratic openness of uncanonized and apocryphal texts. This has tended to produce sectarian and fragmented histories of American literatures (in the plural) instead of American literary history. The literary series that are constructed in new American historical narratives are sometimes single-sex and single-ethnic-group series. In the absence of a pope, what are we to do about the problem of the canon in rewriting American literary history? Let me raise some questions here.

Is exclusionary canonization merely a matter of bad attitude or of prejudice? Are we likely to produce a more comprehensive literary history if we are dutifully penitent of ethnoreligious, regional, and sexual biases? The example of Thomas Wentworth Higginson suggests that this is not necessarily the case. Though Higginson, a Civil War colonel in the first Negro regiment, can hardly be described as insensitive toward blacks, he never mentions Frederick Douglass's *Narrative* or any other African American text in his *Reader's History of American Literature* (1903).

Is lack of awareness the problem? Will we overcome our flaws and biases once we recognize them in other literary histories? Here the example of V. F. Calverton is discouraging; in *The Liberation of American Literature* (1932), Calverton includes a pretty strong antiexclusionary footnote:

> In this connection it is important to remark that, despite this interest in the Negro by many Southern writers and despite the rise of many Negro writers, the hostility felt for the Negro is just as active to-day in the South as it was twenty years ago. This hostility is just as pronounced in many ways in literature as in life. *In the sixteen-volume library of Southern Literature, for example, not a single Negro writer's work is included.* While the biographical section gives mention to Frederick Douglass, Booker T. Washington, and W.E.B. Du Bois, it does not quote a single selection from their works. Paul Laurence Dunbar is not even mentioned in the entire sixteen volumes. Needless to add, dozens of Southern writers whose works are greatly inferior to those of Douglass, Washington, and Du Bois are included, with ample space provided for their ofttimes inferior selections. Equally revealing is the fact that Professor Fred L. Pattee in his recent volume, *American Literature Since 1870*, does not even mention a single Negro writer, although he discusses hundreds of white writers, many of whose works are of no more than microscopical importance. Such promising Negro poets as Langston Hughes and Countee Cullen are not even mentioned in the index; Eddie Guest, on the other hand, is given two pages of discussion—and partial praise.[5]

Yet Calverton himself, aware though he was of the issue, never mentions Douglass (except in this footnote). Incidentally, despite his good anti-Southern intentions, Calverton adheres to an exoticist definition of

Negro art that views actual Negro poets as unfortunately Westernized compromisers of some *real* Negro spirit that seems to exist only outside of bourgeois forms. Dunbar, he tells us, "was at his best when he wrote in the language of his people and not in the language of the poets."[6]

Is it a matter of defining literature? If only we can define literature broadly enough, will we be able to be more catholic in writing literary history? Yet another Douglass example tells us that this is not necessarily the case. Arthur Hobson Quinn's *History of American Literature* (1951), which emphasizes non-belles-lettres writing throughout the periods, contains a huge chapter on "Literature, Politics, and Slavery" that fails to mention Douglass.

I have used *The Narrative of Frederick Douglass* (1845) as an example because it is so conspicuously absent from past literary histories—mentioned neither in Barrett Wendell's *Literary History of America* (1905) nor in Robert Spiller's *Literary History of the United States* (1947)—and yet so unavoidable a text in a literary history of our days. The case of its neglect illustrates that exclusionary canonization is not necessarily correlated to bias in the manner in which Calverton correlated Southern racism and the *Library of Southern Literature* and Weixlmann ascribed racism and sexism to the *Oxford Companion*. My three literary historians, Higginson, Calverton, and Quinn, would have found fuel for their basic contentions in Douglass's work, yet it did not enter their notions of a "canon."

One further example may suggest that this case is not an exception. Granville Hicks's *The Great Tradition* (1935) ignores Abraham Cahan's *The Rise of David Levinsky* (the inclusion of which would have strengthened Hicks' case), whereas the *Cambridge History of American Literature*—which started to appear virtually at the same time as Cahan's novel (1917)—does devote a paragraph to the book. Ironically, this paragraph appears in a section on Yiddish writing, yet the contributor points out that the English-language *Levinsky* far surpasses all Yiddish-American prose publications taken together. The apocryphal text *Levinsky* thus is excluded when it would support the argument, and discussed when it undermines the rationale for a chapter.

Mosaics from the Heart

Structuring or reconstructing an American literary canon is not necessarily a matter of good intentions or moral probity. Yet the contexts that are, consciously or unconsciously, accepted as guidelines for a massive history do influence our principles of inclusion, which are inevitably also principles of exclusion. The contemporary attacks on bigoted exclusionists—as we saw, prefigured by critics like Calverton—have encouraged the creation of new contexts according to previously excluded categories. The pluralistic demands are quite audible in discussions surrounding literary historiography. In an issue of the journal *MELUS*, Marco A. Portales makes a plea to give "Space" to "other literary Traditions" (and not only to Anglo-American writers) in order to arrive at a new type of American literary history,

> one that would detail the stories of writers who have not made it into the canon as the editors of the [*Literary History of the United States*] and their predecessors defined it, but who nevertheless are as American and the study of which would subtly serve not to continue divisions among our people, but to teach all of us to appreciate the rich cultural diversity that we *should* have been stressing since American Literature was brought into existence shortly before the turn of the century.[7]

It is Portales's declared (and laudable) intention to deprovincialize the teaching of American literature, but what is offered as the alternative is theoretically problematic. The proposal rests on the identification of assimilation with white Anglo-Saxon Protestant hegemony—which can thus be opposed in a wholesale fashion—and on the belief in "traditions" which just continue because of the power of descent. The remedy of "space" is seen in what might appear a very American way; not a finite outer limit of, say, a selective five-thousand-page history with certain minimal shares for different writers, but as a flexibly limitless and ultimately all-inclusive thing. Yet a literary history now could not be more inclusive than those of the past without being explicitly exclusive, too; and it is here that more theoretical statements have to be made to offset the unrealistic combination of pluralist faith and the idea of limitless space, which ethnic literature might traverse like Frederick Jackson Turner's frontier. Reference books will not just grow bigger and bigger in the near future, so we must think about the way limited space can be used to accommodate both new trends and traditional expectations. Of course, writers should not be excluded by virtue of race, region, or gender; but at the same time, should the very same categories on which previous exclusions were based really be used as organizing concepts? How, then, can literary histories become more responsive to the changes in canonization? How can they suit the needs of teachers of American literature and general readers?

The dominant assumption among serious scholars who study ethnic literary history seems to be that history can best be written by separating the groups that produced such literature in the United States. The published results of this "mosaic" procedure are the readers and compendiums made up of diverse essays on groups of ethnic writers who may have little in common except so-called ethnic roots while, at the same time, obvious and important literary and cultural connections are obfuscated. As James Dormon wrote in a review of such a mosaic collection of essays on ethnic theater, "there is little to tie the various essays together other than the shared theme 'ethnic American theater history,' as this topic might be construed by each individual author."[8] The contours of an ethnic literary history are beginning to emerge that views writers primarily as "members" of various ethnic and gender groups. James T. Farrell may thus be discussed as a pure Irish-American writer, without any hint that he got interested in writing ethnic literature after reading and meeting Abraham Cahan, and that his first stories were set in Polish America—not to mention his interest in Russian and French writing or in Chicago sociology. Or conversely, Carl Sandburg may be dismissed from the Scandinavian-American part of the mosaic for being "too American."

Taken exclusively, what is called "the ethnic perspective"—which often means, in literary history, the emphasis of a writer's descent—all but annihilates polyethnic art movements, moments of individual and cultural interaction, and the pervasiveness of cultural syncretism in America. The widespread acceptance of the group-by-group approach has not only led to unhistorical accounts held together by static notions of rather abstractly and homogeneously conceived ethnic groups but has also weakened the comparative and critical skills of increasingly timid interpreters who sometimes choose to speak with the authority of ethnic insiders rather than that of readers of texts. (Practicing cultural pluralism may easily manifest itself in ethnic relativism.)

Yet if anything, ethnic literary history ought to increase our understanding of the cultural interplays and contacts among writers of different backgrounds, the ethnic innovations and cultural mergers that took place in America; and the results of the critical readings should not only leave room for, but actively invite, criticism and scrutiny by other readers (outsiders or insiders) of the texts discussed. This can only be accomplished if the categorization of writers and literary critics as members of ethnic groups is understood to be a very partial, temporal, and insufficient characterization at best. Could not an openly transethnic procedure that aims for conceptual generalizations and historicity be more daring, profitable, and conceptually illuminating than that of simply adding to the sections on "major writers" chapters on "the popular muse," "Negro voices," "the immigrant speaks," "generations of women," "mingling of tongues," and the rest of it?

Is it possible now to rewrite Quinn's chapter and include Douglass, or do we need separate chapters for each ethnic group to be written by "insiders"? Can we construct a chapter on intellectual life in the early twentieth century in which ideas entertained by Anglo-American, Irish-American, Jewish-American, and African American figures can be discussed together, or do we have to separate men and women, immigrants and American-born authors? Is it possible to connect Alain Locke, who ended his introduction to *The New Negro* (1925) with the hope for "a spiritual Coming of Age"[9] with his Harvard classmate and author of *America's Coming of Age* (1915), Van Wyck Brooks, or are two heterogeneous ethnic experiences at work in them? These questions apply not only to the synchronic analysis of a period, but also to the construction of diachronic "descent lines." Do we have to believe in a filiation from Mark Twain to Ernest Hemingway, but not to Ralph Ellison (who is supposedly descended from James Weldon Johnson and Richard Wright)? Can Gertrude Stein be discussed with Richard Wright or only with white women expatriate German-Jewish writers? Is there a link from the autobiography of Benjamin Franklin to those of Frederick Douglass and Mary Antin, or must we see Douglass exclusively as a version of Olaudah Equiano and a precursor to Malcolm X? Is Zora Neale Hurston only Alice Walker's foremother? In general, is the question of influence, of who came first, more interesting than the investigation of the constellation in which ideas, styles, themes, and forms travel?

In order to pursue such questions, I have set myself a double task. I shall review significant criticisms of the shortcomings of the concept of cultural pluralism in the hope that the arguments made by intellectual historians may affect thinking about American literature; and I shall attempt to suggest the complexities of polyethnic interaction among some of the intellectuals who were involved in developing the term "cultural pluralism." It is ironic that the story of the origins of cultural pluralism I shall tell could not have been told in the "pluralistic mosaic" format of group-by-group accounts of American cultural life: one protagonist would illustrate what the current fashion calls "the Jewish experience," another "the black experience," a third "the white Anglo-Saxon Protestant experience." But the fact is that it was not any monoethnic "experience" that led to the emergence of the concept of cultural pluralism. It was the protagonists' troubled interaction with each other. Pluralism had a fairly monistic origin in a university philosophy department in the first decade of this century; yet it is a notion whose very mobility challenges the concept's central tenet of the permanent power of ethnic boundaries.

Ku Klux Pluralism?

From its inception, the term "pluralism" has been used contrastively against racist ogres. When Horace Meyer Kallen, apparently for the first time in print, used "Cultural Pluralism" in his essay collection *Culture and Democracy in the United States* in 1924, he offered his capitalized phrase as the redemptive alternative to a forced concept of hierarchical homogeneity as envisioned by the Ku Klux Klan:

> In manyness, variety, differentiation, lies the vitality of such oneness as they may compose. Cultural growth is founded upon Cultural Pluralism. Cultural Pluralism is possible only in a democratic society whose institutions encourage individuality in groups, in persons, in temperaments, whose program liberates these individualities and guides them into a fellowship of freedom and cooperation. The alternative before Americans is Kultur Klux Klan or Cultural Pluralism.[10]

In his opposition to racial myths and dreams of the Klan—which was newly revived after the success of *Birth of a Nation* (1915)—Kallen goes so far as to reject all concepts of American cultural cohesion as "Kultur Klux Klan," even nonracist and nonhierarchical ones such as the melting pot, the target of his most famous essay, "Democracy Versus the Melting-Pot." Kallen's antithetical spirit often manifested itself in such puns. In 1906 he disparaged "Cultur-Zionism";[11] and in 1930, invoking E. Boyd, he described Stuart Sherman as a "Ku Klux Kritic."[12] The phrase "cultural pluralism" was born in a literary polemic that equated all forms of assimilation and acculturation with hard-core racism. This rhetorical strategy is still operative in the many attacks on the melting pot today, attacks that silently identify melting pot and Anglo-conformity and that delight in antitheses.

When it comes to defining cultural pluralism positively (and not merely contrastively against hierarchically conceived notions of oneness), Kallen is lyrically evasive. His invocations of "the outlines of a possible great and truly democratic commonwealth" are vague to the point of contentlessness, unpolitical, and sustained by faith in musically harmonious diversity. Speaking about his ideal commonwealth, Kallen sets the tone for our continuing confusions with cultural pluralism:

> Its form would be that of the federal republic; its substance a democracy of nationalities, cooperating voluntarily and autonomously through common institutions in the enterprise of self-realization through the perfection of men according to their kind. The common language of the commonwealth, the language of its great tradition, would be English, but each nationality would have for its emotional and involuntary life its own peculiar dialect or speech, its own individual and inevitable esthetic and intellectual forms. The political and economic life of the commonwealth is a single unit and serves as the foundation and background for the realization of the distinctive individuality of each *natio* that composes it and of the pooling of these in a harmony above them all. Thus "American civilization" may come to mean the perfection of the cooperative harmonies of "European civilization"—the waste, the squalor and the distress of Europe being eliminated—a multiplicity in a unity, an orchestration of mankind. (*C.* 124)

The buzzwords that permeate today's ethnic discourse are all there, as a static notion of eternal groups—cast as pseudoindividuals—is made the basis of a lofty prophecy of an orchestrated American harmony. The abstract contrast with the squalor of Europe evokes little more than Walt Disney's International Village at Epcot Center with its permanent background music and country-of-origin waiters.[13]

Contrasted by Kallen against old-world hierarchies and squalor as well as monoethnic domination in America, cultural diversity appears as something redemptive in itself, as an ideal to maintain and preserve, though the survival of its ingredients seems threatened in America. Kallen and his successors assume that while the whole concert of cultural pluralism is open-ended, the stable quality of each instrument must be preserved. Kallen's definition of cultural pluralism rests on quasi-eternal, static units, on the "distinctive individuality of each *natio*" (*nationes* are thereby removed from the history of their own emergence), on "ancestry," "homogeneity of heritage, mentality and interest," and mankind's "psycho-physical inheritance." Kallen writes: "In historic times so far as is known no new ethnic types have originated, and from what is known of breeding there comes no assurance that the old types will disappear in favor of the new" (*C.* 119).[14] In an earlier essay he had argued: "To preach assimilation is to preach the absurd and is an unworthy abasement, possibly only to the spiritually degenerate."[15] Kallen's polemically antiassimilationist metaphors direct the pluralists' attention to unhistorical ethnic persistence rather than to historical change and to group survival rather than to group emergence (now termed "ethnogenesis"). Whereas the melting-pot image is eminently dynamic and accommodates the continuous processes of assimilation and ethnogenesis, both mosaic and orchestra are static.

At the root of cultural pluralism is a notion of the eternal power of descent, birth, *natio*, and race that Kallen shares with his worst antagonist, the racist E. A. Ross, against whom he polemicizes, but with whom he also agrees, sometimes explicitly (*C.* 119).[16] John Higham concluded that both the pluralist Kallen and the racist Ross "asserted that ethnic character was somehow rooted in the natural order."[17] Philip Gleason fully explored the racist component in Kallen's cultural pluralism, and his conclusions deserve the serious attention of cultural pluralists:

> Kallen's racialism was romantic in that he valued diversity as such and did not attempt to rank human groups as superior or inferior according to any absolute scale of racial merit. But he also resembled the romantics in attributing the distinctive characteristics of peoples to inborn racial qualities whose origin and nature were obscure. [. . .] Kallen's racialism was also central to his conviction that ethnic nationalities would perpetuate themselves indefinitely. [. . .] Kallen's whole handling of race was extremely ambiguous. He was certainly not a strict biological racist like Madison Grant, but neither did he systematically distinguish between biological and cultural elements in the manner of Franz Boas. [. . .] Kallen talked about "nationalities" as embodying this undifferentiated inheritance in such a way as to make it virtually impossible to determine which elements of an ethnic group's identity were genetically determined and which were culturally transmitted.
>
> Kallen never clarified these issues, and those who came after him in the pluralist tradition apparently failed to recognize them [. . .] and certainly failed

> to address them. Therefore the crucial role of Kallen's ambiguous racialist assumptions still constitutes a major theoretical problem in the cultural pluralist interpretation of ethnicity and American identity.[18]

The current polemics in the name of cultural pluralism notwithstanding, Kallen's concept was not even a good theoretical basis for inclusiveness. One would expect that Kallen's system was not exactly hospitable to the many melting-pot Americans, and he did write in 1906: "We have to crush out the [. . .] chameleon and spiritual mongrel. [. . .] For of all things, the realization of the race-self is the central thing."[19] Yet even within his racialist group-by-group approach, there was sufficient ethnic exclusiveness to deserve mention. Kallen's pluralist orchestra did not have any room for African Americans among others.[20] It could play neither *Shuffle Along* nor *Rhapsody in Blue*. As Isaac Berkson's *Theories of Americanization* (1920) illustrates, the shortcomings of cultural pluralism did not escape Kallen's contemporaries. Berkson perceptively remarked that Kallen's theory was "based on the assumption of the ineradicable and central influence of race."[21] It is worth reconsidering the intellectual foundations on which even some current claims for the American literary mosaic are made. By accepting Kallen's antiassimilationist bias that is so persuasively directed against the (equally antiassimilationist) Ku Klux Klan, the new ethnic literary historians may inadvertently become well-intentioned practitioners of Pluralism Klux Klan.

Another Look at the Origins of Cultural Pluralism

The term "cultural pluralism" first appeared in print in 1924, but this was long after Horace Kallen started using it conversationally. The story of the origins of the coinage "cultural pluralism," in part irrevocably lost and in part intriguingly suggestive, does little to detract from the theoretical criticism of the concept. However, it provides us with an exemplary tale of ideas crisscrossing not only ethnic lines but originating from and traversing the color line at the height of racism.[22]

The son of Esther Rebecca and Jacob David Kallen (a rabbi of the German-speaking Orthodox congregation Hevra ha-Moriah in Boston), Horace Kallen was born on August 11, 1882, in the German Silesian town Bernstadt and came to America at age five.[23] Kallen "felt close to his mother" but "was alienated from his father, whom he remembered as [. . .] proud, demanding, [and] domineering."[24] As a youngster, Kallen (like his contemporary, Mary Antin)[25] explored the Boston sites of American history textbooks, Bunker Hill and Tea Wharf, and later remembered the syncretistic overlay of Jewish and American lore in his mind:

> In our household the suffering and slavery of Israel were commonplaces of conversation; from Passover to Passover freedom was an ideal ceremonially reverenced, religiously aspired to. The textbook story of the Declaration of Independence came upon me, nurtured upon the deliverance from Egypt and the bondage in exile, like the clangor of trumpets, like a sudden light. What a resounding battle cry of freedom! And then, what an invincible march of Democracy to triumph over every enemy—over the English king, over the American Indian, over the uncivilized Mexican, over the American champions of slavery betraying American freedom, over everything, to the very day of the history lesson![26]

When Kallen entered Harvard at eighteen he was a religious renegade, thought of the Old Testament as a "narrow, bigoted" book (S. 38), and was ready to absorb the teachings of Josiah Royce, George Santayana, and most especially, of William James and Barrett Wendell—all of whom Kallen got to know well personally. One could sketch Kallen's interaction with all of these teachers (he even wrote poems about his philosophy professors), but a brief consideration of (Anglo-American) Wendell and a cursory reference to (Irish-American) James will suffice here.

Kallen remembered that Wendell emphasized "the role of the Old Testament as a certain perspective, a certain way of life. He showed how the Old Testament had affected the Puritan mind, traced the role of the Hebraic tradition in the development of the American character" (S. 38). Kallen reluctantly accepted the challenge of this approach:

> I was an alienated intellectual being suddenly challenged in his alienation. [. . .] And the challenge turned not on anything in the Hebraic tradition at all [but . . .] on what Americanism came to mean to me [. . .] in terms of the philosophical pluralism with which [William] James was identified and [. . .] in terms of the interpretation of the American tradition and the literary tradition of America by Barrett Wendell. [. . .] The [Zionist] meanings came to me rather in terms of the American Idea than in terms of what I had learned of *Torah* [Jewish law] at home or in *Cheder* [Hebrew school]. (S. 40)

The result was that in 1902 Kallen became a Zionist at Harvard, "where a Yankee, named Barrett Wendell, re-Judaized" him (S. 36). Sarah Schmidt's excellent analysis of Kallen's Judaization stresses the compatibility of his Zionism with what Wendell (echoing Theodore Parker) called "the American idea." "To be a Zionist was to be a good American" (S. 39). Kallen's activities in the Menorah Society and as a self-styled Zionist permitted him to have it two ways, "to retain," or, perhaps more accurately, to reinvent, "his Jewish identity and to become, thereby, a better American" (S. v). Americanization and ethnicization went hand in hand as Kallen developed a modern ethnic identity that continued to remain at odds with his father's traditional faith. Kallen's transformation can be seen in the context of what Herbert Gans has termed "symbolic ethnicity" that goes along with assimilation: Kallen absorbed concepts from the surrounding culture (the American idea) but gave it an ethnic name (the Jewish idea). Kallen's own life story illustrates Higham's generalization that pluralism "has unconsciously relied on the assimilative process which it seemed to repudiate."[27]

If Kallen's new outlook was not traditionally Jewish, it also was not the result of a collective momentum. "Kallen's decision to become a Zionist was entirely a personal, abstract, one, not influenced by the Jewish community or by the fledgling American Zionist movement" (S. 39). The pervasive metaphors of individualism in Kallen's group thinking may point to this individual moment of his own ethnic rebirth, his personal ethnogenesis in an assimilative context. The orchestra image, too, recurs when Kallen remembered the influence of William James's philosophical pluralism, which stressed

> the reality of manyness, the refusal to accept the proposition that the many are appearance and only the one is reality. When I accepted this idea I didn't have to think of it as an image that could be dissipated. I could think of it as a present perduring reality which, in my personal history, all my experiences joined and with which they orchestrated and made the me that I was becoming. [...]
>
> What it [James's pluralism] released me from was an attitude which shut out operational working of my past. It opened opportunities. Zionism became a replacement and reevaluation of Judaism which enabled me to respect it [...] which allowed me to see an ongoing pattern, a group personality, called Jew. (S. 40)

Through the intellectual contact with James and Wendell, Kallen underwent dramatic changes in ethnic outlook, yet began to formulate static and abstract notions of an "ongoing pattern," of ethnic persistence—imagining the individual as a collectivity and the collectivity as an individual.

Kallen's relationship to Wendell must have been complicated by Wendell's anxieties about the influx of immigrants who, like Mary Antin, made claims to a full American identity. Moreover, Wendell appears to have suffered from some physical revulsion caused by commensality with blacks and Jews, a form of psychosomatic racism. Barbara Solomon called attention to Wendell's daughter's recollections.[28] Edith Wendell Osborne writes that her father, a "great believer in tradition," honored the annual recipient of the Jacob Wendell Scholarship, given out "for merit only," by "asking the scholar to dine at his house, inviting, amongst others, the President of Harvard to meet him." Wendell's daughter dwells on her father's fear "that eventually the scholar would be either an Ethiopian or a Hebrew, holding he would then permanently abandon the dinners." Yet she concludes with the comforting note that "up to the present they have all been Americans, and, with hardly an exception, gentlemen."[29] It is this narrow and exclusive definition of "Americans," of course, that we might expect to have startled Kallen. Wendell revealed at least some of his difficulties to Kallen, and the former student, far from taking the broader approach to Americanness, sounded just like his mentor when he criticized Antin for her American claims, describing her as "intermarried, 'assimilated' even in religion, and more excessively, self-consciously flatteringly American than the Americans" (*C.* 86). However, Kallen deflected the critique from nativist exclusion from the category "American" toward antiassimilationism.

Kallen dedicated *Culture and Democracy* to the memory of Barrett Wendell with whom he had had an intensive exchange of letters up until Wendell's death in 1921. As Moses Rischin has shown in a thoroughly detailed and glowing account of Kallen's contribution to American pluralism, Kallen incorporated a Wendell letter into "Democracy Versus the Melting-Pot." This excerpt also makes clearer what Wendell feared about Antin: "Your Jewish race," Wendell writes to Kallen in December of 1914, "is less lost than we, of old America. For all [its] sufferings [. . .] it has never lost its identity, its tradition, its existence. As for us, we are submerged beneath a conquest so complete that the very name of us means something not ourselves. [. . .] I feel as I should think an Indian might feel, in the face of ourselves that were."[30] Kallen used the last sentence anonymously, ascribing it merely to "a great American man of letters, who has better than any one else I know of interpreted to the world the spirit of America as New England" (*C.* 93).

The pluralist plot begins to thicken in the years 1905–1908. Kallen, who graduated in 1903, worked as a teaching fellow for Santayana and James in 1905–1907 and received a Sheldon fellowship to go to Oxford in 1907–1908, the same academic year during which William James delivered the Hibbert lectures at Oxford, later published under the title *A Pluralistic Universe.* The lectures were full of references that must have been meaningful to Kallen.[31] James used the image of the "federal republic" that recurred in Kallen (*C.* 124);[32] significantly, James's use takes the American political system as a philosophical model for the universe: "The pluralistic world is thus more like a federal republic than like an empire or a kingdom."[33] James also posits a clear alternative between "pluralism" and "monism," and in a form that has persisted in the rhetoric of pluralism since Kallen:

> Is the many-ness-in-oneness that indubitably characterizes the world we inhabit, a property only of the absolute whole of things, so that you must postulate that one-enormous-whole indivisibly as the *prius* of there being any many at all—in other words, start with the rationalistic block-universe, entire, unmitigated, and complete?—or can the finite elements have their own aboriginal forms of manyness-in-oneness, and where they have no immediate oneness still be continued into one another by intermediary terms—each one of these terms being one with its next neighbors, and yet the total 'oneness' never getting absolutely complete?[34]

Meanwhile, the Philadelphia-born black intellectual Alain Locke, who had taken Kallen's section in a Santayana class, graduated from Harvard in 1907 and became the first (and until 1962, the only) black Rhodes scholar at Oxford in the academic year of James's Hibbert lectures.[35] When Locke applied for the scholarship, Clare Bloodgood Crane writes, he noted

> sardonically that although Rhodes had acquired a huge fortune in Africa, no one of African descent had ever been awarded one of his scholarships. Physically small and prone to heart trouble, Locke met the athletic requirement for the Rhodes Scholarship by serving as coxswain on the Harvard crew; and his extracurricular activities in public speaking and music qualified him as an all-round student. [. . .] In his personal interview with the committee, Locke

> stated that he wanted to go to Oxford not only to continue his studies in literature, but also because he wished to "see the race problem from the outside [. . .] to see it in perspective." Locke's "maturity of purpose" and brilliant college record resulted in his appointment.[36]

It was from Kallen's encounters with Locke that the idea of cultural pluralism germinated. Kallen remembered:

> It was in 1905 that I began to formulate the notion of cultural pluralism and I had to do that in connection with my teaching. I was assisting both Mr. James and Mr. Santayana at the time and I had a Negro student named Alain Locke, a very remarkable young man—very sensitive, very easily hurt—who insisted that he was a human being and that his color ought not to make any difference. And, of course, it was a mistaken insistence. It *had* to make a difference and it *had* to be accepted and respected and enjoyed for what it was.
>
> Two years later when I went to Oxford on a fellowship he was there as a Rhodes scholar, and we had a race problem because the Rhodes scholars from the South were bastards. So they had a Thanksgiving dinner which I refused to attend because they refused to have Locke.
>
> And he said, "I am a human being," just as I had said it earlier. What difference does the difference make? We are all alike Americans. And we had to argue out the question of how the differences made differences, and in arguing out those questions the formulae, then phrases, developed—"cultural pluralism," "the right to be different." (S. 49)

The remembered story of Kallen's coming to Locke's rescue has been retold several times as the myth of origins of "cultural pluralism," and it was occasionally expanded to include Wendell's attempts to dissuade Kallen from making a public gesture for a black person (S. 49).[37] A closer look at the Wendell-Kallen correspondence, however, yields a much more complex situation. The "Locke affair"—that inspired Kallen to speak of "cultural pluralism"—begins with a letter from Kallen to Wendell, dated October 22, 1907, which as far as I know has not previously been cited:

> Now I want to ask a favor of you. You will perhaps remember little Locke, the yellow boy who took [. . .] English 42. He is here as a Rhodes scholar; and some people have been in America officious and mean-spirited enough to

> draw "the color-line" for the benefit of Englishmen. The boy earned his scholarship in an open competition. He has said nothing to me himself. Others have deprecated his being here. But he is here, one of America's scholars, and a Harvard man. He finds himself suddenly shut out of things,—unhappy, and lonely and doesn't know how or why.[38]

Whether merely to placate Wendell (as Moses Rischin suggested in a personal letter) or to express his own feelings, Kallen, the father of cultural pluralism, adds:

> As you know, I have neither respect nor liking for his race—but individually they have to be taken, each on his own merits and value, and if ever a negro was worthy, this boy is. I have remembered your warning and have been silent on the matter, but I listened with great anger and I have said all that I could concerning what was commendable in him, and now I want you to write a word to Dyer and others, if you can, to help right this wrong.[39]

Wendell answered on November 3, 1907, with a frank and detailed account of his own race repugnance:

> As to Locke, I really feel regretfully unable to write as you would like me to. My own sentiments concerning negroes are such that I have always declined to meet the best of them—Booker Washington, a man whom I thoroughly respect,—at table. Had Locke won my father's scholarship, I should have given up my plan of an annual dinner at which the former Wendell scholars have, so far, come together here to greet the new one. Professionally, I do my best to treat negroes with absolute courtesy. It would be disastrous to them, if they are gentlemen at heart, to expose them in private life to such sentiments of repugnance as mine, if we were brought into anything resembling personal relations.[40]

Wendell then mused about the meaning of Rhodes scholarships and held Locke as well as the Pennsylvania board in error because the terms of the scholarship included wide comprehensive representation of what was "best in the state" that sent the scholar:

> At least for many years to come, no negro can take just this position anywhere in America. Before he can, the kind of American which unmixed nationhood

has made me must be only a memory. It is sad, I admit—not least so to me for the reason that I am passing, perhaps of the past altogether.[41]

After reiterating that he simply did not attend dinners with Booker T. Washington, adding that hosts should not let their guests guess who is coming to dinner, Wendell gave his student the following advice:

> Some such kindness to Locke is perhaps in your own power. There is no reason, I think, why you should not invite some of your Oxford friends to meet him at tea; though to do so without intimation that he was coming might be inconsiderate. To make a 'cause' of the matter would be, at this juncture, deeply inexpedient.[42]

Wendell's term "repugnance"—a classic case of what another William James student , the sociologist Robert Park in 1928 termed "racial antipathy" in the essay "The Bases of Race Prejudice"[43]—is faithfully echoed by Kallen in his letter to Wendell of November 12, 1907:

> As to Locke—you have phrased my own feeling toward the race, so well that I don't see that there is anything more to say. I have already done the thing you suggested. I have had him to tea—he has met a Rhodes scholar from Princeton,—an old pupil of mine,—Dyer, and the Diceys.
>
> One of my Princeton colleagues, Harper, whom you may have met, is here and has expressed spontaneously a wish to meet the boy. So he is to come to tea again tho' it is personally repugnant to me to eat with him. Shylock's disclaimer [*Merchant of Venice* I.iii.35ff.] expresses my feeling exactly; but then, Locke is a Harvard man and as such he has a definite claim on me. I think he is going to do us credit. Already he has 'cox'd a boat to victory and won a silver cup.[44]

The birth of cultural pluralism was beset by ironies: a nonreligious Jewish student was converted to Zionism by a Boston Brahmin professor who suffered from spells of repugnance brought about by race contact during dinners; the student denounces assimilation and endears himself to his professor by claiming the same feelings of repugnance toward a black fellow student whom, with the help of his professor, he yet wants to protect against racism; and he views the young black intellectual, perhaps tongue-in-cheek, not as a fellow philosophy student but as an athlete and credit to the university. It seems strange, indeed, that Kallen singled out the early contact with Locke as the stimulus for pluralism when his own letters at the time of the incident make Kallen such an unlikely ancestor for contemporary pluralists. Uppercase "Cultural Pluralism" emerged in a world that also contained lowercase "negroes."

Alain Locke, whose personal statements and letters might reveal another dimension of the story or another story altogether, contributed some philosophical essays to collections edited by Kallen or dedicated to him in later years—essays that are curiously omitted in collections of Locke's works—and described his own conversion to cultural pluralism in a longer autobiographical statement published in 1935:

> Verily paradox has followed me the rest of my days: at Harvard, clinging to the genteel tradition of Palmer, Royce and Münsterberg, yet attracted by the disillusion of Santayana and the radical protest of James: again in 1916 I returned to work under Royce but was destined to take my doctorate in Value Theory under Perry. At Oxford, once more intrigued by the twilight of aestheticism but dimly aware of the new realism of the Austrian philosophy of value; socially Anglophile, but because of race loyalty, strenuously anti-imperialist; universalist in religion, internationalist and pacifist in world-view, but forced by a sense of simple justice to approve of the militant counter-nationalisms of Zionism, Young Turkey, Young Egypt, Young India, and with reservations even Garveyism and current-day "Nippon over Asia." Finally a cultural cosmopolitan, but perforce an advocate of cultural racialism as a defensive counter-move for the American Negro and accordingly more of a philosophical mid-wife to a generation of younger Negro poets, writers, artists than a professional philosopher. Small wonder, then, with this psychograph, that I project my personal history into its inevitable rationalization as cultural pluralism and value relativism, with a not too orthodox reaction to the American way of life.[45]

Alain Locke, though he adopted Kallen's term here, saw the dynamic of "cultural racialism" as a countermove for black intellectuals and interpreted it in a broad international context. In the introduction to his famous anthology *The New Negro* (1925), he called Harlem the "home of the Negro's 'Zionism.'"[46] Incidentally, Locke also once mentioned that he had written a study entitled "Frederick Douglass; a Biography of Anti-Slavery" (1935).[47]

Beyond Pluralism

The point of this documentation was not to malign Horace Kallen—whose correspondence with Wendell deserves study beyond the uses that were made of it here[48]—but to ask new questions about some problems at the very source of cultural pluralism. Pluralism is not a redemptively transcendent category that removes its advocates from prejudice. Few champions of pluralism today share the racist sentiments expressed in the Wendell-Kallen correspondence, but Kallen's antiassimilationist bias has remained pervasive in the many diatribes against melting pot and intermarriage. In the current cultural debates, pluralism often implies purism.

The tradition of pluralism from 1924 to the present discussions of literary histories is, of course, characterized by more shifts and changes. Most notably, the terms pluralism and cultural pluralism came into high fashion in the period during and after World War II, when the antithesis against totalitarianism made pluralism a desirable (though still largely undefined) concept. Though Kallen's influence has not been universally acknowledged, Kallen, too, participated in providing Cold War definitions of pluralism against totalitarianism. In the essay "Alain Locke and Cultural Pluralism" (1957), for example, Kallen writes:

> There persists in the sciences of man and nature and in philosophies as they have developed in our country, a disposition to assert and somehow to establish the primacy of totalitarian unity at the beginning, and its supremacy in the consummation, of all existence. It is, of course, conceded that multitude and variety seem pervasive, always and everywhere. But it is denied that they are real. It is the One that is real, not the Many.[49]

Kallen thus substituted "totalitarian unity" for James's "monism" and instrumentalized the pluralist tradition for political purposes of the 1950s. As America was pitted against its "monolithic" adversaries, there was some ideological necessity to reconstruct the United States as the culture of the many.

Albert Murray has very forcefully argued that the "mainstream is not white but mulatto,"[50] but literary pluralists of our time would like to construct a mosaic of ethnic stories that relies on the supposed permanence, individuality, and homogeneity of each ancestral tradition and has no space for the syncretistic nature of so much of American literary and cultural life. Ironically, while the pluralist argument is often phrased against a racist target, literary pluralists share their dislike of mixings and "impurities" with the old nativists who, too, worked very hard at ignoring not only certain ethnic groups but also the polyethnic mixings in American culture.[51] Instead of accepting the possibility of a text's many mothers, pluralists often settle for the construction of one immutable grandfather. Pluralists may thus surprisingly stress oneness when it concerns the origins of all the diverse groups. This bias in favor of purity and monoethnic myths of origins makes it far from unusual now for Americanists to publically profess the belief that only ethnic insiders are entitled to criticize literature from a given "ethnic tradition"; yet is this "biological insiderism"—advanced in the name of pluralistic diversity—not merely a timid approach that freezes ethnicity not only in the texts but also in the interpreters themselves? Despite his claims for static ethnic persistence, Kallen was ethnicized in a modern environment, as a result of reading and by an act of will rather than in the spirit of his own father. His ethnicity was a product of a transethnic experience of modernity, not of any tradition or "ethnic experience."

If we approach American literature, ethnic or mainstream, with an awareness of the dynamic nature of ethnogenesis, we might arrive at an understanding of writing as more than a reflection of ethnically diverse "experiences." Instead, literature could become recognizable as a productive force that may Americanize *and* ethnicize (as well as internationalize) readers, listeners, or other cultural participants. It is precisely this aspect that has often been emphasized by American writers who, from the Jewish-American assimilationist Mary Antin to the black nationalist Malcolm X,[52] have stressed the importance of reading in their ethnic conversion experiences.[53]

The additive approach that puts group after group into a volume not only avoids generalizations and synthesis but also cannot come to terms with American culture that abounds in ethnogenesis on the basis of transethnic contacts like the ones that were sketched here. Many other models of new transethnic approaches exist that focus on cultural interaction and ethnicization, and avoid static and abstract uses of ethnic groups. A growing number of literary scholars are pursuing postpluralist, postethnic approaches in studying American literature. Ethnogenesis, the emergence of ethnic groupings, sometimes with the help of literary texts, is now being studied together with efforts at constructing myths of persistence. Ethnicity is being recognized as a dynamic phenomenon that needs theoretical and practical understanding—without the reified nativist and belligerently antithetical closures of the past.

Because the omission of Frederick Douglass's *Narrative* from American literary historiography was the point of departure here, the book may now serve as a concluding illustration for the process of ethnogenesis that transcends popular constructions of purism. There is an often-analyzed individual development that culminates in Douglass's creation of an American Christlike hero who undergoes a rebirth experience despite his enslavement; and there is a collective, and ethnic, aspect to Douglass's growing sense of selfhood as a living man, part of a living community of people who should not be slaves. The collective aspect is best grasped as the development of a sense of sacred peoplehood through a shared cultural activity. It is most clearly spelled out by Douglass when he describes the effects of the slaves' songs at the Great House Farm:

> They would then sing most exultingly the following words:—
>
> "I am going away to the Great House Farm!
> O, yea! O, yea! O!"
>
> This they would sing, as a chorus, to words which to many would seem unmeaning jargon, but which, nevertheless, were full of meaning to themselves . . . [These songs] told a tale of woe which was then altogether beyond my feeble comprehension; [. . .] they breathed the prayer and complaint of souls boiling over with the bitterest anguish. Every tone was a testimony against slavery, and a prayer to God for deliverance from chains. [. . .] To those songs I trace my first glimmering conception of the dehumanizing character of slavery.[54]

As Douglass's account makes clear, the songs contribute to the process of ethnogenesis, of emerging peoplehood. Though the texts need contain no specific reference to freedom (many songs did) and though the songs need not be of "pure" African origins (Lawrence Levine wrote about the "irrelevancy" of the question of origins "for an understanding of consciousness"),[55] the very act of collective singing is a revelation about the nature of things and a bonding process for the heterogeneous slaves who are united in a feeling of brotherhood through the ritual of singing. The sense of a dynamically emerging group identity is acquired, in a precise historical setting, and on the basis of words and music. Many other observers, among them ethnic outsiders like the literary historian and collector of spirituals Thomas Wentworth Higginson, noticed the centripetal force of "these peculiar but haunting slave songs."[56] Higginson's observation interested Alain Locke, on whose materials Margaret Just Butcher's book *The Negro in American Culture* was based, which includes this reference. Butcher/Locke also stressed that Douglass "was far in advance of any narrowly racialist stand"[57]—including, we might add, that of many later literary historians and pluralists. For the new literary histories that are in the making, the time has come to follow Douglass's lead and to go beyond pure pluralism.

	The Problem of Cultural Diversity and National Unity		
Foci of Human Relations	Emphasis on American Group Differences	Emphasis on American Group Likenesses	Differences and Likenesses in Balance
Anglo-Domination	A social hierarchy with relative group status		
The Melting Pot		Assimilation of groups into one inclusive pattern	
Pluralism and Tolerance	Culture groups enjoying autonomy and equality		
Dynamic Democracy			Diversity and unity in intergroup relationship

FIGURE 5 *The Problem of Cultural Diversity and National Unity*. Adapted from Stewart G. Cole and Mildred Wiese Cole, *Minorities and the American Promise: The Conflict of Principle and Practice*, 1954.

5

The Multiculturalism Debate as Cultural Text

A debate is going on in the world of American higher education. It is a debate that concerns educational contents, forms of instruction, and the changing composition of the student and faculty bodies. It revolves around such terms as "the canon" and "political correctness" (or PC for short) and such policies as affirmative action. There is said to be a conflict between a "traditional," "conservative" emphasis on keeping established values of liberal arts education and a "radical," "ethnic," or "feminist" demand for such changes as the "diversification" of faculty and of reading lists. The word that has most galvanized these discussions is "multiculturalism." It is a word that seems omnipresent now but has been part of debates in the United States for only a short time. It seems to have come into use in the wake of reactions, on the one hand, to the traditionalist assertions by Allan Bloom and William J. Bennett or, somewhat differently, E. D. Hirsch and, on the other hand, to the vehement public reactions to a modification in

SOURCE Wendy Katkin, Ned Landsman, and Andrea Tyree, eds. *Beyond Pluralism: Essays on the Conception of Groups and Group Identities in America*. Champaign: University of Illinois Press, 1998, 63–104. By permission of the University of Illinois Press.

the Stanford core curriculum, a substitution in one of eight tracks that permitted the inclusion of non-Western literature in a great books course.

"Multiculturalism" as an "-ism" word apparently originated in discussions about Africa,[1] Australia, and Canada. As a key term of the official Canadian government policy introduced by Pierre Trudeau on October 8, 1971, multiculturalism included various features, such as giving "grants to ethnic organizations to help them preserve their culture," with an annual budget that increased from 1.5 million dollars in 1971 to 10 million dollars in 1973; and the appointment of a cabinet minister, Dr. Stanley Haidasz, "whose exclusive responsibility was multiculturalism."[2] John Porter's essay "Ethnic Pluralism in Canada" may have helped transport the new "-ism" into the context of US academics. This contribution to the widely read *Ethnicity* collection of 1975 contains a section entitled "Multiculturalism within a Bilingual Framework" in which Porter outlines Trudeau's policy.[3]

"Multiculturalism" came into wider use in the United States only in the late 1980s. Of course, there are probably many earlier isolated instances, such as Edward F. Haskell's *Lance: A Novel About Multicultural Men* (1941) whose hero Major Campbell is, as the *New York Herald Tribune* reviewer noted, "polyglot, bi-national, tied to no patriotic loyalties but ardently a servant of science and of social science particularly" who feels happy only with people who "are 'multicultural' like himself."[4] The reviewer put the brand new term in quotation marks here and when she assessed the book as a "fervent sermon against nationalism, national prejudice and behavior in favor of a 'multicultural' way of life and a new social outlook more suited to the present era of rapid transport and shifting populations."[5] Haskell was the son of a Swiss-American couple of missionaries and grew up in the United States, Turkey, Greece, Bulgaria, and Switzerland, before going to Oberlin, Columbia, and Harvard and becoming an activist aiding political prisoners and an investigator of political trials. As the dust jacket tells the reader, Haskell regarded his novel "not only as the statement of a problem, but also its partial theoretical solution." His mouthpiece, Major Campbell, states at a dramatic point in the novel, "Men in all climes and all times live by the narrow little things they know. [. . .] Their contact has been with one language, one faith, and one nation. They are unicultural. [. . .] But we, being children of the great age of transportation and communication, have contacts with *many* languages, *many* faiths, and *many* nations. We are *multi*cultural." Haskell's characters whose life stories transcend the confines of individual nation states, of one language, or of a single religion, may be representative harbingers of what has happened in the world at a much larger scale since World War II. Haskell anticipated the anxieties that multiculturalism could unleash in readers accustomed only to the unicultural model of the nation state, readers who might suspects Haskell's "multicultural men" of disloyalty and lack of patriotism. Thus he also let Campbell stress the similarities between multiculturalists and uniculturalists: "Multicultural people [. . .] are just like unicultural people. They develop faith and loyalty and patriotism too: faith in science, loyalty to world organization, and patriotism for mankind."[6]

Edward Haskell's 1941 novel introduced the word "multicultural" to describe the pioneering quality of a few exceptional men. Before the wider dissemination of "multiculturalism," the issues with which the term has become associated were usually debated under such terms as "cultural pluralism," introduced by Horace Kallen in 1924,[7] or "ethnicity," a 1941 coinage by W. Lloyd Warner that slowly replaced the older, compromised word "race."[8]

Utopian and Ideological Aspects of Multiculturalism

Now that it exists lexically, what does the word "*multiculturalism*" mean? Definitions are not always easy to come by, and they differ widely. In 1990, for example, the Ford Foundation gave nineteen grants to universities "to broaden cultural and intellectual diversity in American higher education," reflecting the "rapid demographic changes under way in American society," yet the Ford Foundation spokesman refused to provide a definition, giving the reason that "the Foundation does not define multiculturalism."[9]

Critical definitions resemble reactions that the "new ethnicity" received in the 1970s. Michael Walzer and Richard Bernstein call it "the new tribalism."[10] Isaiah Berlin speaks of "the return of the *Volksgeist*."[11] Yet the proponents Wahneema Lubiano and Ted Gordon distance multiculturalism expressly from ethnicity—as well as from "Western culture"—when they write: "Multiculturalism is not a tourist's eye view of 'ethnicity,' nor is it a paean to the American mythology defining this nation as a collection of diverse and plural groups living happily together and united by their knowledge of, and proper respect for, something called 'Western culture.'"[12] According to Arthur Schlesinger Jr.'s book *The Disuniting of America*, multiculturalism is quite unlike and much more sinister than cultural pluralism because "instead of referring as it should to all cultures, [multiculturalism] has come to refer only to non-Western, nonwhite cultures. The former president of the Modern Language Association even wonders why 'we cannot be students of Western culture and multiculturalism at the same time,'" as if they were opposites.[13] Lewis Feuer also distinguishes between multiculturalism and cultural pluralism when he asks, "Why was 'multiculturalism' chosen to replace the already existing expression 'cultural pluralism?' The answer is a simple one. 'Cultural pluralism' was invented by supporters of liberal democracy who had a strong faith in American civilization."[14] By contrast, Mortimer Adler, the senior defender of the "great books" concept, writes: "Multiculturalism is cultural pluralism," but he advocates a "*restricted* cultural pluralism."[15] According to the Afrocentrist Molefi Kete Asante, "either you support multiculturalism in American education, or you support the maintenance of white supremacy."[16]

Roger Kimball, whose book *Tenured Radicals* sharply criticizes multiculturalism,[17] calls the word "an omnibus term for the new academic orthodoxy" that "has provided common cause and something of a common vocabulary for a profession otherwise riven by an allegiance to competing radicalisms."[18] The term "multiculturalism" is sufficiently ambiguous to contain different and, indeed, incompatible programs and ideas. Paul Berman, the editor of an anthology of essays entitled *Debating P.C.*, concludes, "no three people agree about the meaning of central terms like . . . 'multiculturalism'. [. . .] Every participant carries around his own definitions, the way that on certain American streets every person packs his own gun. [. . .] The debate is unintelligible. But it is noisy!"[19] Larry Yarbrough finds that the debate "may seem as interminable as some faculty meetings."[20] A sense of fatigue is palpable in the "interminable" debate.

If the battle is indeed one between traditionalists and radicals, then the image that multiculturalism evokes as a promise for a better future is particularly important. In the interest of a utopian vision, Henry Giroux, for example, advocates a pedagogy "which refuses to reconcile higher education with inequality."[21] Such rhetoric of hope is certainly present in the discussion. Less strongly pronounced is what Karl Mannheim saw as a feature of utopias, that is, that they work as "wish-images which take on revolutionary functions."[22] One of the essays that comes closest to such wish-images is Ishmael Reed's "America: The Multinational Society," which has as its motto a clipping from the *New York Times*: "At the annual Lower East Side Jewish festival yesterday, a Chinese woman ate a pizza slice in front of Ty Thuan Duc's Vietnamese grocery store. Beside her a Spanish-speaking family patronized a cart with two signs: 'Italian Ices' and 'Kosher by Rabbi Alper.' And after the pastrami ran out, everybody ate knishes."[23] Reed's essay continues in the same vein: "[A] poet called me to describe a city he had just visited. He said that one section included mosques, built by the Islamic people who dwelled there. Attending his reading, he said, were large numbers of Hispanic people, forty thousand of whom lived in the same city. He was not talking about a fabled city located in some mysterious region of the world. The city he'd visited was Detroit."[24]

This strategy of making the familiar strange and of presenting the American experience as an increasingly syncretistic give-and-take multiculturalism is, of course, a well-known feature from the traditions of melting pot and pluralist rhetoric; it is also worth remembering that Reed's essay was written before multiculturalism had become such a central term. Yet the exciting research that has been undertaken by scholars who have explored such polyethnically interactive features of American culture has not been drawn on much for multicultural utopianism. Berndt Ostendorf, for example, has investigated and theorized the creolization of American culture.[25] Donald Weber has worked on the subtle ways ethnic difference made itself felt in such national television series as *The Goldbergs*; he cites, for example, a character who said, "America I love you. If I didn't hear an accent every day I'd think I was in a foreign country."[26] Christopher Newton studied the linguistic mix in the Italian-American commedia dell arte tradition: the play *Iammo a Connailanda* (Let's go to Coney Island), for example, contains such lines as "Ai brecche iu fesse" and a comment on the ridiculous notion that in America *femmine* are called "uomini" (women).[27] The absence or weakness of such visions is illustrated by the fact that Cornel West has to make the following plea in the multiculturalism debate: "If you're Afro-American and you're a victim of the rule of capital, and a European Jewish figure who was born in the Catholic Rhineland and grew up as a Lutheran, by the name of Karl Marx, provides certain analytical tools, then you go there."[28] Utopian vision seems in decline at this moment in history; and even when critics articulate a hopeful model, they may add disastrous qualifiers—as does Isaiah Berlin who develops a concept of nonhegemonic pluralism only to conclude that "there is little historical evidence for the realizability of such a vision."[29] John Higham rightly mentions that the question of whether multiculturalism should present divergence or convergence is rarely addressed in the debate,[30] which is often looking backward to various ethnic histories and rarely looking forward to a polyethnic future.

Perhaps one of the last areas for utopian thinking is the belief that multiculturalism will increase the self-esteem and hence the performance of some students,[31] a belief that is also seriously questioned in the literature.[32]

What we are more likely to find in the debate about multiculturalism than wish-images of future interactions of many cultures and languages are demographic projections according to which in fifty years half of all US citizens will be nonwhite. Such journalistic statistical estimates, Stephan Thernstrom argues, simply project high birthrates of rural populations into the future. There is, however, reason to expect birthrates to decline in cultural environments where children signal high costs rather than wealth. Thernstrom also points out that such visions of the coming "minority majority" resemble the American "race suicide" predictions in the face of the fertile South and East European immigrants a century ago. He cites Lothrop Stoddard who "calculated that after 200 years 1,000 Harvard men would have left only 50 descendants, while 1,000 Romanian immigrants would have produced 100,000." Yet whereas then such predictions were made in order to argue for immigration restrictions, the current projections "are trotted out as evidence of the need for bigger and better social programs."[33] In a different way of reflecting on these demographic forecasts, Joel Perlmann wondered why US Census population predictions of the 1990s were based on "the bizarre assumption that there will be no further intermixing of peoples across racial lines."[34]

Demographic predictions may not make much of a utopia, but the discussion of the changing composition of the United States and of higher education in this country is a factor that has animated the debate. Yet, as several observers have also pointed out, such statistics do not translate into an increase in cultural activities. Not all ethnic groups are interested in multiculturalism, and many of the new immigrants have shown restraint in their endorsement of multicultural education.[35] Gerald Early suggests three reasons why the rhetoric of demography is not convincing in supporting claims of a growing diversity: first, there is no increased interest in foreign languages; second, the multicultural reform efforts seem directed at the present rather than the future; and third, there is no indication that power relations would be changing as well.[36]

Whatever may explain the thinness of utopianism (or its substitution by demographic prophecy) in the debate on multiculturalism, there is no paucity of ideological energy that makes itself felt in commodification and exporting, ethnicization and identity politics, top-down approaches and compromise strategies. No matter what one's definition or position on the subject, multiculturalism may be an excellent marketing device. Benetton set the tone for multicultural commercials, and the academy, too, has moved closer than ever to the marketplace in the context of multiculturalism. Upon closer inspection, some battles turn out to involve such earthshaking issues as the choice between two widely marketed literary anthologies for classroom use. Michael Bérubé noted that prominent cultural conservatives Allan Bloom and Roger Kimball "now occupy the front covers of each other's books" since mutual endorsements are no longer uncommon."[37]

Arthur Schlesinger Jr.'s book *The Disuniting of America* also received an enthusiastic promotional comment from Kimball and was marketed in unusual ways.[38] When it was widely cited in the press it was not yet available in bookstores, only by mail order from Whittle Direct Books in Knoxville, Tennessee. Having sent my check for $11.95, I was surprised to receive the book by return mail via Federal Express. Opening it, I was even more surprised to find a hardback book that was interrupted by nine two-page color ads for Federal Express which counted in the pagination of the ninety-eight-page book and which had such pertinent slogans as "We didn't start an air express service. We started a revolution," and "We know our way around like the natives. Because we *are* the natives"—in Japanese and in English translation.[39]

The debate itself may be a commodity, too. This is certainly true for the articles that are hectically marketed in widely disseminated mass-market paperback collections, as the back cover of Paul Berman's collection *Debating P.C.* demonstrates:

> WHITE MALE EUROCENTRISM . . . OR AN ESSENTIAL CULTURAL HERITAGE?
> The debate [. . .] is the most important discussion in American education today and has grown into a major national controversy raging on the covers of our top magazines and news shows. This provocative anthology gives voice to the top thinkers of our time.

The public debate performances on college campuses, radio, and television, are at least partly also forms of "orchestrated" marketing devices that bridge political differences: Thus conservative Dinesh D'Souza and radical Stanley Fish "put themselves on the market—for a fee of $10,000 per debate," engaged in "orchestrated verbal fisticuffs," yet still could "have a drink afterward."[40]

After the end of the cold war multiculturalism could also be offered and propagated politically as America's new trademark. The question of whether Japan is open enough to multiculturalism to justify an academic association meeting there or the notion that American multiculturalism can be (or ought to be) a model for a world torn by nationalisms is occasionally voiced.[41] It is, of course, a consensus model of multiculturalism that is thus being advocated for export.

Multiculturalism may reduce participants to self-interested articulators of predictable points; it may inhibit not only cross-ethnic critique but also intraethnic critique among creative writers as well as critics and scholars. Many discussions are turned into autobiographies.[42] Such autobiographic forms may look more like talk shows, Oprah Winfrey–style confessions that are quickly followed by the next one, and each autobiography itself may just be a list of generalized items and clichés; individuals seem to fall into categories carved out by "corporate pluralism"[43] and feel obliged to assert and express themselves through ethnic identity. Thus the talk about diversity may actually strengthen a shared frame; there are few unpredictable divisions, only the familiar groupings on grounds of race, gender, and sexual orientation (not *politics*, which is a theme that a new student Right may be beginning to claim, and not *class*, though it is often invoked by name).

Such identity politics is intellectually flabby. The term "identity" (which may go back only to Erik Erikson in 1950) in connection with "ethnic," is omnipresent today.[44] A sense of belonging to a race, ethnic group, or gender is generally permitted, at times even encouraged, to "hypercathect" itself upon all other social categories to which an individual may also belong—a phenomenon George Devereux has analyzed in the extreme case of Fascism.[45] Multiculturalism as an educational policy is based on *very* soft social science and has been criticized for its weak anthropological foundations—for example, in blurring the distinctions between culture and race[46]—and for its poor philosophical underpinnings.[47]

Racial incidents, and instances of interethnic hostility (as well as of sexual harassment) have increased in the multicultural years.[48] The notion of ethnos has been reinstated; as Higham points out, ethnic mobilization tends to spread rapidly,[49] and it can reach dominant majorities, too. Ethnicization also is likely to direct discussions to ethnic origins rather than to a possible polyethnic future—which may be a reason why there seems to be more ideology than utopia in the debate. A new flurry of cultural production generates an often shrill debate focusing on the dividing line between permissible "free speech" and what is now called "hate speech," to be banned from college campuses. The areas in which conflicts erupt have undoubtedly proliferated, and the boards and committees deciding disciplinary matters are busier than ever.

Critiques of these aspects of multiculturalism are on the rise. David Hollinger compellingly articulated the need to construct a new, "postethnic" universalism that is informed—but not stymied—by the particularist challenges: "A postethnic perspective recognizes the psychological value and political function of bounded groups of affiliation, but it resists a rigidification of exactly those ascribed distinctions between persons that various universalists and cosmopolitans have so long sought to diminish."[50] In a similar vein, Kwame Anthony Appiah argues, "The task is not to replace one ethnocentrism with many or to reject old ideals of truth and impartiality as intrinsically biased. Rather it is to recognize that those ideals have yet to be fully lived up to in our scholarship, that the bias has derived not from scholars who took Western standards (which often turn out to be everybody's standards) of truth for granted, but from those who did not take them seriously enough."[51] In *On Human Diversity* (1993), Tzvetan Todorov considers untenable the opinion that universalism is necessarily ethnocentric. He reminds readers that today ethnocentrism is not the only or even the most important perversion of universalism: one only has to think of relativism and scientism.[52] For him the key question is how we can fend off the dangers of perverted universalism and of relativism.

The Australian anthropologist Marie de Lepervanche considered the possibility as early as 1980 "that where racist behavior and ideologies were convenient to ruling class interests one hundred years ago, the apparent opposite—the promotion of ethnicity—performs a similar role today."[53] In that sense, the distinction between "conservatives" and "radicals" may, in fact, be one between two interest groups. One does not have to agree with Robert Hughes's general harangue to appreciate his point that in cultural matters "we can hardly claim to have a left and a right anymore. Instead we have something more akin to two puritan sects, one masquerading as conservative, the other posing as revolutionary but using academic complaint as a way of evading engagement in the real world."[54] Instead, Hughes portrays one possible background of the multiculturalism debate as the arrival of a new elite: "Though élites are never going to go away, the composition of those élites is not necessarily static. The future of American ones, in a globalized economy without a cold war, will rest with people who can think and act with informed grace across ethnic, cultural, linguistic lines."[55] Robert Christopher's book *Crashing the Gates*, tellingly subtitled *The De-WASPing of America's Power Elite*, gives a vivid account of the dramatic changes the United States has undergone and expresses the author's belief that a new American ruling class has emerged "in which with each year that passes ethnicity becomes less and less of a touchstone, and the distinctions between 'them' and 'us' become more and more blurred."[56] He views America as "far more inclusionary than most contemporary Americans assume."[57] Christopher explicitly includes black Americans in this vision, and his book opens with a chapter significantly entitled "Room at the Top."

The push for multicultural changes, in such a view, does not necessarily come from the populace but may come from the top; and what is sometimes noteworthy is a "top-down" approach in multicultural education, too.[58]

Multiculturalism may be attractive to governments and agencies because it is cheap. As Louis Menand writes, "Changing the curriculum is the cheapest social program ever devised."[59] It is certainly much cheaper than a full social security, medicare, and unemployment insurance system in a society that is also increasingly polarized by class. Thus, from 1977 to 1989—the period of the rise of multiculturalism—pretax income of the rich grew sharply:

> In the top 1 percent it grew by 77 percent to an average annual income of $559,800;
> in the top fifth by 29 percent to $109,400;
> in the second fifth by 9 percent to $47,900;
> the income of the third fifth grew by only 4 percent to $32,700;
> that of the fourth fifth sank by 1 percent to $20,100;
> and annual income in the bottom fifth declined by 9 percent to $8,400.[60]

This shift is all the more dramatic since all efforts by other statisticians to deflect from its essentials have failed,[61] and since philanthropic efforts also declined very dramatically in the Reagan and Bush years.[62] The situation has only worsened since then.

Multiculturalism may be less expensive than social equalization, but it is by no means "free." The idea of multiculturalism is often articulated as if it were phrased against the controlling powers of the status quo, but it is, in fact, endorsed by many presidents of major universities and the Rockefeller and Ford foundations, whereas Olin, Mobil, Earhart, Smith-Robertson, Sarah Scaife, and Bradley support the conservatives. (The debate may thus also be a battle of foundations.) Many institutions have assigned large amounts of money to offices, foundations, fellowships, and so forth through which efforts are channeled. Neil Rudenstine, then the president of Harvard University, for example, declared that nothing is higher on his priority list than diversifying the faculty.[63] A special 1992 issue of *Change* magazine, sponsored by a grant from the Ford Foundation and devoted to multiculturalism, listed some rather startling statistics, according to which more than a third of all colleges in the United States have a multicultural requirement; more than a third offer black, Hispanic, Native-American, or Asian-American studies courses; more than half have increased departmental course offerings; half have multicultural advising programs; 60 percent offer recruitment and retention programs for multicultural faculty; more than 40 percent offer faculty development programs focusing on multicultural issues; and more than a third have multicultural institutes or centers.[64] Arthur Levine and Jeanette Cureton conclude: "The sheer quantity of multicultural activity [. . .] belies the belief that the traditional curriculum has been largely impermeable to, or has simply marginalized, diversity. [. . .] Multiculturalism today touches in varying degrees a majority of the nation's colleges and universities."[65] It may thus constitute a firmly launched but segmental and top-heavy experience, rather than promise a utopian vision for a whole society.

John Porter has argued that for the United States and Canada the dilemma is between mobility and ethnicity: "[O]n the one hand if they value and emphasize ethnicity, mobility and opportunity are endangered, on the other hand if they emphasize mobility and opportunity, it will be at the cost of submerging cultural identity."[66] Here multiculturalism could work as a compromise: by simultaneously emphasizing ethnicity and visibly incorporating representatives of the most important ethnic groups into elites without having to make changes in the social structure, multiculturalism might combine a stress on ethnicity with a symbolic demonstration of mobility. The two lines come together most plausibly in the biographical format of widely circulating success stories of previously excluded Americans.

Formal and Thematic Features of the Debate

A persistent paradox in the debate about multiculturalism is that the assertion of diversity is expressed in a rather homogeneous fashion because only a limited arsenal of formal strategies and recurrent motifs and themes are employed. It is thus tempting to take the debate as if it were a text and review some of its formal and thematic characteristics. Formally, many contributions to the discussion have generic affinities with the "*jeremiad*" (Schlesinger, Bloom, Kimball); they tend to be critical or vituperative as Puritan sermons once were, yet they end on a note of hope and promise. This affinity is recognized and thematized in the debate itself: Fish, for example, refers to D'Souza and Kimball as "our modern Jeremiahs."[67] The nature of the debate may be responsible for a smaller formal feature that recurs with some frequency, the Whitmanian "*catalogue*" of ingredients that proponents or opponents tend to ascribe to multiculturalism. Roger Kimball, for example, having observed a Modern Language Association meeting, listed the following items he regards as "substitutes for literature": "Marxism, feminism, what we might call homosexualism, 'cultural studies,' ethnic studies, and any number of indeterminate mixtures of the above leavened with dollops of deconstructivist or poststructuralist theory—in other words, multiculturalism *de luxe*."[68] The recurrence of such cataloguing has also been noted in the debate. Henry Louis Gates Jr. speaks ironically of the "trinity" of race, class, and gender.[69] Barbara Ehrenreich writes, "Too often [multiculturalism] [. . .] leads to the notion of politics as a list. Political 'theory' becomes a list of all the groups, issues, and concerns that you must remember to check off lest you offend somebody with no larger perspective connecting them. But a list does not define a political outlook."[70]

The smallest defining formal unit of the debate is probably the anecdote. With its cultural origins in such champions of anecdotal writing as Franklin and Emerson, its master in the debate on multiculturalism is undoubtedly D'Souza, whose anecdotes of incidents on campuses are often retold, varied upon, and corrected by other readers. The issues that led to Thernstrom's decision to discontinue offering a course called "The Peopling of America" have been told and retold in so many fashions since D'Souza highlighted his version of the story that printed interpretations are beginning to reach the indeterminacy threshold. Even when there is agreement about (or only one printed source of) an anecdote, interpretations in the context of race and gender may veer into different directions because the assessment of human motives can be difficult. Shelby Steele, a black opponent of affirmative action, stylizes some episodes in such a way as to show the outline of a world in which race may matter less. He frames a scene in a California supermarket as follows:

> When we [Steele is speaking of blacks here] first meet, we experience a trapped feeling, as if we had walked into a cage of racial expectations that would rob us of our individuality by reducing us to an exclusively racial dimension. We are a threat, at first, to one another's uniqueness. I have seen the same well-dressed black woman in the supermarket for more than a year now. We do not speak, and we usually pretend not to see each other. But, when we turn a corner suddenly and find ourselves staring squarely into each other's eyes, her face freezes and she moves on. I believe she is insisting that both of us be more than black—that we interact only when we have a reason other than the mere fact of our race. Her chilliness enforces a priority I agree with—individuality over group identity.[71]

Yet as one reviewer pointed out, this woman may actually be miles ahead of Steele in the struggle for individuality. She, too, might not be thinking of race at all and only find Shelby Steele to be not likeable enough individually to thaw her chilliness. She might also have recognized him and be showing her disapproval of his widely publicized political views by snubbing him. It is good to remember that much of the debate rests on the plausibility of anecdotes that no one can possibly verify. This again strengthens the autobiographical format of the debate.

A variant of the anecdote—which at least purports to be based on facts—is the fable, or parable, which derives its point or moral from an admittedly hypothetical scenario. John Searle used such a "counterfactual situation" to review the assumptions of the "traditionalists" and the identity politics of the multicultural challengers:

> Suppose it was discovered by an amazing piece of historical research that the works commonly attributed to Plato and Aristotle were not written by Greek males, but by two Chinese women who were cast ashore on the coast of Attica when a Chinese junk shipwrecked off the Piraeus in the late fifth century B.C. What difference would this make to our assessment of the works of Plato and Aristotle. From the traditionalist point of view, none whatever. It would just be an interesting historical fact. From the challengers' point of view, I think it

> would make a tremendous difference. Ms. Plato and Ms. Aristotle would now acquire a new authenticity as genuine representatives of a previously underrepresented minority, and the most appropriate faculty to teach their works would be then Chinese women.[72]

Searle uses this fable to drive home the following moral: "Implicit in the traditional assumptions [. . .] is the view that the faculty member does not have to exemplify the texts that he or she teaches. They assume that the works of Marx can be taught by someone who is not a Marxist, just as Aquinas can be taught by someone who is not a Catholic, and Plato by someone who is not a Platonist. But the challengers assume, for example, that women's studies should be taught by feminist women, Chicano studies by Chicanos committed to a certain set of values, etc."[73]

An often-repeated suffix is on the borderline between formal and thematic features of the multiculturalism debate. Whereas a *Rhyming Dictionary* from 1936[74] lists only ten words rhyming with "-centric," our own age is so much richer for poets who are looking for words ending with "-centric" and "-centrism." The fashion may go back to William Graham Sumner's coinage "ethnocentrism" of 1906. For Sumner, "ethnocentrism" is "the technical name for [a] view of things in which one's own group is the center of everything, and all others are scaled and rated with reference to it. [. . .] [E]thnocentrism leads a people to exaggerate and intensify everything in their own folkways which is peculiar and which differentiates them from others. It therefore strengthens the folkways."[75] Now "centric" and "centrism" are common in many words that have become familiar, from "Afrocentric" to "Eurocentric." The catalogue has been further enriched by "Amerocentric" or "Americentric."[76] Jean Devisse uses the less familiar "Mediterraneocentrism."[77]

Some recurrent thematic elements in the multiculturalism debate also deserve attention. There is, for example, a decided preference for the term "discontents," often an allusion to Freud's *Unbehagen an der Kultur*.[78] We find panels and essays on "multiculturalism and its discontents," and the word is used pervasively. Catharine Stimpson writes, for example, "Even though multiculturalism has [. . .] discontents, it is a great, defining feature of our historical moment."[79] Interestingly, critics of the multiculturalism debate, such as Ostendorf and Marshall Sahlins, have been drawn to Freud's work for the expression "narcissism of minor differences," which Freud applied to the "phenomenon that it is precisely communities with adjoining territories, and related to each other in other ways as well, who are engaged in constant feuds and ridiculing each other—like the Spaniards and the Portuguese, for instance, the North Germans and the South Germans, the English and Scotch, and so on."[80] According to Sahlins, Freud was concerned about balkanization when he spoke of this particular narcissism, and "balkanization" is another thematic cluster that traverses the multiculturalism debate.[81] There is also a widespread desire to explore the semantic possibilities of a word like "canon" through repeated punning. Thus we read of "loose canons" (Todd Gitlin, Adam Yarmolinsky, and Henry Louis Gates Jr.); canons of the past simply become "canon-fodder" of the present (Irving Louis Horowitz); and there is talk of firing the canon (Bryan Wolf).[82]

E Pluribus Unum

Probably no phrase is used as much in the multiculturalism debate as *E pluribus unum* (out of many, one). It has been connected with the discussion of American diversity for some time, for example, in Arthur Mann's 1979 book *The One and the Many*.[83] Schlesinger book *The Disuniting of America* contains a long meditation on this theme: "The national ideal had once been *e pluribus unum*. Are we now to belittle *unum* and glorify *pluribus*? Will the center hold? Or will the melting pot yield to the Tower of Babel? [. . .] The question poses itself: how to restore the balance between *unum* and *pluribus*?"[84] Yet Schlesinger has no monopoly on wordplays with *e pluribus unum*. Ravitch gave her essay on multiculturalism the subtitle "E pluribus plures."[85] "More pluribus, more unum," a *New York Times* editorial followed suit.[86] "*E pluribus* what?" an *American Studies Newsletter* asked as a lead-in to a special section. "E Pluribus nihil," Midge Decter answered, followed by Stanley Schmidt's editorial "E pluribus zero."[87] Or the other way around: "Ex uno, plus," as a *National Review* editorial put it.[88] In this company, the title of one of Albert Shanker's ad columns in the *New York Times* sounds modest as it only adds a question mark and asks: "E Pluribus Unum?"[89]

Given the wide circulation the phrase *e pluribus unum* enjoys in multiculturalism, it is regrettable that its origins have been largely ignored. To my knowledge, no participant in the debate on multiculturalism—with the exception of the internationally pitched *American Studies Newsletter*—has paid attention to the source of this saying, which appears on coins and is immortalized on the back of each dollar bill, reproducing the Great Seal of the United States. The motto was, as Kenneth Silverman writes, part of the original proposal for the seal that a committee (which included Benjamin Franklin, Thomas Jefferson, Thomas Paine, and John Adams) had made on August 20, 1776. In 1782 Congress adopted a design by William Barton, who "made the central image of the seal a large eagle displaying a reduced shield of thirteen stripes on its chest. In its talons the eagle would grip an olive branch and a bundle of arrows. In its beak would be a scroll reading *e pluribus unum*. Above the eagle would hover a cloud shrouding a constellation of thirteen stars."[90] The "one" was clearly meant to signify the confederation, the "many" its united thirteen colonies; but how and where did the founders find this neat Latin phrase? The most plausible source is the title page of the popular London *Gentleman's Magazine* where the motto *e pluribus unum* promised "a variety of literary texts" under one cover.[91] A poem of 1734 explained: "To your motto most true, for our monthly inspection, / You mix various rich sweets in *one* fragrant collection."[92] The epigraph had been copied from the *Gentleman's Journal or the Monthly Miscellany*, originally edited by the Huguenot refugee Pierre Antoine Motteux from 1691 to 1694.[93]

Ultimately, the phrase goes back to Horace's *Epistle to Florus* (circa 20 BC) or to the poem "Moretum," ascribed to Vergil. Horace's exhortative epistle asks at the end: "Do you grow gentler and better, as old age draws near. What good does it do you to pluck out *a single one of many* thorns? If you know not how to live aright make way for those who do."[94] Horace provided the motto for the *Spectator* of August 20, 1711; but Horace meant "one selected from many," not "one composed of many."[95] The "Moretum" (or Ploughman's Lunch) is a short poem about the farmer (perhaps former slave) Simulus who, with some help from the African woman Scybale, prepares a meal, a dumpling made of something resembling pesto or, according to another reader, a salad.[96] Having added hard cheese, salt, and herbs, and having mashed the garlic, he pounds everything: "Round and round went his hand; gradually the original ingredients lost their own properties and *one* colour emerged *from several*, not wholly green, since the milky fragments held out, nor shining milk-white, being variegated by all the herbs."[97] "E pluribus unus," one source of *e pluribus unum* comes from the same metaphoric realm as do such alternatives to the melting pot as stew or salad bowl; and an African woman is involved in it. Monroe Deutsch's conclusion of 1929 deserves to be remembered: "And so a Frenchman adapted and published on the title-page of a magazine issued in England a group of three Latin words which became the national motto of this composite people, the United States of America."[98] All the interest in cultural studies has not redirected academics toward this truly ironic story of origins of the noble motto which had nothing to do with political federalism, let alone ethnic diversity. In this instance, the multiculturalism debate also continues to canonize a few words an Englishman adapted from Horace or Vergil.

Matthew Arnold

Similar canonization processes take place with other snippets of Western culture. Giroux, for example, writes in the course of his democratic critique of canons, "The liberal arts curriculum, composed of the 'best' that had been said or written, was intended, as Elizabeth Fox-Genovese has observed, 'to provide selected individuals with a collective history, culture, and epistemology so that they could run the world effectively.'"[99] The phrasing, "the best that has been said or written," is favored by many contributors to the multiculturalism debate and goes back, of course, to Matthew Arnold.[100] To my knowledge the multicultural "left" has not yet claimed and defended Matthew Arnold against his "conservative" admirers who have appropriated him; yet a look at Arnold's "platitude" could actually be helpful at this moment. (Morris Dickstein has written a brief for Arnold's radicalism that I shall relate a little later.) In his essay "The Function of Criticism at the Present Time," first published in 1864, Arnold distinguishes a practical, "English" tradition from a "French" world that cherishes ideas. He takes up the demand for critical "disinterestedness" (perhaps derived from Goethe's term *Uneigennützigkeit* in *Dichtung und Wahrheit*, used to characterize Spinoza).[101] Criticism can show this

> by resolutely following the law of its own nature, which is to be a free play of the mind on all subjects which it touches. By steadily refusing to lend itself to any of those ulterior, political, practical considerations about ideas, which plenty of people will be sure to attach to them, which perhaps ought often to be attached to them, which in this country at any rate are certain to be attached to them quite sufficiently, but which criticism has really nothing to

> do with. Its business is, as I have said, simply to know the best that is known and thought in the world, and by in its turn making this known, to create a current of true and fresh ideas.[102]

Arnold repeats the famous phrase when he praises the *Revue des deux mondes* as an organ that—unlike the practical and partisan English journals—has chosen "for its main function to understand and utter the best that is known and thought in the world."[103] Baudelaire's *Fleurs du mal* had appeared in the *Revue* a few years earlier, and Arnold points out that "as England is not all the world, much of the best that is known and thought cannot be of English growth."[104] Hence he demands that the "English critic of literature must dwell much on foreign thought, and with particular heed on any part of it, which, while significant and fruitful in itself, is for any reason specially likely to escape him."[105]

When Arnold put the essay into his collection, he added a passage addressing the reader's possible complaint that his observations lacked practical use and were not enough devoted to "the current English literature of the day."[106] He responded, "I am sorry for it, for I am afraid I must disappoint these expectations. I am bound by my own definition of criticism: a disinterested endeavor to learn and propagate the best that is known and thought in the world. How much of current English literature comes into this 'best that is known and thought in the world?' Not very much, I fear; certainly less, at this moment, than of the current literature of France and Germany."[107] He concludes with his vision of a contemporary criticism that transcends national boundaries and "regards Europe as being, for intellectual purposes, one great confederation, bound to a joint action and working to a common result; and whose members have, for their proper outfit, a knowledge of Greek, Roman, and Eastern antiquity, and of one another."[108]

Arnold's "overquoted" phrase (overused perhaps even by Arnold himself) comes from a context that is not irrelevant to the multicultural discussions of today, as Arnold was concerned not with a static canon of the past, as his conservative adherents claim at times, but with the open exploration of fresh ideas in a cosmopolitan spirit of disinterestedness that went beyond predictable *parti pris* positions and national boundaries. Hence he could be cited to strengthen calls for reading "the best that is known and thought in the world," with a stress on "world," not just the works of one country or in one language.[109]

It is noteworthy that for twentieth-century American Jewish intellectuals who moved into the humanities, Matthew Arnold was a central subject of interest. Horace M. Kallen, Ludwig Lewisohn, and Lionel Trilling chose Arnold as an important topic for their reflections.[110] Inspired by Trilling, Dickstein has articulated his own appreciation of Arnold, stressing Arnold's originality in demanding "relevance" in literary studies and the fact that Arnold's "canon" was "anti-canonical, existential."[111] Dickstein notes the irony (vividly illustrated by the multiculturalism debate) that Arnold's "attacks on English insularity . . . became the ground of a new traditionalism, the justification for a new insularity, not very different from the insularity he attacked."[112] Dickstein summarizes: "Mistaken for a conservative, Arnold belongs if anything to this great tradition of cultural radicalism which recoiled from the alliance between liberalism and 'progress,' and hence did much to establish the modern humanist critique of industrial society."[113] Contrasting Arnold with his present-day detractors who see in his striving for "disinterestedness" a "mask for specific social interests: white, male, and middle-class," Dickstein, whose most famous earlier book was a sympathetic account of the 1960s, points out that for Arnold, "disinterestedness" "was a social as well as literary goal—really a utopian ideal"[114]—of which we have found so little in the multiculturalism debate.

George Orwell

The English writer who has been most frequently invoked is George Orwell, as an exploration of the term "political correctness" suggests.[115] Though the term "*politically correct*" does not literally appear in George Orwell's novel *Nineteen Eighty-Four* it might come from the ambience of this work. When Julia asks Winston Smith about his wife Katharine, for example, he answers:

> "She was—do you know the Newspeak word *goodthinkful?* Meaning naturally orthodox, incapable of thinking a bad thought?"
>
> "No, I didn't know the word, but I know the kind of person, right enough."[116]

In "The Principles of Newspeak," the appendix to the novel, Orwell states that "a Party member called upon to make a political or ethical judgment should be able to spray forth the correct opinions as automatically as a machine gun spraying forth bullets."[117] Even though Orwell said "goodthinkful" to characterize Winston's wife and legitimate his adultery, and though he placed the words "political" and "correct" in the same sentence without actually saying "politically correct," the multiculturalism debate is suffused with nothing more than allusions to Orwell—with whose works many intellectuals refamiliarized themselves, starting in the year 1984.

First, there is the general sense of "newspeak" about all the new words that have emerged as a result of the desire to be more sensitive and gender neutral.[118] If the conservatives call the liberals' pleas for more sensitive language "newspeak," the liberals retaliate in kind. "Hate speech" is the term generally used now to describe offensive or insensitive language. Orwell readers will recognize the echo of "Hate Week"[119] and the "Hate Song" that people intone during this event. Bérubé uses the word "doubleplusungood" to describe the media campaign against political correctness:[120] in Orwell it refers to pornography in Pornosec of the Ministry of Truth Records Department.[121] Paula Rothenberg writes, "But in the end, war is *not* peace, slavery is *not* freedom, and no matter what the N.A.S. [the conservative National Association of Scholars] may believe, ignorance is *not* strength." She is, of course, alluding to the inscriptions on the ministries in *Nineteen Eighty-Four*.[122] Patricia Williams distinguishes the "joy of multiculturalism" from "the oppression of groupthink and totalitarianism."[123]

The most frequently circulating Orwellian term may be "Thought Police," used by Right, center, and Left.[124] George Will employs the term to denounce politically correct thinking at American universities;[125] Michael Novak uses it in *Forbes* in 1990;[126] Camille Paglia deplores women's studies programs and finds that they have "hatched the new thought police of political correctness";[127] Henry Louis Gates Jr. adds his voice: "We must not succumb to the temptation to resurrect our own version of the thought police, who would determine who, and what, is 'black.'"[128] Robert Hughes argues against comparisons between McCarthyism and political correctness by pointing out that the "number of conservative academics fired by the lefty thought police [. . .] is zero."[129]

The elusive nature of "truth" and "reality" has also been seen in terms of *Nineteen Eighty-Four*. Thus *Speaking for the Humanities* (a controversial pamphlet produced by the American Council of Learned Societies) stated, without giving evidence: "As the most powerful modern philosophies and theories have been demonstrating, claims of disinterest, objectivity, and universality are not to be trusted and themselves tend to reflect local historical conditions."[130] When Tzvetan Todorov reviewed and rightly criticized this pamphlet in the *New Republic*, he pointed out that it is "awkwardly reminiscent" of O'Brien's speech to Winston Smith in Orwell's *Nineteen Eighty-Four*: "You believe that reality is something objective, external, existing in its own right. [. . .] But I tell you, Winston, that reality is not external. Reality exists in the human mind and nowhere else."[131]

In Orwell's novel the dialogue in question takes place in the feared torture chamber 101 of the Ministry of Truth about the Party's right to history. O'Brien shows Winston a photograph of three one-time Party members that constitutes proof that they were later executed for trumped-up charges; then he destroys it in the memory hole:

> "Ashes, he said. "Not even identifiable ashes. Dust. It does not exist. It never existed."
>
> "But it did exist! It does exist! It exists in memory. I remember it. You remember it."
>
> "I do not remember it," said O'Brien.[132]

In teaching Winston "doublethink," O'Brien forces him to recite the Party slogan about the past: "Who controls the past controls the future; who controls the present controls the past."[133] Then O'Brien lectures Winston as he responds to the question of how one can control memory that is involuntary, and it is from this passage that some sentences were taken:

> Only the disciplined mind can see reality, Winston. You believe that reality is something objective, external, existing in its own right. You also believe that the nature of reality is self-evident. When you delude yourself into thinking that you see something, you assume that everyone else sees the same thing as you. But I tell you, Winston, that reality is not external. Reality exists in the human mind, and nowhere else. Not in the individual mind, which can make mistakes, and in any case soon perishes; only in the mind of the Party, which is collective and immortal.[134]

Of course, Orwell may seem concerned just as much about individual resistance to collective power as about metaphysical realism; yet the reading that casts O'Brien as a protodeconstructionist interestingly suggests the totalitarian aspects of relativism that leaves all room for arbitration to pure power, as Erich Fromm stressed when he discussed the term "mobile truth," then used to describe corporate America, in his 1961 afterword to the novel.[135] (And as I am about to send this essay collection to the publisher, the coinage "alternative truth" is continuing in this tradition.)

Rereading Orwell, one notices his strange misrepresentation of totalitarianism that one might expect would collide with multiculturalism. Orwell, for example, strongly stresses sexual freedom yet portrays Julia as generally uninterested in politics and as a rebel only "from the waist downwards,"[136] which should make the book somewhat problematic to today's multicultural readers. Indeed, Daphne Patai discussed Orwell's novel under the label "androcentrism" and focused on narrative comments that make women the embodiment of what we would now call political correctness: "It was always the women, and above all the young ones, who were the most bigoted adherents of the Party, the swallowers of slogans, the amateur spies and nosers-out of unorthodoxy."[137] Amazingly, racial (but not sexual) integration is ascribed to the realm of totalitarianism—which is strange if one remembers that *Nineteen Eighty-Four* depicts a conglomerate of Communism and Fascism. Thus Orwell writes, "In principle, membership [. . .] is not hereditary. Admission to either branch of the Party is by examination, taken at the age of sixteen. Nor is there any racial discrimination. [. . .] Jews, Negroes, South Americans of pure Indian blood are to be found in the highest ranks of the Party."[138] This might give a reader the impression that fighting for racial integration might be fighting for the world of *Nineteen Eighty-Four*, for the Party, and for totalitarianism.

No matter how incompatible the issues of the multiculturalism debate and of Orwell's novel may be, the present debate is a form of "living Orwell." Like multiculturalism, Orwell has become a compromise term that can be used for contrary political purposes. In the United States, he has been taken up by radicals, liberals, neoconservatives, old conservatives, and the John Birch Society,[139] and he has been marketed successfully as a commodity: Orwell's two most famous novels sold 40 million copies worldwide, "more than any other pair of books by a serious *or popular* postwar author."[140] Thus Orwell is a white male English author whose canonical status (however recently acquired) all sides in the multiculturalism debate reinforce by taking general knowledge of his work for granted. John Rodden calls the posthumous adoption of "St. George" Orwell "Assimilation Through Canonization"[141] and points out that

> "Big Brother," "1984," "doublethink," "Newspeak," "Orwellian," and even "Orwell" *are* obfuscatory language. [. . .] Whether hurled with intent to confuse or in ignorance of Orwell's life and work, they have become charged code words, easily manipulated to call up reflexively all sorts of (often widely exaggerated) associations with a police state.[142]

This way, Rodden says, Orwell has become the Dr. Frankenstein of the twentieth century. Yet all sides in the multiculturalism debate find it useful to define themselves against totalitarianism, as represented by Orwell, in order to characterize their opponents.

Whether through Orwell or not, all factions in the multiculturalism debate evoke Hitler, National Socialism, and the Holocaust to make their points. American students demonstrating for gay rights wear buttons imitating the pink triangles homosexuals were forced to wear in German concentration camps. In an instance in which Ishmael Reed uses the word "monocultural" (before "multiculturalism" had come into vogue), he asks whether Adolf Hitler wasn't "the archetypal monoculturalist who, in his pigheaded arrogance, believed that [. . .] one blood was so pure that it had to be protected from alien strains at all costs?"[143] This raises the question of how theories of group relations were affected by totalitarianism, especially by the Nazi extermination policies of the 1940s.

A Forgotten History of Multicultural Education

Historians have for a long time emphasized the significance of totalitarianism and World War II for the development of integrationist policies in the United States. Richard Polenberg has described the discrediting of racialism that took place in American scholarship of the 1940s;[144] Philip Gleason has carefully traced the effect of the war years on such central terms of group relations as "*identity*," "*minorities*," and "*pluralism*";[145] Arthur Mann noted that the assumptions of post–World War II cultural pluralism rested on the notion of a shared national culture;[146] and in his survey of pluralistic thinking John Higham formulated memorably the relationship between

European totalitarianism and American pluralism: "If the enemy was totalitarian, America would have to be pluralistic."[147]

This connection may have been constitutive for the origins of multiculturalism. (Perhaps it is an inversion of this maxim that characterizes the cultural logic of this moment: If America is multicultural, then those Americans who question such ascriptions—or those countries who fail to follow this model—may be called totalitarian.) "The unique fact that characterizes America is that it is a multiculture society. Consider at random almost any community in the country. Its social structure reveals a variety of culture groups, which differ widely in pattern, enlisting more or less distinctive racial folkways, religious faiths, languages, Old-World or indigenous household practices, social mores, and economic class status."[148] This observation was made in a chapter entitled "Disunity Among Americans," and the discussion proceeds to mention Crèvecœur and Zangwill, distinguishing such concepts as "Anglo-Conformity," "Melting Pot," and "Pluralism"; yet the text is not from the multiculturalism debate but from the year 1954. It is one of the earliest fully developed instances of the term "multiculture" that I have found, apart from Haskell's 1941 novel about "multicultural men." Hence what is now being debated under the label "multiculturalism" may not be all that new.

Though participants in the debate speak about the importance of history, the relatively short history of the concept of America as a multicultural society has largely remained ignored. I offer here only a brief consideration of some of the works that appeared from the mid-1940s to the mid-1950s—roughly contemporary with Orwell's novel—to suggest the need for further investigations. I focus on the sociologists around Robert MacIver at Columbia University, on Robin Williams and the Social Science Research Council, and on the movement for "intercultural education" surrounding the Coles, and I present their tenets and recommendations with extensive excerpts from their works. Donald R. Young, the sociologist who helped propagate the term "minority" for American use,[149] articulated in Robert McIver's 1945 book, *Civilization and Group Relationships*, what was the goal of many studies of that moment:

> A practical program to reduce the social visibility of our minorities would reverse Hitler's measures to increase anti-Semitism in Germany. He increased awareness of the Jews and assured their identification by marking their clothing and their places of business, by designating special areas where they could live.

> He increased fear of the Jews by a constant stream of propaganda emphasizing their success and their wealth, asserting that they monopolized the professions, ran the government, held all the best jobs, and so threatened the welfare of all the rest of the population. His campaign was very effective in Germany and in a good part of Europe; its influence reached across the ocean to this country.[150]

Young's response to the Holocaust was to work for better group assimilation because the Nazis had based their program on exaggerating difference. He discusses how this would work with various immigrant groups and Indians; then he proceeds to consider the case of African Americans:

> In the single case of the Negro, both numbers and visibility are such that awareness and fear are less easily decreased. But fear can be reduced by seeing to it that white people become familiar with the fact that Negroes can do and are doing everything that anyone else does. A campaign to make Negro activities of all kinds usual and matter-of-fact will both allay fears and reduce social visibility in spite of great numbers and biological visibility. But such a campaign must emphasize differences neither by stressing alleged special abilities and accomplishments, even though they are considered to be of high social value, such as dancing, musical, or dramatic talent, nor by needlessly overemphasizing mistreatment and conflict. The former unconsciously lends support to theories of race differences. The latter sharpens issues, increases visibility and fears, and can do little more than increase general awareness that there is a "Negro problem." We have too great a tendency, in our efforts to prove that there is no basis for discrimination, to stress the exceptional qualities and achievements of all minority groups instead of concentrating on making their participation in all the ordinary aspects of life so commonplace that it does not cause concern. The current campaign against anti-Semitism is wise in that it does not accentuate special Jewish contributions to modern civilization, does not needlessly publicize cases of discrimination, and does as little as possible to bring Jews to the attention of the nation as Jews.[151]

For Young, as for other social scientists of that time, things could not just be left to the wisdom of the populace; what was needed was a program, formulated in opposition to the Nazis: "The Nazis and the Fascists [. . .] had a racial goal for a purpose and they knew what had to be done to achieve it. It is incredible that we should help them do it simply because we can only state that the integration of democratic principles and intergroup behavior is our goal and vow to hold to it, when we should be actually blazing the trail by work on a planned program of practical accomplishments."[152] This is the emphatic ending of Young's essay of 1945. In his demand for a program, and his suggestion that de-emphasizing difference should be a constitutive part of it, he shared beliefs widely held by social scientists of that era.

Robert M. MacIver, an eminent Columbia University sociologist, similarly advocated, in 1945, a "line" of "social re-education" for Americans (and the word "re-education" was certainly in the air elsewhere!). His principle was, "What we do for one [group], we are doing for all, we are doing for ourselves. The accent must not be on difference, because that is already our trouble."[153] MacIver—who also called attention to the motto *e pluribus unum*—was interested in finding a middle way between pluralism and assimilation. As Higham writes, MacIver "made a significant effort to give that middle way some conceptual coherence [and] [...] developed a fundamental distinction between culture and coercion."[154] MacIver wrote, "What we have to advance toward is the common rights of all groups, and we can help by showing how some are denied these common rights, and proceeding to indicate these rights in the name of all rather than in the name of any group."[155] He saw the danger of distorted ideas about groups, because "they exaggerate the differences between the group that makes them and the group they are supposed to represent. They give the one group many virtues, and, of course, they give the other groups many less favorable qualities. Thus they exaggerate the differences between groups, and, even more, they exaggerate the likeness within the single group."[156]

This sense of crisis was also evident in the Social Science Research Council. Its freshly appointed Committee on Techniques for Reducing Group Hostility, under the direction of the sociologist Robin M. Williams Jr., produced a most interesting report in 1947, *The Reduction of Intergroup Tensions: A Survey of Research on Problems of Ethnic, Racial, and Religious Group Relations*, which cited numerous empirical studies that support the MacIver group's approach.[157] Williams's findings led him to formulate a careful program toward positive changes in group relations that is particularly concerned about possible unintended side effects. His research findings and suggestions include the following:

> Simultaneous direct attack on every form of intergroup discrimination is likely to intensify the reaction it attempts to stop. [...] Generally speaking, any policy which tends to make Jews as Jews more conspicuous, and

> particularly those Jews who are at the same time vulnerable symbols in other respects, would tend to be an invitation to anti-Semitic reaction. Thus, indiscriminate attack on every form of existent discrimination, regardless of anything but the immediate effectiveness of the means, is not likely to achieve the actual elimination of anti-Semitism, but on the contrary to intensify the reactions it attempts to stop.
>
> [P]roblems of group conflict are usually most readily resolved by indirection than by frontal assault.
>
> Where strong prejudice is present in a group which is highly self-conscious, and strongly bound together, outside criticism of its prejudice is likely to be taken as an attack on the group; and *one* immediate effect is to strengthen the prejudice, which by virtue of the attack becomes a symbol of in-group membership and solidarity.
>
> Propaganda which appeals for minority rights on the basis of the group's achievements tends beyond a certain point to arouse insecurity-hostility in the dominant group by stressing group differences and competitive success.
>
> An effective propaganda approach in intergroup relations is that which emphasizes national symbols and common American achievements, sacrifices, destinies, etc., while unobtrusively indicating the common participation of minority group members.
>
> Hostility is reduced by arranging for reverse role-taking in public drama or ceremony (e.g., an anti-Negro person plays a realistic Negro role).
>
> The likelihood of conflict is reduced by education and propaganda emphases upon characteristics and values *common* to various groups rather than upon intergroup *differences*.[158]

Yet Williams is also alert to the problems inherent in such an approach and makes two important qualifications: "But there is danger that attitudes thus created may lead to expectation of greater similarity than later experience demonstrates, and this can lead to disillusionment and secondary reinforcement of hostility. A second qualification is that some persons holding to a doctrine of cultural pluralism advocate awareness of differences on the assumption that acceptance of differences comes only after a transitional period, which may involve temporary intensification of hostilities."[159] Williams's paradigm is clearly designed to deemphasize difference; yet he is open to the possible workings of a pluralistic program, too. The tradeoff is an intensification of hostilities (hopefully a "transitional" one) that might lead toward acceptance of differences.

Another way of reconciling the integrationist reactions to World War II with more pluralism than was suggested in Young's essay came with the concept of intercultural education, advocated by a group of educators and sociologists in the 1940s and 1950s. The Bureau for Intercultural Education in New York published a series of monographs on such topics as prejudice, race relations, and assimilation.

Cole and Cole's *Minorities and the American Promise: The Conflict of Principle and Practice* is characteristic of a balanced approach toward the shortcomings and merits of both assimilationist and pluralist strategies. Looking today at this text from 1954 makes a good part of the current debate look like a slightly touched-up déjà-vu. The Coles were the authors of the sentence quoted earlier: "The unique fact that characterizes America is that it is a multiculture society."[160] I have not found any recognition or mention of this even semantically interesting precursor text in the literature on multiculturalism.

After a rejection of "Anglo-conformity," the approaches of "melting pot" and "pluralism and tolerance" are weighed against each other: the practice of assimilation is criticized for sacrificing the "significance of ethnic differences," overemphasizing "social likeness and cultural solidarity of the people," and for often being "impracticable in human relations."[161] Pluralism, however, "tends to border indecisively on the shaky rim of intolerance" and tends to exaggerate "the social separateness of peoples and the individuality of their subcultures."[162] Hence they conclude, "A multiculture society needs a more comprehensive conception of democratic human relations."[163] In diagrams and discussions they search for principles of democratic human relations that combine the advantages and eschew the shortcomings of both melting pot and pluralism. (See Figure 5.) The Coles saw the need for and the drawbacks of thinking about unity and diversity; and their book is also clearer than many contributions to the current debate about what is at stake in stressing or in deemphasizing difference. Thus they describe their project of an educational philosophy adequate for a "multiculture society" in ways that differentiate "pluralism" from education for "dynamic democracy" (which includes assimilation and shared values). Finally, they view American education in a global context and demand that students should learn not only to negotiate ethnic and American identities but also to be prepared as citizens of the world.

Things have changed so radically that neither a reasoned choice between pluralism and assimilation nor the hope for a synthesis of the two would seem to be present in the multiculturalism debate. A 1992 report entitled *Meeting the Challenges of Multicultural Education* seems representative in its overwhelming focus on teaching "cultural identity," and "racial or ethnic pride and self-esteem" as the mission of schooling.[164] Multiculturalism seems largely unaware of its precursors and has worked out its own rhetorical conventions and hopes.

How did we get from the 1950s to the present? Milton Gordon has offered an account that illuminates the transformation from liberal pluralism, which gives no formal recognition to categories of people on the basis of race or ethnicity, to corporate pluralism, which recognizes ethnic entities.[165] More than the social sciences, it was probably black political language of the 1960s that helped to change things, redefining "assimilation" and "melting pot" as if they were associated with the Holocaust. We saw how Donald R. Young had suggested the promotion of ethnic assimilation in response to the Holocaust. The following passage from Malcolm X's bestselling *Autobiography* signals the collapse of the assimilationist paradigm:

> "Integration" is called "assimilation" if white ethnic groups alone are involved: it's fought against tooth and nail by those who want their heritage preserved. Look at how the Irish threw the English out of Ireland. The Irish knew the English would engulf them. Look at the French-Canadians, fanatically fighting to keep their identity.
>
> In fact, history's most tragic result of a mixed, therefore diluted and weakened, ethnic identity has been experienced by a white ethnic group—the Jew in Germany.
>
> He had made greater contributions to Germany than German themselves had. Jews had won over half of Germany's Nobel Prizes. Every culture in Germany was led by the Jew; he published the greatest newspaper. Jews were the greatest artists, the greatest poets, composers, stage directors. But those Jews made a fatal mistake—assimilating.
>
> From World War I to Hitler's rise, the Jews in Germany had been increasingly intermarrying. Many changed their names and many took other religions. Their own Jewish religion, their own rich Jewish ethnic and cultural roots, they anesthetized and cut off [...] until they began thinking of themselves as "Germans."
>
> And the next thing they knew, there was Hitler, rising to power from the beer halls—with his emotional "Aryan master race" theory. And right at hand

> for a scapegoat was the self-weakened, self-deluded "German" Jew. Most mysterious is how did those Jews—with all of their brilliant minds, with all of their power in every aspect of Germany's affairs—how did those Jews stand almost as if mesmerized, watching something which did not spring upon them overnight, but which was gradually developed—a monstrous plan for their own *murder*. The self-brainwashing had been so complete that not long after, in the gas chambers, a lot of them were still gasping, "It *can't* be true!" If Hitler *had* conquered the world, as he meant to—that is a shuddery thought for every Jew alive today. The Jew will never forget that lesson. Jewish intelligence eyes watch over every neo-Nazi organization. Right after the war, the Jews' Haganah mediating body stepped up the longtime negotiations with the British. But this time, the Stern gang was shooting the British.
>
> And this time the British acquiesced and helped them to wrest Palestine away from the Arabs, the rightful owners, and then the Jews set up Israel, their own country—the one thing that every race of man in the world respects, and understands.[166]

For Malcolm X, in this passage at least,[167] "Jew" was a stand-in for "Negro" and "German" for "American";[168] the lesson of the Holocaust had become an opposition to racial integration; and militant Zionism was seen as the model for black Americans—the very opposite of Young's conclusions. Malcolm stands for many other cultural figures of the 1960s that have similarly opposed racial integration in the name of the Holocaust. One only needs to think of LeRoi Jones, later to become Amiri Baraka, who in the essay "What Does Nonviolence Mean?" also draws an analogy between the situation of black Americans and the fate of German Jews under Hitler.[169] In a universe in which assimilation of blacks or Jews becomes culturally linked to the Holocaust, the image of the melting pot could become as threatening as that of a gas chamber. Assimilation now could be viewed as if it were annihilation, and the careful weighing of pluralism and assimilation gave way to a strong assertion of difference, first in the "new ethnicity" of the 1970s, and later in multiculturalism.

It seems quite disturbing that much of the multiculturalism debate reinvents—and reintroduces with less scholarly evidence—what has been discussed for more than half a century and has often led earlier scholars to recommendations that differ dramatically from the ones that are now being institutionalized, practiced, and simply taken for granted. Is it an expression of the postmodern moment that the debate is based on weak empirical analysis of the present and pits "radicals" without a utopian vision of the future against "conservatives" with no deep concern for the past they wish to preserve? That the endless debates about "the canon" are flanked by implicitly enacted canonizations of a Latin motto, phrases by Matthew Arnold and George Orwell, and a belated and displaced opposition to totalitarianism?

Perhaps the pluralists' hope is well founded that intensification of hostilities may only be a temporary stage toward greater intergroup understanding. (It was mentioned by Robin Williams in an aside.) But what if it is not? What if the racist and sexist incidents that keep being reported in the literature of multicultural anecdotes signal an increase in hostilities that are at least partly a reaction to the top-down enactment of multiculturalism itself? Is American life going through a "transitional period" at the end of which mutual acceptance will be greater—or is it at an explosive crisis point, made all the more volatile by the far-reaching institutional support that is being extended to difference in a social system in which classes are drifting further apart, and quite dramatically so?

Challenges of Diversity

In the last few years, concerns about multiculturalism seem to have receded somewhat, while the term has become so omnipresent that Nathan Glazer's 1997 book *We Are All Multiculturalists Now* constitutes a perfect counterpoint to Edward Haskell's 1941 novel that introduced the word "multicultural" in order to describe the quality of a few exceptional men. Glazer's new endorsement of multiculturalism comes as the result of his recognition that it is the price America has to pay for having failed to integrate blacks. Against that historical backdrop multiculturalism may be the next best thing to universalism, he argues; in fact, it may be the only way to go. Glazer cites approvingly the most detailed brief for multiculturalism published, Lawrence Levine's *The Opening of the American Mind*, a 1996 response to Allan Bloom. In *Achieving Our Country* (1998) Richard Rorty offered a much more cautious endorsement of the various movements that later became known under the slogan multiculturalism as having helped to reduce the forms of social sadism (against women, against members of ethnic minorities, against homosexuals, against handicapped people, and so forth) that were still commonplace in American life of the 1950s, including the academic world. This is no small accomplishment. Yet Rorty also sees the danger that the international world of cultural politics has helped to eclipse the pressing issues of growing social inequality in the United States and around the globe. There may now be many multicultural men and women who are completely disconnected from any proletariat anywhere, and multicultural internationalism may even serve as the marker that separates these intellectuals from people, making multiculturalists instead part of a global ruling class. How can new social movements be built, Rorty therefore asks, that would (as did precursors from the 1930s to the 1960s) attempt to fight the crimes of (social) selfishness with the same vigor that multiculturalists have focused on the crimes of sadism?[170]

Notes

Introduction

1 Odysseus to Nausikaa, trans. Richmond Lattimore (New York: Harper Perennial Classics, 1967), 105. Odysseus uses the same formulation in his speech to his men in the land of the Cyclopes, IX:174–176, ibid., 141.
2 *United Nations International Migration Report 2015*, at http://www.un.org/en/development/desa/population/migration/publications/migrationreport/docs/MigrationReport2015_Highlights.pdf.
3 Different terms can thus refer to the same person. The Danish-born Jacob Riis, for example, would be considered an "emigrant" in Europe, an "immigrant" in America, and a "migrant" by the United Nations or scholars studying movements of people.
4 Cotton Mather, *Magnalia Christi Americana*, ed. Thomas Robbins (Hartford: S. Andrews and Son, 1853), II, 86-88. Quoted by Sacvan Bercovitch, "Fusion and Fragmentation: The American Identity," in *The American Identity: Fusion and Fragmentation*, ed. Rob Kroes, vol. 3, European Contributions to American Studies (Amsterdam: Amerika Instituut, Universiteit van Amsterdam, 1980), 19-45, here 21.
5 Benjamin Franklin, "Proposal for the Great Seal of the United States [before August 14, 1776]," at *Founders Online,* https://founders.archives.gov/documents/Franklin/01-22-02-0330.
6 John Adams's letter of August 14, 1776, to Abigail Adams, on the design of the Great Seal, at https://www.masshist.org/digitaladams/archive/doc?id=L17760814ja. See also *Founders Online,* at https://founders.archives.gov/documents/Jefferson/01-01-02-0206-0002.
7 "Annuit" is both the present and the present perfect tense. Vergil also used the expression "adnue coeptis" in *Georgics* I:40, where it is addressed to Caesar.
8 US Census 2010, Table 42, "Foreign-Born Population by Citizenship Status and Place of Birth: 2009."
9 US Census 2010, Table 6, "Resident Population by Sex, Race, and Hispanic Origin Status: 2000–2009." Because Hispanics are not considered a race by the Census, they describe themselves by race separately; thus 44 million of 47 million Hispanics consider themselves white and are added to the total white population of 200 million. About 2.5 million couples were interracially married, an enormous growth from 1980, when there were 650,000 interracially married couples, but a relatively small figure in a total of 60 million married couples. (US Census 2010, Table 60, "Interracially Married Couples by Race and Hispanic Origin: 1980–2010.")
10 US Census 2010, Table 52, "Population by Selected Ancestry Group: 2009."
11 Among 286 million Americans over the age of five, 229 million (or 80 percent) indicated that they speak only English at home; among the 50 million Americans of German ancestry only 1 million still speak German; and among 18 million Italian Americans there are only three-quarters of a million Italian speakers. By contrast, about 35 million of 48 million Hispanics speak Spanish at home, and among 14 million Asians about 8.5 million speak Chinese, Tagalog, Korean, Vietnamese,

Japanese, or another Asian language at home. (US Census 2010, Table 53, "Language Spoken at Home: 2009.")

12 Benjamin Franklin, *Observations Concerning the Increase of Mankind, Peopling of Countries, &c.* (Boston: S. Kneeland, 1755), 10. At https://archive.org/details/increasemankindoofranrich.

13 Alexander Hamilton, "Examination of Jefferson's Message to Congress of December 7, 1801," viii, January 7, 1802, in Henry Cabot Lodge, ed., *The Works of Alexander Hamilton*, Vol. 8 (New York: Putnam's, 1904) at http://oll.libertyfund.org/titles/hamilton-the-works-of-alexander-hamilton-federal-edition-vol-8. Hamilton also feared that giving foreigners full rights of citizenship upon arrival "would be nothing less than to admit the Grecian horse into the citadel of our liberty and sovereignty."

14 Alexis de Tocqueville, quoted in Werner Sollors, *Beyond Ethnicity: Consent and Descent in American Culture* (New York and Oxford: Oxford University Press, 1986), 3.

15 Edgar Allan Poe, "MS. Found in a Bottle," *Poetry and Tales,* ed. Patrick F. Quinn (New York: Library of America, 1983), 189.

16 Walt Whitman, *Complete Poetry and Collected Prose*, ed. Justin Kaplan (New York: Library of America, 1982), 372.

17 *Moby-Dick; or, The Whale,* ed. Luther S. Mansfield and Howard P. Vincent (New York: Hendricks House, 1951), ch. XVI, 80; digital text at http://web.archive.org/web/20030110125800/http://etext.lib.virginia.edu:80/etcbin/toccer-new2?id=Mel2Mob.sgm&images=images/modeng&data=/texts/english/modeng/parsed&tag=public&part=16&division=div1.

18 *White-Jacket; or, The World in a Man-of-War* (Evanston & Chicago: Northwestern University Press), ch. xxxvi, p. 150; quoted in Bercovitch, "Fusion and Fragmentation," 23.

19 "Introduction," *The Promised Land* (Boston: Houghton Mifflin, 1912), xi.

20 Ralph Ellison, *Invisible Man* (1952; repr. New York: Vintage Books, 1972), 16.

21 Jacob Riis, *The Making of an American* (1901; repr. New York: Macmillan, 1904), 7.

22 Horace M. Kallen, *Culture and Democracy in the United States: Studies in the Group Psychology of the American Peoples* (New York: Boni and Liveright, 1924), 122.

23 Kwame Anthony Appiah, "Afterword: How Shall We Live as Many?" in *Beyond Pluralism: Essays on the Conception of Groups and Group Identities in America*, ed. Wendy Katkin, Ned Landsman, and Andrea Tyree (Champaign: University of Illinois Press, 1998).

24 John Higham, *Send These To Me: Jews and Other Immigrants in Urban America* (New York: Atheneum 1975), 208.

25 Still, residential and educational segregation continued with real-estate redlining and discriminatory treatment of minority mortgage seekers. And minorities are dramatically overrepresented in the criminal justice system and incarceration rates.

26 See Eduardo Porter, "A Bigger Economic Pie, but a Smaller Slice for Half of the U.S.," *New York Times* (December 7, 2015), B1.

27 See "Just 8 Men Own Same Wealth as Half the World," Oxfam International press release, January 16, 2017, https://www.oxfam.org/en/pressroom/pressreleases/2017–01–16/just-8-men-own-same-wealth-half-world.

Divided by income and poverty rates the US population figures show that sharp class divergences exist both among and within different groups. Though the

American median income in 2014 was $53,657, for Asian Americans it was $74,297, for non-Hispanic whites $60,256, for Hispanics (any race) $42,491, and for African Americans $35,398. Among African American families, the success of the top fifth, with a mean annual income of $165,382, an amount that is more than four-fifths of the black families below them combined, contrasts sharply with the situation of the bottom fifth, with an income of a mere $9,399. US Census Data 2015, Historical Income: Families. Table F-3. Mean Income Received by Each Fifth and Top 5 Percent of Black Families: 1966 to 2015. At http://www.census.gov/data/tables/time-series/demo/income-poverty/historical-income-families.html. About 14.3 percent of the population, or 42.7 million Americans, had incomes below the poverty line; but for American Indians the poverty rate was 27 percent, for blacks 25.8 percent, and for Hispanics it ranged widely from 16.2 percent for Cubans to 26.3 percent for Dominicans. Suzanne Macartney, Alemayehu Bishaw, and Kayla Fontenot, *Poverty Rates for Selected Detailed Race and Hispanic Groups by State and Place, 2007–2011*. American Community Survey Briefs, February 2013. See also the comparable figures for family income in US Census 2010. Table 36. Selected Characteristics of Racial Groups and Hispanic or Latino Population. On average noncitizens in each group earn significantly less than citizens. US Census 2010. Table 40. Native and Foreign-Born Populations by Selected Characteristics: 2010. Here figures given for median annual earnings were $41,480, but for non-US citizens only $27,170. See also Carmen DeNavas-Walt and Bernadette D. Proctor, *Income and Poverty in the United States: 2014*, Current Population Reports, US Census: September 2015.

28 Richard Rorty, *Achieving Our Country: Leftist Thought in Twentieth-Century America* (Cambridge, MA: Harvard University Press, 1998).

29 David A. Hollinger, "How Wide the Circle of the 'We'? American Intellectuals and the Problem of the Ethnos since World War II," *American Historical Review* 98 (April 1993): 335–336.

30 John Higham, "The Redefinition of America, 1910-1930," ms. 1989, 25–29.

31 See United Nations General Assembly resolution 429(V) of December 14, 1950, at http://www.unhcr.org/refworld/docid/3b00f08a27.html; and http://www.refworld.org/cgi-bin/texis/vtx/rwmain?page=search&docid=57ceb74a4&skip=0&query=new%20york%20declaration%202015.

32 See Peter Mesenhöller, *Augustus F. Sherman: Ellis Island Portraits 1905-1920* (New York: Aperture, 2005), https://publicdomainreview.org/collections/portraits-of-ellis-island-immigrants/ and https://digitalcollections.nypl.org/search/index?utf8=%E2%9C%93&keywords=augustus+f.+sherman.

Chapter 1. Literature and Ethnicity

1 Among the best essays concerned with questions of ethnicity and literature are Daniel Aaron, "The Hyphenate Writer and American Letters," *Smith Alumnae Quarterly* (July 1964): 213–217; Jules Chametzky, "Our Decentralized Literature; A Consideration of Regional, Ethnic, Racial, and Sexual Factors," *Jahrbuch für Amerikastudien* 17 (1972): 56–72; Henry Pochmann, "The Mingling of Tongues," *Literary History of the United States*, ed. Robert E. Spiller, rev. ed. (New York: Macmillan, 1953), 676–693; and the appropriate sections in Carl Wittke, *We Who Built America: The Saga of the Immigrant* (New York: Prentice-Hall, 1939). A thematic survey of the literature of immigration is given by Carter

Davidson, "The Immigrant Strain in Contemporary American Literature," *English Journal* 25 (December 1936): 862–868. Malcolm Cowley, "Where Writers Come From," *The Literary Situation* (New York: Viking Press, 1954), 152–161, raises interesting questions about ethnic, regional, and educational backgrounds of American writers; Brom Weber, "Our Multi-Ethnic Origins and American Literary Studies," *MELUS* 2 (March 1975): 5–19, is a suggestive address given at the Modern Language Association. Volume 9 of the Proceedings of the Comparative Literature Symposium at Texas Tech University is a two-part reader on *Ethnic Literature since 1776: The Many Voices of America* (Lubbock, TX: Interdepartmental Committee on Comparative Literature, Texas Tech University, 1978). Of further interest are Randolph S. Bourne, "Trans-National America," *War and the Intellectuals: Essays 1915–1919*, ed. Carl Resek (New York: Harper & Row, 1964), 107–123; Van Wyck Brooks, "Transnationalism," *The Writer in America* (New York: Dutton, 1953), 86–108; Howard Mumford Jones, "American Literature and the Melting Pot," *Ideas in America* (Cambridge, MA: Harvard University Press, 1944), 185–204; and several essays in David F. Bowers, ed., *Foreign Influences in American Life: Essays and Critical Bibliographies* (Princeton, NJ: Princeton University Press, 1944). The most complete bibliography of ethnicity, arranged by ethnic groups and with many entries on literature and criticism, is *A Comprehensive Bibliography for the Study of American Minorities*, ed. Wayne Charles Miller and others, 2 vols. (New York: New York University Press, 1976). A more easily usable reference tool is *The Image of Pluralism in American Literature: An Annotated Bibliography on the American Experience of European Ethnic Groups* (New York: Institute for Pluralism and Group Identity of the American Jewish Committee, 1974) by Babette F. Inglehart and Anthony R. Mangione; it includes lists of literary works of eleven ethnic groups, brief plot summaries, and a thematic index. Further bibliographies are Joseph S. Roucek, *The Immigrant in Fiction and Biography* (New York: Bureau for Intercultural Education, 1945); and Nancy S. Prichard, *A Selected Bibliography of American Ethnic Writing* and *Supplement* (Champaign, IL: National Council of Teachers of English, 1969).

Several literary anthologies contain important selections from major texts, introductory and interpretive materials, as well as bibliographic references. Katharine D. Newman, *The American Equation: Literature in a Multi-Ethnic Culture* (Boston: Allyn and Bacon, 1971), arranges and interprets wellselected literary works under illuminating chapter headings. Edward Ifkovic, *American Letter: Immigrant and Ethnic Writing* (Englewood Cliffs, NJ: Prentice-Hall, 1975), organizes the literature, with introductions and study questions, in thematic units. Lillian Faderman and Barbara Bradshaw, *Speaking for Ourselves: American Ethnic Writing*, 2nd ed. (Glenview, IL: Scott, Foresman, 1975); and Wayne Miller, *A Gathering of Ghetto Writers: Irish, Italian, Jewish, Black, and Puerto Rican* (New York: New York University Press, 1972), are arranged by ethnic groups.

Chapter 2. National Identity and Ethnic Diversity

1 Urs Bitterli, ed., Die *Entdeckung und Eroberung der Welt: Dokumente und Berichte* (München: C. H. Beck, 1980), 43.

2 "J. Hector St. John" de Crèvecœur, *Letters from an American Farmer* (1782; New York: Dutton, 1957), 39.
3 Earl Jeffrey Richards, "European Literature and the Labyrinth of National Images: Literary Nationalism and the Limits of Enlightenment" (dissertation, Universität Aachen, 1989).
4 Henry James, *The American Scene* (1907; Bloomington and London: Indiana University Press, 1968), 124.
5 Robert Park, cited in Charles S. Johnson, *Shadows of the Plantation* (1934; Chicago and London: University of Chicago Press, 1979), xxi.
6 Maxine Hong Kingston, *Tripmaster Monkey: His Fake Book* (New York: Knopf, 1989), 317.
7 David G. Croly, *Glimpses of the Future: Suggestions as to the Drift of Things*. New York and London: Putnam's, 1888), 22–24. See Sidney Kaplan, "The Miscegenation Issue in the Election of 1864," *Journal of Negro History* 34.3 (1949): 274–343.
8 Hamilton Holt, ed., *The Life Stories of Undistinguished Americans: As Told by Themselves* (New York: J. Pott, 1906).
9 Anonymous (David G. Croly, George Wakeman, and E. C. Howell), *Miscegenation: The Theory of the Blending of Races, Applied to the American White Man and Negro* (New York: H. Dexter, Hamilton & Co., 1864), 63–64.
10 Rodman Gilder, *Statue of Liberty Enlightening the World* (New York: New York Trust Company, 1943), 17; Marvin Trachtenberg, *The Statue of Liberty* (Harmondsworth and New York: Penguin, 1977), 60.
11 Martha Banta, *Imaging American Women: Idea and Ideals in Cultural History* (New York: Columbia University Press, 1988), 125-130, 206-213.
12 John Greenleaf Whittier, *Complete Poetical Works* (Boston and New York: Houghton, Mifflin and Co., 1904), 295–296.
13 Emma Lazarus, *Poems of Emma Lazarus*, vol. 1 (Boston and New York: Houghton, Mifflin and Co., 1888), 202–203.
14 Oscar Handlin, *Statue of Liberty* (New York: Newsweek Book Division, 1971), 61, 63; Heinrich Eduard Jacob, *The World of Emma Lazarus* (New York: Schocken Books, 1949), 179.
15 Karl Baedeker, *The United States, with Excursions to Mexico, Cuba, Porto Rico, and Alaska* (Leipzig: Baedeker, 1909), 72.
16 John Higham, *Send These to Me: Jews and Other Immigrants in Urban America* (New York: Atheneum 1975), 82–83.
17 Lecture at Columbia University, 1976; see also Higham, *Send These to Me*, 85–86.
18 James H. Patten, *The Immigration Problem and the South* (Raleigh, NC: [1906?]), 16; Barbara Miller Solomon, *Ancestors and Immigrants: A Changing New England Tradition* (1956; Chicago: University of Chicago Press, 1972), 126.
19 Zola Levitt Ministries, www.levitt.com/newsletters/1995–07 (accessed May 8, 1998). See also http://www.jta.org/1957/12/23/archive/new-york-airport-deletes-line-from-plaque-of-emma-lazarus-poem.
20 Gunnar Thander, "*Valkyrian*, a Mediator Between Cultures" (lecture, Emigrant Institute Växjö, Sweden, June 2, 1991).
21 Maxine Hong Kingston, *China Men* (New York: Knopf, 1980), 67.
22 Emma Goldman, *Living My Life: An Autobiography* (1931; Salt Lake City: Peregrine Smith, 1982), 11; see Bernhard Giesen, ed., *Nationale und kulturelle Identität:*

Studien zur Entwicklung des kollektiven Bewußtseins in der Neuzeit (Frankfurt: Suhrkamp, 1991), 513.

23 Giesen, ed., *Nationale und kulturelle Identität*, 515.

24 Banta, *Imaging American Women*, 28.

25 Thomas Bailey Aldrich, "Unguarded Gates," *Atlantic Monthly* 70 (1892): 57; cf. Israel Zangwill, *The Melting-Pot* (New York: Macmillan, 1910), 199–200.

26 Solomon, *Ancestors and Immigrants*, 88.

27 Arthur W. Calhoun, "Race Sterility and Race Suicide," in *A Social History of the American Family from Colonial Times to the Present*, vol. 3, *Since the Civil War* (Cleveland: Arthur H. Clark Company, 1919), 225–254.

28 Lothrop Stoddard, *The Revolt Against Civilization: The Menace of the Under Men* (New York: Scribner's, 1923), 113. Cited in Stephan Thernstrom, "The Minority Majority Will Never Come," *Wall Street Journal*, July 26, 1990.

29 Oliver Wendell Holmes, *Elsie Venner: A Romance of Destiny* (1861; Cambridge, MA: Riverside Press, 1891), 1–5.

30 William Taylor, *Cavalier and Yankee: The Old South and American National Character* (1957; Cambridge, MA: Harvard University Press, 1979), 43–44.

31 John McPhee, "Travels of the Rock," *New Yorker*, February 26, 1990, 108–117, here 112, 114, 117.

32 William Bradford, *Of Plymouth Plantation 1620–1647*, ed. Samuel Eliot Morison (New York: Modern Library 1952), 72n; see also McPhee, "Travels," 115.

33 McPhee, "Travels," 113.

34 Alexis de Tocqueville, *Democracy in America* (1835), Henry Reeve text, ed. Phillips Bradley, vol. 1 (New York: Knopf, 1951), 34n8; see Charlotte Sears, *The Peregrinations of Plymouth Rock* (Plymouth, MA: Antiquarian Society, 1985), 16.

35 L. H. Sigourney, *National Era*, May 20, 1852, n281.

36 Burton Egbert Stevenson, ed., *Poems of American History* (1908; Boston and New York: Houghton, Mifflin and Co., 1922), 46–47.

37 See, e.g., Benson J. Lossing, *A Common-School History of the United States; From the Earliest Period to the Present Time* (New York: Sheldon and Co., 1873), 36.

38 E. Digby Baltzell, *The Protestant Establishment: Aristocracy and Caste in America* (1964; New York: Vintage, 1966), 115.

39 Mrs. Joseph Rucker Lamar, *A History of the National Society of the Colonial Dames of America from 1891 to 1933* (Atlanta, GA: Walter W. Brown Publishing Co., 1934), 19–44, 132–143.

40 Samuel Adams Drake, *A Book of New England Legends and Folk Lore in Prose and Poetry* (1884; rev. ed., Rutland, VT: Tuttle Company, 1906), 380.

41 A. S. Burbank, *Guide to Historic Plymouth: Localities and Objects of Interest* (Plymouth, MA: A. S. Burbank, 1916), 8.

42 Horace M. Kallen, *Culture and Democracy in the United States: Studies in the Group Psychology of the American Peoples* (New York: Boni and Liveright, 1924), 98–99.

43 Mary Antin, *They Who Knock at Our Gates: A Complete Gospel of Immigration* (Boston and New York: Houghton, Mifflin and Co., 1914), 25–26.

44 Ibid., 98.

45 Georges Perec, *Récits d'Ellis Island: Histoires d'errance et d'espoir* (Paris: Editions du Sorbier , 1980), 16; August C. Bolino, *The Ellis Island Source Book* (Washington, DC: Kensington Historical Press, 1985).

46 Antin, *They Who Knock*, 69.

47 Dag Blanck, "An Invented Tradition: The Creation of a Swedish-American Ethnic Consciousness at Augustana College," in *Scandinavia Overseas: Patterns of Cultural Transformation in North America and Australia*, ed. Harald Runblom and Dag Blanck, 2nd ed. (Uppsala: Center for Multiethnic Research, 1990), 90; Orm Øverland, *The Western Home: A Literary History of Norwegian America* (Northfield, MN: Norwegian American Historical Association, distr. University of Illinois Press, 1996), 288.

48 *American and Other Poems*, cited in Øverland, *Western Home*, 340.

49 Doris Sommer, *Foundational Fictions: The National Romances of Latin America* (Berkeley: University of California Press, 1991).

50 Richard Polenberg, "Progressivism and Anarchism: Judge Henry D. Clayton and the Abrams Trial," *Law and History Review* 3.2 (Fall 1985): 397–408, here 397, 407; Lawrence H. Fuchs, *The American Kaleidoscope: Race, Ethnicity, and the Civic Culture* (Middletown, CT: Wesleyan University Press, 1990), 68.

51 M. A. DeWolfe Howe, *Barrett Wendell and His Letters* (Boston: Atlantic Monthly Press, 1924), 282.

52 Ibid., 6–11.

53 Lamar, *History of the National Society*, 135, 119, 14.

54 Howe, *Barrett Wendell*, 282.

55 Agnes Repplier, *Counter-Currents* (Boston and New York: Houghton, Mifflin and Co., 1916), 226–227.

56 Ibid., 219–220.

57 Ibid., 205.

58 Ibid., 197–201; see James Russell Lowell, *Literary Essays*, vol. 3. (Boston and New York: Houghton, Mifflin and Co., 1892), 220–254.

59 Kallen, *Culture and Democracy*, 86.

60 Ibid., 106.

61 Sui Sin Far (Maude Eaton), *Mrs. Spring Fragrance* (New York: A. C. McClurg & Co., 1912), 12, 3.

62 Arthur Mann, *The One and the Many: Reflections on the American Identity* (Chicago: University of Chicago Press, 1979), 142.

63 Cited in Øverland, *Western Home*, 469.

64 John Higham, "The Redefinition of America, 1910–1930," ms. 1989, 23–26.

65 Randolph S. Bourne, *The Radical Will: Selected Writings, 1911–1918*, ed. Olaf Hansen (New York: Urizen Press, 1977), 249.

66 Thomas Bender, *New York Intellect: A History of Intellectual Life in New York City, from 1750 to the Beginnings of Our Own Time* (Baltimore: Johns Hopkins University Press, 1987), 246–249.

67 Bourne, *Radical Will*, 249.

68 F. H. Matthews, "The Revolt Against Americanism: Cultural Pluralism and Cultural Relativism as an Ideology of Liberation," *Canadian Review of American Studies* 1.1 (1970): 4–31.

69 David A. Hollinger, *In the American Province: Studies in the History and Historiography of Ideas* (Bloomington: Indiana University Press, 1985), 56–73.

70 Øverland, *Western Home*, 469.

71 Bourne, *Radical Will*, 262.

72 Ibid., 249.

73 Philip Gleason, "Americans All: Ethnicity, Ideology, and American Identity in the

Era of World War II," in *The American Identity: Fusion and Fragmentation*, ed. Rob Kroes, vol. 3, European Contributions to American Studies (Amsterdam: Amerika-Instituut, Universiteit van Amsterdam, 1980), 235–264, here 248–254.

74 Higham, *Send These to Me*, 208.

75 Higham, "Redefinition of America," 25–29.

76 Bourne, *Radical Will*, 254.

77 Ibid.

78 Louis Adamic, *My America 1928–1938* (New York and London: Harper and Brothers, 1938), 195; Louis Adamic, *From Many Lands* (New York and London: Harper and Brothers, 1940), 292. See Higham, *Send These To Me*, 85; and Gleason "Americans All," 244.

79 Adamic, *From Many Lands*, 299.

80 Walt Whitman, *Complete Poems and Collected Prose* (New York: Library of America, 1982), 5; see also Louis Adamic, *A Nation of Nations* (New York and London: Harper and Brothers, 1945).

81 Judith Smith, "Celebrating Immigration History at Ellis Island," *American Quarterly* 44.1 (March 1992): 82–100, here 84.

82 Alessandra Stanley, "Ellis Island Will Reopen in a Subdued Mood," *New York Times*, September 3, 1990, 1, 32; Deborah Sontag, "Immigrants Find Immorality, but at a Price" *New York Times*, January 14, 1993, B3.

83 "Indian Ceremony on Ellis Island," *New York Times*, June 29, 1987, B3.

84 Kingston, *China Men*, 52–53.

85 Him Mark Lai et al., eds., *Island: Poetry and History of Chinese Immigrants on Angel Island 1910–1940* (San Francisco: HOC DOI [History of Chinese Detained on Island], Chinese Cultural Foundation, 1980), 141. See also Xiao-huang Yin, *Chinese American Literature since the 1850s* (Urbana: University of Illinois Press, 2000); and Te-Hsing Shan, "Redefining Chinese-American Literature from a LOWINUS Perspective: Two Recent Examples," in *Multilingual America: Transnationalism, Ethnicity, and the Languages of American Literature*, ed. Werner Sollors (New York: New York University Press, 1998), 112–123.

86 Nathan Irvin Huggins, "Introduction: The Deforming Mirror of Truth," *Black Odyssey: The African American Ordeal in Slavery* (New York: Pantheon, 1990), xliv–xlvi.

87 Anonymous [Nathaniel Hawthorne], "Chiefly about War-Matters. By a Peaceable Man," *Atlantic Monthly* 10 (July 1862): 43–61, here 50.

88 Malcolm X, with the assistance of Alex Haley, *The Autobiography of Malcolm X* (1965; New York: Grove Press, 1966), 201. This is the quote from the autobiography, though at Michigan State University on January 23, 1963, Malcolm X actually said, "this twentieth-century Uncle Tom, he'll stand up in your face and tell you about when his fathers landed on Plymouth Rock. His father never landed on Plymouth Rock; the rock was dropped on him." Malcolm X, *The Last Speeches*, ed. Bruce Perry (New York: Pathfinder Press, 1989), 40.

89 Mark Twain, *Collected Tales, Sketches, Speeches, & Essays 1852–1890*, ed. Louis J. Budd (New York: Library of America, 1992), 782.

90 Ibid., 782–784.

91 Ibid., 784–785.

92 William Wells Brown, *Clotel; or, The President's Daughter* (1853; New York: Collier Books, 1970), 147.

93 Ibid., 177
94 Huggins, "Deforming Mirror," xlvii.
95 W.E.B. Du Bois, *Writings*, ed. Nathan I. Huggins (New York: Library of America, 1986), 424, 545.
96 Richard Wright, *12 Million Black Voices* (1941; New York: Thunder's Mouth Press, 1988), 14.
97 Charles E. Hatch, *Jamestown, Virginia: The Townsite and Its Story* (1949; Washington, DC: National Park Service, 1957), 23–24; *The 350th Anniversary of Jamestown, 1607–1957: Final Report* (Washington, DC: National Park Service, 1958), 78; *Significant Addresses of the Jamestown Festival, 1957*, ed. Ulrich Troubetzkoy, with addresses by Queen Elizabeth, President Eisenhower, Richard Nixon, and others (Richmond, VA: United States Jamestown-Williamsburg-Yorktown Celebration Commission, 1958); Ransom B. True, *Jamestown: A Guide to the Old Town* (Richmond, VA: Association for the Preservation of Virginia Antiquities, 1983); Theodore Roosevelt, "The Settlement of Jamestown" (1907), in *The Works of Theodore Roosevelt*, Memorial Edition, vol. 12 (New York: Charles Scribner's, 1924), 585–596, here 585n, 585, 589.
98 "Africans in Early Virginia," *New York Times*, August 7, 1994, travel section, 3.
99 Booker T. Washington, *The Story of the Negro: The Rise of the Race from Slavery*, vol. 2 (London: T. Fisher Unwin, 1909), 293–294; Mary White Ovington, *Portraits in Color* (New York: Viking Press, 1927), 222.
100 See Adamic, *Nation of Nations*, 195.
101 James Edwin Campbell, *Echoes from the Cabin and Elsewhere* (Chicago: Donohue and Henneberry, 1895), 82.
102 Melvin B. Tolson, "Rendezvous with America," *Common Ground* 2.4 (Summer 1942): 3.
103 Ibid., 4–5.
104 Ibid., 7.
105 Ibid., 3.
106 Jack Salzman et al., ed., *Social Poetry of the 1930s: A Selection* (New York: Burt Franklin, 1978), 314–320.
107 Richard Wright, *Native Son* (New York: Harper and Brothers, 1940), 332.
108 Wright, "I Choose Exile," MS 1948, James Weldon Johnson Collection, Beinecke Library, Yale University.
109 Wright, *White Man, Listen!* (1957; Garden City, NY: Doubleday and Co., 1964), 16.
110 W.E.B. Du Bois, *The Autobiography of W.E.B. Du Bois: A Soliloquy on Viewing My Life from the Last Decade of Its First Century* (New York: International Publishers, 1968), 182.
111 Goldman, *Living My Life*, 11, 663.
112 Ibid., 717.
113 "Chronicle" *New York Times*, December 8, 1990.
114 "Chronicle," *New York Times*, March 24, 1992, B18.

Chapter 3. Dedicated to a Proposition

1 Henry James, *Collected Travel Writings: Great Britain and America*, ed. Richard Howard (New York: Library of America, 1993), 594.

2 Jefferson to Henry Lee, May 8, 1825, in *Writings*, ed. Merrill Peterson (New York: Library of America, 1984), 1500. Cited in Sacvan Bercovitch, *The Rites of Assent: Transformations in the Symbolic Construction of America* (New York: Routledge, 1993), 84.

3 Pauline Maier, *American Scripture: Making the Declaration of Independence* (New York: Knopf, 1997), 132.

4 Ibid., 132.

5 *Proceedings and Debates of the Virginia State Convention of 1829–30* (1830; Maier, *American Scripture*), 134.

6 Maier, *American Scripture*, 239. Maier gives the elided text as follows: "[H]e has waged cruel war against human nature itself, violating it's most sacred rights of life & liberty in the persons of a distant people, who never offended him, captivating and carrying them into slavery in another hemisphere, or to incur miserable death in their transportation thither. [T]his piratical warfare, the opprobrium of *infidel* powers, is the warfare of the *Christian* king of Great Britain. determined to keep open a market where MEN should be bought & sold, he has prostituted his negative for suppressing every legislative attempt to prohibit or to restrain this execrable commerce: and that this assemblage of horrors might want no fact of distinguished die, he now is now exciting those very people to rise in arms amongst us, and to purchase that liberty of which *he* has deprived them, by murdering the people upon whom *he* also obtruded them: thus paying off former crimes committed against the *liberties* of one people, with crimes which he urges them to commit against the *lives* of another."

7 Thomas Jefferson, *Autobiography by Thomas Jefferson* (New Haven, CT: The Avalon Project at Yale Law School, 2006), http://www.yale.edu/lawweb/avalon/jeffauto.htm.

8 John Trumbull, *Independence Hall, Philadelphia, on July 4, 1776*, 1819, oil on canvas, 12' x 18', in Rotunda, Capitol Complex. From *The Architect of the Capitol* (Washington, DC: Architect of the Capitol, 2006), http://www.aoc.gov/cc/art/rotunda/declaration_independence.cfm.

9 Jamaica Kincaid, "A Little Revenge from the Periphery," *Transition* 73 (1997): 68–73, here 70–71.

10 Ibid., 71.

11 Ibid., 72.

12 Arthur Zilversmit, "Quok Walker, Mumbet, and the Abolition of Slavery in Massachusetts," *William and Mary Quarterly* 25.4 (3rd ser., October 1968): 614–624, here 615.

13 Catherine Sedgwick, "Slavery in New England," *Bentley's Miscellany* 34 (1853): 417–424, here 421.

14 Zilversmit, "Quok Walker," 617.

15 David Walker, *Appeal, in Four Articles; Together with a Preamble, to the Coloured Citizens of the World, but in Particular, and Very Expressly, to Those of the United States of America*, ed. William Loren Katz (New York: Arno Press, 1969), 85–86. Originally published as *Walker's Appeal, in Four Articles* (Boston: D. Walker, 1829).

16 Frederick Douglass, "What to the Slave Is the Fourth of July?" excerpted in *My Bondage and My Freedom* (New York: Miller, Orton & Mulligan, 1855). Quoted as "The Meaning of July Fourth for the Negro, speech at Rochester, New York, July 5,

1852," in *The Life and Writings of Frederick Douglass*, ed. Philip S. Foner (New York: International Publishers, 1975), 188–189.

17 Douglass, "The Meaning of July Fourth," 189–190.

18 Ibid., 203.

19 "Frederick Douglass' Paper," *Frederick Douglass' Paper*, September 10, 1852, 1.

20 William Wells Brown, *Clotel, or the President's Daughter* (1853; New York: Citadel Press, 1969), 64.

21 Brown, *Clotel*, 68.

22 Thomas Moore, "To Thomas Hume, Esq. M.D. from the City of Washington," in *The Poetical Works of the Late Thomas Little, Esq.* (London: J. Carpenter, 1822), 295. *English Poetry*, http://collections.chadwyck.com.ezp1.harvard.edu/home/home.

23 Ovid, *Metamorphoses* V:79: Not the least well known among other infernal nymphs.

24 Thomas Moore, footnote to "To Thomas Hume, Esq. M.D. from the City of Washington," *The Poetical Works*, 295. *English Poetry*, http://collections.chadwyck.com.ezp1.harvard.edu/home/home.

25 Henry Adams, *History of the United States of America During the Administrations of Thomas Jefferson*, ed. Earl N. Harbert (New York: Library of America, 1986), 114.

26 Frederick Marryat, *A Diary in America: With Remarks on Its Institutions* (London: Longman, Orme, Brown, Green & Longmans, 1839), vol. 3, 300–301. See also his general remarks, vol. 3, 56–58.

27 Headnote to "Jefferson's Daughter," *The Liberator*, May 26, 1848, 84.

28 Nathan Irvin Huggins, *Revelations: American History, American Myth*, ed. Brenda Huggins (New York: Oxford University Press, 1995), 277. Huggins interestingly generalizes: "Legitimizing myths and myths of national origins are commonly set in illicit sexual unions."

29 Huggins, *Revelations*, 277.

30 Elizabeth Cady Stanton, "Declaration of Sentiments," in *We, the Other People: Alternative Declarations of Independence by Labor Groups, Farmers, Woman's Rights Advocates, Socialists, and Blacks, 1829–1975*, ed. Philip S. Foner (Urbana: University of Illinois Press, 1976), 78.

31 Stanton, "Declaration of Sentiments," 78.

32 Ibid., 79.

33 See ibid., 78.

34 Ibid., 80.

35 Bercovitch, *Rites of Assent*, 49.

36 Ibid., 49.

37 Kincaid, "Little Revenge," 71.

38 Carolyn Porter, "Social Discourse and Nonfictional Prose," in *Columbia Literary History of the United States*, ed. Emory Elliott (New York: Columbia University Press, 1988), 348.

39 Porter, "Social Discourse," 348.

40 Ibid., 348.

41 See Herman Melville, *White-Jacket, or, the World in a Man-of-War* (New York: Harper & Brothers, 1850). Melville also wrote in a letter to Duykinck that even Shakespeare could not be frank to the uttermost because of the muzzle all Elizabethans had to wear: "But the Declaration of Independence makes a difference."

Correspondence, ed. Lynn Horth (Evanston: Northwestern University Press and the Newberry Library, 1993), 122.

42 Lydia Maria Child, *A Romance of the Republic* (Boston: Ticknor and Fields, 1867).

43 See Walt Whitman, "A Poem of Many in One," *Leaves of Grass* (Brooklyn, NY: 1856), 192.

44 Walt Whitman, "Respondez!" *Leaves of Grass* (Boston: Thayer and Eldridge; London: Trübner, 1860–1861), 168, 166.

45 Daniel De Leon, "Declaration of Interdependence" in *We, the Other People*, ed. Foner, 142–143.

46 Ibid., 147.

47 Ibid., 143.

48 Ibid., 144.

49 Ibid., 143.

50 Ibid., 149.

51 "The Life Story of a Lithuanian," quoted in *The Life Stories of Undistinguished Americans as Told by Themselves*, ed. Hamilton Holt (New York: J. Pott, 1906), 25.

52 Holt, *Life Stories*, 15.

53 Ibid., 15.

54 Originally published as Langston Hughes, *Freedom's Plow* (New York: Musette Publishers, 1943). Reprinted in *The Collected Poems of Langston Hughes*, ed. Arnold Rampersad and David Roessel (New York: Vintage, 1994), 264.

55 Hughes, "Freedom's Plow," *The Collected Poems*, 265–266.

56 Ibid., 268.

57 Adam Fairclough, "Civil Rights and the Lincoln Memorial: The Censored Speeches of Robert R. Moton (1922) and John Lewis (1963)," *Journal of Negro History* 82.4 (Autumn 1997): 412.

58 W.E.B. Du Bois, "A Chronicle of Race Relations," *Phylon* 2.4 (1941): 403.

59 Gunnar Myrdal, *An American Dilemma: The Negro Problem and Modern Democracy* (New York and London: Harper & Brothers, 1944); Walter A. Jackson, *Gunnar Myrdal and America's Conscience: Social Engineering and Racial Liberalism, 1938–1987* (Chapel Hill and London: University of North Carolina Press, 1990), 186.

60 Myrdal, *American Dilemma*, 187.

61 Jackson, *Gunnar Myrdal*, xi.

62 Myrdal, *American Dilemma*, 3.

63 Ibid., 3.

64 Ibid., 4.

65 See Myrdal, *American Dilemma*, 5.

66 Myrdal, *American Dilemma*, 6. The point suggests itself how much the theme of wars, World War I, World War II, and the Korean War is intertwined with new thinking about race and ethnicity.

67 Myrdal, *American Dilemma*, 6–7.

68 Jackson, *Gunnar Myrdal*, 199.

69 Ibid., 200.

70 Ibid., 279.

71 As Jackson puts it, Myrdal "had overemphasized social pathologies and had neglected the mechanisms, strategies, beliefs, symbols, and institutions that gave

coherence and meaning to Afro-American communities and enabled blacks to resist oppression" (*Gunnar Myrdal*, 291).

72 Jackson, *Gunnar Myrdal*, 292.

73 Martin Luther King Jr., speech delivered as part of the "March on Washington for Jobs and Freedom" (Lincoln Memorial, Washington, DC, August 28, 1963). Reprinted as "I Have a Dream," in *Basic Readings in U.S. Democracy*, ed. Melvin I. Urofsky (Washington: USIA, 1994), 230–232.

74 Gregory Corso, "The American Way," in *Elegiac Feelings American* (New York: New Directions, 1970), 69.

75 Lawrence Ferlinghetti, "One Thousand Fearful Words for Fidel Castro," in *Starting from San Francisco* (New York: New Directions, 1961), 48–52.

76 Henry Steele Commager, "A Declaration of Interdependence," in *We, the Other People*, ed. Foner, 203.

77 Martin Espada, "Thomas Jefferson and the Declaration of Food Stamps," in *Imagine the Angels of Bread* (New York: W. W. Norton & Company, 1996), 51–52.

78 "A Jazz Lesson," in *Riverdeep Interactive Learning Limited* (San Francisco, CA: Riverdeep Interactive Learning Limited, 2006), https://www.riverdeep.net/current/2000/02/front.160200.jazz.jhtml.

79 H. L. Mencken, "The Declaration of Independence in American," in *The American Language: An Inquiry into the Development of English in the United States* (New York: A. A. Knopf, 1923), 398–402. Originally printed as "Essay in American," *Baltimore Evening Sun*, November 7, 1921.

80 Oliver Jensen, "The Gettysburg Address in Eisenhowerese," in *The Best of Modern Humor*, ed. Mordecai Richler (New York: Knopf, 1983), 199–200. See also "Inside the Funny Business," *New York Times Book Review*, http://www.nytimes.com/books/97/12/21/home/richler-humor.html; and "Dwight D. Eisenhower: Little Known Facts," Trivia-Library.com, http://www.trivia-library.com/b/u-s-president-dwight-d-eisenhower-little-known-facts.htm.

81 Richard "Lord" Buckley, "The Gettysburg Address," *Lord Buckley Live* (Shambhala Lion Editions: 1991), transcribed by Earl Rivers http://www.columbia.edu/~tdk3/gettysbu.txt.

82 James Rado and Gerome Ragni, "Abie Baby," in *Vocal Selections from Hair / Words by James Rado and Gerome Ragni; Music by Galt MacDermot* (New York: Big 3, 1979).

83 Rado and Ragni, "Abie Baby."

Chapter 4. A Critique of Pure Pluralism

1 Horace M. Kallen, *Culture and Democracy in the United States: Studies in the Group Psychology of the American Peoples* (New York: Boni and Liveright, 1924), 122.

2 Joe Weixlmann, review of *Oxford Companion to American Literature, MELUS* 11 (Spring 1984): 10.

3 David Dorsey, "Minority Literature in the Service of Cultural Pluralism," in *Minority Language and Literature: Retrospective and Perspective*, ed. Dexter Fisher (New York: Modern Language Association, 1977), 19.

4 Robert J. Di Pietro and Edward Ifkovic, eds., *Ethnic Perspectives in American Literature: Selected Essays on the European Contribution* (New York: Modern Language Association, 1983), 1, 11.

5 V. F. Calverton, *The Liberation of American Literature* (New York: Scribner's, 1932), 148.

6 Ibid., 143.

7 Marco A. Portales, "Literary History, a 'Usable Past,' and Space," *MELUS* 11 (Spring 1984): 101.

8 James H. Dormon, "The Varieties of American Ethnic Theater: A Review Essay," *Journal of American Ethnic History* 4 (Spring 1985): 88.

9 Alain Locke, ed., *The New Negro* (1925; New York: Atheneum, 1969), 16.

10 Horace M. Kallen, *Culture and Democracy in the United States: Studies in the Group Psychology of the American Peoples* (New York: Boni and Liveright, 1924), 43. All further references to this work appear in the text, cited parenthetically as *C.*

11 Horace M. Kallen, "The Ethics of Zionism," *The Maccabaean* 2 (August 1906): 70.

12 Horace M. Kallen, *Indecency and Seven Arts; and Other Adventures of a Pragmatist in Aesthetics* (New York: Liveright, 1930), 59.

13 As John Higham and Philip Gleason have pointed out, Kallen's vision of cultural pluralism is somewhat problematic. Higham called attention to the "chronic indistinctness of the pluralist idea in ethnic relations" (*Send These to Me: Jews and Other Immigrants in Urban America* [New York: Atheneum, 1975], 196), and Gleason argued that cultural pluralism "has always been more of a vision than a rigorous theory" ("American Identity and Americanization," in *Harvard Encyclopedia of American Ethnic Groups*, ed. Stephan Thernstrom, Ann Orlov, and Oscar Handlin [Cambridge, MA: Belknap Press of Harvard University Press, 1980], 43).

14 One might characterize this position as creationist, and no Scopes monkey in literary history has given evolutionists a foothold: mankind was seemingly created in a fairly finite and stable assortment of ethnic groups (a.k.a. races or stocks). American pluralism attempts to stabilize the existing groups into a state of symphonic bliss. Creationists, however, can hardly explain the emergence of American groups such as Southerners, Mormons, Appalachians, or African Americans in historical times.

15 Kallen, "Ethics," 70.

16 It is also worth noting that the nativist journalist Agnes Repplier (of Franco-German descent) was troubled (as was Barrett Wendell) by Jewish immigrant Mary Antin's presumptuousness in taking "possession of Beacon Street" and calling the Pilgrim Fathers "our forefathers." Repplier significantly associated immigrants with dirt and quoted Elizabeth Robins Pennell, who wrote that "if Philadelphia blossomed like the rose with Mary Antins, the city would be ill repaid for the degradation of her noble old streets, now transformed, into foul and filthy slums. Dirt is a valuable asset in the immigrant's hands" (Agnes Repplier, *Counter-Currents* [Boston: Houghton Mifflin, 1916], 227–228; also see Mary Dearborn, *Pocahontas' Daughters: Gender and Ethnicity in American Culture* [New York: Oxford University Press, 1985], 39–40). Repplier invoked none other than a slightly misquoted Kallen in order to support her nativism. "Mr. Horace Kallen," she writes approvingly, and some pages before the Philadelphia dirt sets in, "has put the case into a few clear conclusive words when he says, 'Only men who are alike in origin and spirit, and not abstractly, can be truly equal, and maintain that inward unanimity of action and outlook which makes a national life'" (Repplier, 203; cf. Kallen, *Culture*, 115). The culture critic Randolph Bourne, however, despite his dislike of assimilation, was more clearly aware of the political implications of

the New Englanders' reaction to Mary Antin. "We have had to watch," Bourne writes in "Trans-National America" (1916), "hard-hearted old Brahmins virtuously indignant at the spectacle of the immigrant refusing to be melted, while they jeer at patriots like Mary Antin who write about 'our forefathers'" (Randolph S. Bourne, *War and the Intellectuals: Collected Essays, 1915–1919*, 2nd ed. [New York: Alfred A. Knopf, 1973], 107).

17 Higham, *Send These to Me*, 207.

18 Gleason, "American Identity and Americanization," 44–45.

19 Kallen, "Ethics," 71.

20 This criticism of Kallen's exclusivism was fully developed by Higham. "[T]here was a fatal elision when he wrote that America could become 'an orchestration of mankind' by perfecting 'the cooperative harmonies of European civilization.' Nothing in Kallen's writing gave away the magnitude of that elision. In the fullest statement of his argument there was only a single obscure footnote on the point. 'I do not discuss the influence of the negro,' Kallen confessed in fine print. 'This is at once too considerable and too recondite in its processes for casual mention. It requires separate analysis' (Kallen, *Culture*, 226). The pluralist thesis from the outset was encapsulated in white ethnocentrism" (Higham, *Send These to Me*, 208).

21 Isaac B. Berkson, *Theories of Americanization: A Critical Study with Special Reference to the Jewish Group* (New York: Teachers College, Columbia University, 1920), 81.

22 Parts of the story have been suggested by Gleason and Higham as well as by Barbara Solomon, Milton Konvitz, Moses Rischin (who views Kallen's role in a very favorable light), Sarah Schmidt, and Clare Crane; others are offered here for the first time.

23 Milton R. Konvitz, "Horace Meyer Kallen: Philosopher of the Hebraic American Idea," *American Jewish Yearbook, 1974–75* (Philadelphia: Jewish Publication Society of America, 1974), 56.

24 Ibid., 56.

25 See Mary Antin, *The Promised Land* (Boston: Houghton Mifflin, 1912), 225–232; and Mary Antin, *They Who Knock at Our Gates: A Complete Gospel of Immigration* (Boston: Houghton Mifflin, 1914), 28–29, 98, and 142. Antin was born in Polotzk in the Jewish Pale of Settlement in 1881 and came to live in Boston at age thirteen.

26 Sarah L. Schmidt, "Horace Kallen and the Americanization of Zionism" (PhD diss., University of Maryland), 1973, 34. All further references to this work appear in the text, cited parenthetically as S.

27 Higham, *Send These to Me*, 198. Also see William Boelhower, *Through a Glass Darkly: Ethnic Semiosis in American Literature* (Venice: Edizioni Helvetia, 1984), 33.

28 Barbara Miller Solomon, *Ancestors and Immigrants: A Changing New England Tradition* (Chicago: University of Chicago Press, 1956), 173.

29 Edith Wendell Osborne, *Recollections of My Father Barrett Wendell* (privately printed, 1921), 17.

30 Moses Rischin, "The Jews and Pluralism: Toward an American Freedom Symphony," in *Jewish Life in America: Historical Perspectives*, ed. Gladys Rosen (New York: Institute of Human Relations Press of the American Jewish Committee and KTAV, 1980), 17.

31 William James drew out the ethnic and relativistic implications of pluralism in the essay "On a Certain Blindness in Human Beings" (1906)—which made a

lasting impression on Robert Park when he was a student at Harvard; see Robert E. Park, *Race and Culture: Essays in the Sociology of Contemporary Man* (New York and London: Free Press and Collier-Macmillan, 1964), vi–vii; occasionally James read this piece to his students. Using the illustration of the difference between his negative perception of a North Carolina wood clearing and the mountaineers' positive image of the same scene—not as denudation of nature, but as a "paean of duty, struggle, and success"—James generalizes: "I had been blind to the peculiar ideality of their conditions as they certainly would also have been to the ideality of mine, had they had a peep at my strange indoor academic ways of life at Cambridge" (William James, *Talks to Teachers on Psychology: and to Students on Some of Life's Ideals* [1906; New York: Holt, 1910], 234).

It should be noted, however, that Kallen was critical of James in a letter written to Wendell shortly before James delivered the Hibbert lectures: "Poor James! victim of a too excellent English style!" (Horace M. Kallen, letter to Barrett Wendell, March 11, 1908, Wendell Papers, Houghton Library, Harvard University).

William James's letter of reference on Kallen, addressed to F.C.S. Schiller at Oxford and dated July 15, 1907, adds another dimension to this story:

> A student of ours named Kallen, candidate for Ph.D., is about writing to you for advice about whether to go to Oxford next year—he has one of our fellowships. He is a Russian Jew by birth, very intense in character, very able and with high potentialities of all round cultivation, an enthusiastic and aggressive 'pragmatist', an active political worker, a *decidedly* original mind, neurotic disposition, but sails indefinitely long close to the wind without losing headway, a man with a positive future and possibly a great one and in good directions: *Revers de la médaille*: sticky, conceited, censorious of all institutions. Nevertheless faithful, candid, goodlooking and in favor of all good things. I shouldn't wonder if these eastern jews formed the chief ferment of ideality in our future America—they seem quite different from the more materialistic German hebrews.
>
> If you want that kind of a man for a famulus—encourage him; if not, discourage. He gains lots from experience and will gain lots from Oxford. I value Kallen very much, but have been disappointed in the portions of his thesis he has got ready this year. Too much general program and denunciation—too little hard work at discriminations.

(William James, *Selected Unpublished Correspondence: 1885–1910*, ed. Frederick J. Down Scott [Columbus: Ohio State University Press, 1986], 443).

32 Also see Higham, *Send These to Me*, 206.

33 William James, *A Pluralistic Universe* (Cambridge, MA: Harvard University Press, 1977), 145.

34 Ibid., 147.

35 Clare Bloodgood Crane, "Alain Locke and the Negro Renaissance" (PhD diss., University of California, San Diego, 1971), 27.

36 Ibid., 27.

37 Also see Rischin, "The Jews and Pluralism," 19.

38 Wendell Papers, Houghton Library, Harvard University.

39 Ibid. Louis Dyer (1851–1908) was a classicist lecturer.

40 Barrett Wendell to Horace Kallen, November 3, 1907, Horace M. Kallen Collection, American Jewish Archives, Cincinnati.

41 Ibid.

42 Ibid.

43 Park, *Race and Culture*, 230–243.

44 Kallen, letter to Barrett Wendell, November 12, 1907, Wendell Papers. Albert Venn Dicey (1835–1922) was a conservative professor of law; his brother Edward (1832-1911) was a writer and journalist.

45 Alain Locke, "Values and Imperatives," in *American Philosophy Today and Tomorrow*, ed. Sidney Hook and Horace Kallen (New York: L. Furman, 1935), 312.

46 Locke, ed., *New Negro*, 14.

47 Locke, "Values, "312.

48 See, for example, M. A. DeWolfe Howe, *Barrett Wendell and His Letters* (Boston: Atlantic Monthly Press, 1924), 183–184; and Kallen, letter to Barrett Wendell, May 2, 1908, Wendell Papers. Drawing on Kallen's 1907 letters to Harvard Professor Ralph Barton Perry, David Weinfeld has offered a more nuanced understanding of Kallen and Locke at Oxford, in "What Difference Does Difference Make? Horace Kallen, Alain Locke, and the Development of Cultural Pluralism in America," PhD diss., New York University, 2014, here 173.

49 Horace M. Kallen, "Alain Locke and Cultural Pluralism," *Journal of Philosophy* 54.5 (February 1957): 119–127, here 119–120. The vogue for indeterminacy in interpretation (sometimes in combination with cultural relativism) may also originate in pluralist thought. Thus James argued that "pluralism involves indeterminism"; and even though he lectured that "if you say 'indetermination,' you are determining just *that*," he was only mocking Hegelian thinking in that passage. (James, *A Pluralistic Universe*, 5, and 48.)

50 Albert Murray, *The Omni-Americans: New Perspectives on Black Experience and American Culture* (New York: Avon, 1970), 112.

51 The writer Jean Toomer is a good example here. He may have been excluded from older literary histories because he was black, but the new concern for Toomer as a black writer does injustice to Toomer's polyethnic ancestry and artistic interests. As Nellie Y. McKay writes persuasively, Toomer "was convinced that in the melting pot of America, the people of this nation were evolving into a racial mixture that would make it not only inaccurate but impossible to select out strains of racial or ethnic heritage eventually" (Nellie Y. McKay, *Jean Toomer, Artist: A Study of His Literary Life and Work, 1894–1936* [Chapel Hill: University of North Carolina Press, 1984], 244).

52 Antin, *Promised Land*, xi–xii; and Malcolm X with the assistance of Alex Haley, *The Autobiography of Malcolm X* (New York: Grove Press, 1966), 169–190.

53 Even contemporary advocates of pluralism and proponents of the power of ethnicity sometimes go further than literary critics in recognizing cultural texts as a shaping force of supposedly "natural" group affiliations. Thus Andrew Greeley writes: "Subscriptions to any two of the following are sufficient to guarantee one membership at least on the margins of this ethnic group: *The New York Times, Commentary, Partisan Review, Saturday Review, The New York Review of Books, The Atlantic* (but not *Harpers), Dissent, The New Republic,* and *The Nation.* In case of doubt, a subscription to *The New York Review of Books* alone will suffice" (Andrew M. Greeley, "Intellectuals as an 'Ethnic Group,'" *New York Times Magazine,* July 12, 1970, 22). Greeley's not altogether facetious ethnic identification-by-subscription, ironically published in *The New York Times Magazine*, was echoed by Michael

Novak who, originally writing in the safety of *Harper's*, defines "ruling classes" parenthetically as "subscribers to the *New Yorker*, I suppose" (Michael Novak, *The Rise of the Unmeltable Ethnics: Politics and Culture in the Seventies* [New York: Macmillan, 1975], 68). Jules Chametzky observed that ethnic identity may not be "what you do or what you are but an image created by what you read or at least know about" (Jules Chametzky, "Styron's *Sophie's Choice*, Jews and Other Marginals, and the Mainstream," *Prospects* 9 [1985]: 435–436). Even Kallen's supposedly instinctual repugnance at interracial dinners may be seen as an extreme form of Shakespeare exegesis, since in his letter to Wendell he explicitly invokes Shylock's disclaimer: "I will buy with you, sell with you, talk with you, walk with you, and so following; but I will not eat with you, drink with you, nor pray with you" (*The Merchant of Venice* I.iii.35ff.).

54 Frederick Douglass, *Narrative of the Life of Frederick Douglass an American Slave, Written by Himself*, ed. Benjamin Quarles (1845; Cambridge, MA: Belknap Press of Harvard University Press, 1960), 36–37.

55 Lawrence W. Levine, *Black Culture and Black Consciousness: Afro-American Folk Thought from Slavery to Freedom* (New York: Oxford University Press, 1977), 24.

56 Margaret Just Butcher, *The Negro in American Culture: Based on Materials Left by Alain Locke*, 2nd ed. (New York: Knopf, 1973), 26. See also Levine, *Black Culture*, 29.

57 Butcher, *The Negro in American Culture*, 148.

Chapter 5. The Multiculturalism Debate as Cultural Text

1 Audrey I. Richards, *The Multicultural States of East Africa* (Montreal and London: McGill-Queen's University Press, 1969), vii.

2 John Porter, "Ethnic Pluralism in Canada," in *Ethnicity: Theory and Experience*, ed. Nathan Glazer and Daniel P. Moynihan (Cambridge, MA: Harvard University Press, 1975), 287–288.

3 Ibid., 284–288.

4 Edward F. Haskell, *Lance: A Novel about Multicultural Men* (New York: John Day, 1941).

5 Iris Barry, "Melodrama, Tract, Good Story," review of Edward F. Haskell's *Lance*, *New York Herald Tribune Books*, July 12, 1941, 3.

6 Ibid.; Haskell, *Lance*, 320–321.

7 Horace M. Kallen, *Culture and Democracy in the United States: Studies in the Group Psychology of the American Peoples* (New York: Boni and Liveright, 1924). See chapter four in the present volume.

8 W. Lloyd Warner and Paul S. Lunt, *The Social Life of a Modern Community*, vol. 1 (New Haven, CT: Yale University Press, 1941).

9 Itabari Njeri, "Multiculturalism," *Los Angeles Times*, January 13, 1991.

10 Michael Walzer, "The New Tribalism: Notes on a Difficult Problem," *Dissent* 39 (Spring 1992): 164–172; Richard Bernstein, "The Arts Catch Up with a Society in Disarray: America's 'New Tribalism' Is Producing a Climate of Cultural Combat," *New York Times*, September 2, 1990.

11 Quoted by Berndt Ostendorf, "The Costs of Multiculturalism" (Working Paper No. 50, John F. Kennedy-Institut für Nordamerikastudien, Freie Universität Berlin, 1992), 19.

12 Ted Gordon and Wahneema Lubiano, "The Statement of the Black Faculty Caucus," in *Debating P.C.: The Controversy over Political Correctness on College Campuses*, ed. Paul Berman (New York: Dell, 1992), 249.
13 Arthur M. Schlesinger Jr., *The Disuniting of America: Reflections on a Multicultural Society* (Knoxville, TN: Whittle Direct Books, 1991), 40.
14 Lewis S. Feuer, "From Pluralism to Multiculturalism," *Society 29 (November/* December 1991): 9.
15 Mortimer Adler, "Multiculturalism, Transculturalism, and the Great Books," in *Beyond P.C.: Towards a Politics of Understanding*, ed. Patricia Aufderheide (St. Paul, MN: Graywolf, 1992), 64.
16 Quoted in Amitai Etzioni, "Social Science as a Multicultural Canon," *Society* 29 (November/December 1991): 15.
17 Roger Kimball, *Tenured Radicals: How Politics Has Corrupted Our Higher Education* (New York: Harper and Row, 1990).
18 Roger Kimball, "The Periphery *v.* the Center: The MLA in Chicago," in *Debating P.C.*, ed. Berman, 64.
19 Paul Berman, "Introduction: The Debate and Its Origins," in *Debating P.C.*, ed. Berman, 6.
20 Larry Yarbrough, "Three Questions for the Multicultural Debate," *Change: The Magazine of Higher Learning* 24 (January/February 1992): 64.
21 Henry A. Giroux, "Liberal Arts Education and the Struggle for Public Life: Dreaming about Democracy," in *The Politics of Liberal Education*, ed. Daryl J. Gless and Barbara Hernstein Smith (Durham, NC: Duke University Press, 1992), 139.
22 Karl Mannheim, *Ideology and Utopia: An Introduction to the Sociology of Knowledge*, trans. Louis Wirth and Edward Shils (New York: Harcourt Brace, 1936), 193.
23 Ishmael Reed, "America: The Multinational Society," in *Graywolf Annual Five: Multicultural Literacy, "Opening the American Mind,"* ed. Rick Simonson and Scott Walker (St. Paul, MN: Graywolf, 1988), 155.
24 Ibid.
25 Berndt Ostendorf, "Creoles and Creolization: Notes on the Multi-Cultural Origins of New Orleans Music," *Rivista di Studi Anglo-Americani* 5.7 (1989): 289–302.
26 Donald Weber, "Gertrude Berg and the Goldbergs," in *The Other Fifties: Interrogating Mid-Century American Icons*, ed. Joel Forman (Urbana: University of Illinois Press, 1997), 144–167.
27 Christopher C. Newton, "Commedia at Coney Island," *Theatre Symposium*, vol. 1 (Tuscaloosa: University of Alabama Press, 1993), 104–115.
28 Cornel West, "Diverse New World," in *Debating P.C.*, ed. Berman, 330.
29 Quoted in Ostendorf, "Cost of Multiculturalism," 17.
30 John Higham, "Multiculturalism and Universalism: A History and Critique," *American Quarterly* 45 (June 1993): 212–213.
31 Gary D. Gottfredson, Saundra Murray Nettles, and Barbara McHugh, eds., *Meeting the Challenges of Multicultural Education: A Report from the Evaluation of Pittsburgh's Prospect Multicultural Education Center* (Baltimore, MD: Johns Hopkins University Center for Social Organization of Schools, 1992), 4–9.
32 See, for example, Diane Ravitch, "Multiculturalism: E Pluribus Plures," in *Debating P.C.*, ed. Berman, 297.
33 Stephan Thernstrom, "The Minority Majority Will Never Come," *Wall Street Journal*, July 26, 1990. See also Stephen Thernstrom, "American Ethnic Statistics,"

in *Immigrants in Two Democracies: French and American Experience*, ed. Donald I. Horowitz and Gerard Noiriel (New York: New York University Press, 1992), 90–91.

34 See Joel Perlmann, "'Multiracials,' Racial Classification, and American Intermarriage – The Public's Interest," *Levy Institute Working Paper* No. 195 (June 1997), at http://www.levyinstitute.org/pubs/wp195.pdf, 35, reprinted in *Interracialism: Black-White Intermarriage in American History, Literature, and Law*, ed. Werner Sollors (New York: Oxford University Press, 2000), 524.

35 Nathan Glazer, "In Defense of Multiculturalism: Why the Sobol Commission Was Right," *New Republic*, September 2, 1991, 19; Gottfredson, Nettles, and McHugh, *Meeting the Challenges of Multicultural Education,* 8.

36 Gerald Early, "American Education and the Postmodern Impulse," *American Quarterly* 45 (June 1993): 220–223.

37 Michael Bérubé, "Public Image Limited: Political Correctness and the Media's Big Lie," in *Debating P.C.*, ed. Berman, 131. Bérube writes: "Allan Bloom (apparently thinking that Kimball is working on a major motion picture) heads Kimball's front cover with the line, 'All persons serious about education should see it.' [. . .] Kimball's salute to Bloom is more rigorous: 'An unparalleled reflection on today's intellectual climate . . . That rarest of documents, a genuinely profound book.'"

38 Kimball's blurb: "*Trenchant* . . . One of the most devastating and articulate attacks on multiculturalism yet to appear." *New York Times Book Review*, March 15, 1992, 20.

39 Schlesinger, *Disuniting of America,* 85, 75.

40 Adam Begley, "Souped-Up Scholar: Prof. Stanley Fish, Duke University's 'Politically Correct' Showman, Never Met a Debate He Didn't Like," *New York Times Magazine*, May 3, 1992, 50. The essay opens with a photomontage by Burk Uzzle of Stanley Fish, the spines of some of his books, and the front of a red sports car.

41 The American Federation of Teachers Union president Albert Shanker, for example, quoted the Czech leader of the Civic Forum Jan Urban as saying: "Do you realize that every country in Europe—Czechoslovakia, Yugoslavia, Bulgaria, Romania—is looking at this great miracle, which is the U.S. We cannot understand how different people can live together for hundreds of years and think of themselves as one. We are trying to understand how to emulate you so we can remain unified and not return to the racism, pogroms and wars of the past."Albert Shanker, "E Pluribus Unum?" *New York Times*, February 23, 1992.

42 Elizabeth Fox-Genovese, "The Self-Interest of Multiculturalism," in *Beyond P.C.*, ed. Aufderheide, 231, writes: "At the core of the multicultural agenda lies a commitment to education—and, indeed, culture itself—as primarily the quest for an acceptable autobiography."

43 See Milton M. Gordon, "Toward a General Theory of Racial and Ethnic Group Relations," in *Ethnicity*, ed. Glazer and Moynihan, 106–110; and Milton M. Gordon, *The Scope of Sociology* (New York: New York University Press, 1988), 157–166.

44 See Philip Gleason, "Identifying Identity," in *Theories of Ethnicity: A Classical Reader*, ed. Werner Sollors (Basingstoke: Macmillan / New York: New York University Press, 1996), 460–487. In a 1926 B'nai Brith address, Sigmund Freud had opposed religious faith and national pride but described his sense of Jewishness as the result of unconscious elements and what he called "the secret familiarity of identical psychological construction" (Heimlichkeit der gleichen inneren

Konstruktion). In *Childhood and Society* (1950), Erikson offered the term "*identity*" as a shortened English formula for Freud's notion. It was a formula that took.

45 George Devereux, "Ethnic Identity: Its Logical Foundations and Its Dysfunctions," in *Ethnic Identity: Cultural Continuities and Change*, ed. George De Vos and Lola Rornanucci-Ross (1975; Chicago: University of Chicago Press, 1982), 66–68.

46 Richard J. Perry, "Why Do Multiculturalists Ignore Anthropologists?" *Chronicle of Higher Education*, March 4, 1992.

47 John R. Searle, "Is There a Crisis in American Higher Education?" (lecture at the American Academy of Arts and Sciences, Cambridge, MA, May 1992).

48 United States Commission on Civil Rights, *Civil Rights Issues Facing Asian Americans in the 1990s* (Washington, DC: United States Commission on Civil Rights, 1992); Richard de Silva, "The Race Crisis on Campus," *Harvard Crimson Commencement Issue*, June 4, 1992.

49 Higham, "Multiculturalism and Universalism," 195–219.

50 David A. Hollinger, "How Wide the Circle of the 'We'? American Intellectuals and the Problem of the Ethnos since World War II," *American Historical Review* 98 (April 1993): 335–336. David A. Hollinger, *Postethnic America: Beyond Multiculturalism* (New York: Basic Books, 1995), 107.

51 Kwame Anthony Appiah, "Afterword: How Shall We Live as Many?" in *Beyond Pluralism: Essays on the Conception of Groups and Group Identities in America*, ed. Wendy Katkin, Ned Landsman, and Andrea Tyree (Champaign: University of Illinois Press, 1998).

52 Tzvetan Todorov, *On Human Diversity: Nationalism, Racism, and Exoticism in French Thought*, trans. Catherine Porter (Cambridge, MA: Harvard University Press, 1993), 353–399.

53 Marie de Lepervanche, "From Race to Ethnicity," *Australian and New Zealand Journal of Sociology* 16 (March 1980): 34.

54 Robert Hughes, "The Fraying of America," *Time Magazine*, February 3, 1992, 46.

55 Ibid., 47.

56 Robert C. Christopher, *Crashing the Gates: The De-WASPing of America's Power Elite* (New York: Simon and Schuster, 1989), 283.

57 Ibid., 22.

58 Thus the chair of the Institute for Educational Management, Arthur Levine, gives the following advice to administrators in a pro-multiculturalist, yet conservative-sounding magazine: "Vigorous support must come from the top. Avoid politicization. The effort must be faculty-driven. [. . .] Try to avoid a top-down emphasis, but offer support (moral and fiscal)." Arthur Levine, "A Time to Act," *Change: The Magazine of Higher Learning 24* (January/February 1992): 5.

59 Louis Menand, "Illiberalisms," in *Beyond P.C.*, ed. Aufderheide, 233.

60 Sylvia Nasar, "Even Among the Well-Off, the Richest Get Richer," *New York Times*, March 5, 1992. See the introduction to this volume for more recent statistical information.

61 Sylvia Nasar, "However You Slice the Data the Richest Did Get Richer," *New York Times*, May 11, 1992.

62 Felicity Barringer, "Giving by the Rich Declines, on Average," *New York Times*, May 24, 1992.

63 Michele K. Collison, "Angry Protests over Diversity and Free Speech Mark Contentious Spring Semester at Harvard," *Chronicle of Higher Education*, May 6, 1992.

64 *Change: The Magazine of Higher Learning* 24 (January/February 1992): 4.
65 Arthur Levine and Jeanette Cureton, "The Quiet Revolution," in ibid., 29.
66 Porter, "Ethnic Pluralism in Canada," 294.
67 Quoted in Begley, "Souped-Up Scholar," 52.
68 Kimball, "Periphery v. the Center," 66.
69 Personal notes.
70 Barbara Ehrenreich, "The Challenge for the Left," in *Debating P.C.*, ed. Berman, 337.
71 Shelby Steele, *The Content of Our Character: A New Vision of Race in America* (1990; New York: Harper, 1991), 22–23.
72 Searle, "Is There a Crisis in American Higher Education?," 9.
73 Ibid.
74 Clement Wood, *The Complete Rhyming Dictionary and Poet's Craft Book* (Garden City, NY: Doubleday, 1936), 368.
75 William Graham Sumner, *Folkways: A Study of the Sociological Importance of Usages, Manners, and Morals* (1906; Boston: Ginn, 1940), 13.
76 Thus Diane Ravitch, "Multiculturalism," 289, writes: "American education is not centered on anything, is centered on itself. It is 'Americentric.' Most American students know very little about Europe, and even less about the rest of the world. [. . .] When the Berlin Wall was opened in the fall of 1989, journalists discovered that most American teenagers had no idea what it was, nor why its opening was such a big deal. Eurocentrism provides a better target than Americentrism."
77 Jean Devisse, in *The Image of the Black in Western Art: From the Early Christian Era to the Age of Discovery,"* vol. 2, part I, series ed. Ladislas Bugner, trans. William Granger Ryan (n.p.: Menil Foundation; distributed by Harvard University Press, 1979), 249.
78 Sigmund Freud, "Civilization and Its Discontents" (1930), *Standard Edition of Complete Psychological Works*, vol. 21, trans. James Strachey (London: Hogarth, 1961).
79 Catharine R. Stimpson, "The White Squares," *Change: The Magazine of Higher Education* 24 (January/February 1992): 77–78.
80 Freud, "Civilization and Its Discontents," 114. See Freud's "The Taboo of Virginity" (1918), in *Standard Edition of Complete Psychological Works*, trans. James Strachey, vol. 11 (London: Hogarth, 1957), 199; and Freud's "Group Psychology" (1921), in *Standard Edition of Complete Psychological Works*, vol. 18, trans. James Strachey (London: Hogarth, 1955), 101.
81 Marshall Sahlins, "Goodbye to Tristes Tropes" (paper presented at National Identity and Ethnic Diversity, Greater Philadelphia Philosophy Consortium, March 7, 1992). Steele, *Content of Our Character*, 132, feels that as "racial, ethnic, and gender differences become forms of sovereignty, campuses become balkanized." Dinesh D'Souza and Robert MacNeil, "The Big Chill? D'Souza's opinion of the new university politics, characterized by affirmative action, is summed up in this way: "I think this is a formula for racial division, for Balkanization, and ultimately for racial hostility." (Interview with Dinesh D'Souza," in *Debating P.C.*, ed. Berman, 35.) Itabari Njeri, "Multiculturalism," writes, "Schlesinger and other critics see [multiculturalism] as a kind of tribalism, a dangerous balkanization of American society." Todd Gitlin, "On the Virtues of a Loose Canon," in *Beyond P.C.*, ed. Aufderheide, 190, finds in "group narcissism" "a perfect recipe for a home-grown Yugoslavia."
82 Todd Gitlin, "Toward a Loose Cannon," *Dissent* 37 (Spring 1990): 254; Adam

Yarmolinsky, in *Change: The Magazine of Higher Learning* 24 (January/February 1991); Henry Louis Gates Jr., *Loose Canons: Notes on the Cultural Wars* (New York: Oxford University Press, 1992); Irving Louis Horowitz, "The New Nihilism," *Society* 9 (November/December 1991): 27; Bryan Wolf, "Firing the Canon," *American Literary History* 3 (Winter 1991): 707–752.

83 Arthur Mann, *The One and the Many: Reflections on the American Identity* (Chicago: University of Chicago Press, 1979).

84 Schlesinger, *Disuniting of America*, 2, 80.

85 Ravitch, "Multiculturalism."

86 *New York Times*, June 23, 1991.

87 Decter, in *Commentary* (September 1991). Schmidt, *Analog Science Fiction & Fact* 112 (April 1992): 4.

88 *National Review* editorial, July 29, 1991, 16.

89 *New York Times*, February 23, 1992.

90 Kenneth Silverman, *A Cultural History of the American Revolution* (New York: Crowell, 1976), 417.

91 Ibid., 658.

92 Monroe Deutsch, "E Pluribus Unum," *Classical Journal 18* (1922–1923): 392.

93 Ibid.

94 Horace, Epistles II, in *Satires, Epistles and Ars Poetica*, trans. by H. Rushton Fairclough (Cambridge, MA: Harvard University Press, 1956), 211–213. Fairclough translated from "Lenior et melior fis accedente senecta? Quid te exempta iuvat spinis *de pluribus una*. Vivere se recte nescis, decede peritis" (emphasis added).

95 Deutsch, "E Pluribus Unum," 391.

96 Edward Kennard Rand, *The Magical Art of Virgil* (Cambridge, MA: Harvard University Press, 1963), 59–60.

97 E. J. Kenney, ed., *The Ploughman's Lunch Moretum: A Poem Ascribed to Virgil* (Bristol: Bristol Classical Press, 1984), 8–9. Kenney translated from "it manus in gyrum: paula tim singula uires / deperdunt proprias, color est *e pluribus unus,* / nec totus uiridis, quia lactea frusta repugnant, / nec de lacte nitens, quia tot uariatur ab herbis" (emphasis added).

98 Deutsch, "E Pluribus Unum," 406.

99 Giroux, "Liberal Arts Education and the Struggle for Public Life," 131.

100 D'Souza and MacNeil, "The Big Chill?" in *Debating P.C.*, ed. Berman, 31: "I'm in favor of a multicultural curriculum that emphasizes what Matthew Arnold called the best that has been thought and said." Kimball, quoted in Bérubé, "Public Image Limited," 134, thinks that Arnold "had looked to the preservation and transmission of the best that had been thought and written as a means of rescuing culture from anarchy in a democratic society." Gertrude Himmelfarb describes a better past, when "it was considered the function of the university to [. . .] liberate [students] intellectually and spiritually by exposing them, as the English poet Matthew Arnold put it, to 'the best which has been thought and said in the world.'" Himmelfarb is quoted in Alexander Nehamas, "Serious Watching," in *Politics of Liberal Education*, ed. Gless and Smith, 163, and Alexander Nehamas responds (163-164) by calling attention to an inaccuracy in such uses of Arnold:

> Nostalgia has colored [. . .] Professor Himmelfarb's [. . .] recollection of Arnold, who actually wrote that the 'business' of criticism is 'to know the best that is known and thought in the world.' [. . .] Himmelfarb's replacement of Arnold's

> present-tense 'is' by the perfect tense 'has been' [. . .] allows her to appeal to Arnold's authority in order to insinuate, if not to argue outright, that the university's concern is with the past and that the present, at least in connection with the humanities, lies largely outside the scope of its function.

Some advocates of multiculturalism have criticized conservative uses of Arnold more generally by declaring him irrelevant to democratic education or to the electronic age. John Searle, "The Storm over the University," in *Debating P.C.*, ed. Berman, 88, observes that what were once undisputed educational platitudes have now become contested, for example, the demand that students should, "in Matthew Arnold's overquoted words, 'know the best that is known and thought in the world.'"

101 Matthew Arnold, "The Function of Criticism at the Present Time" (1864), in *Lectures and Essays in Criticism*, ed. R. H. Super (Ann Arbor: University of Michigan Press, 1962), 477.

102 Ibid., 270.

103 Ibid. Arnold chastises the notion "that truth and culture themselves can be reached by the processes of this life," a notion advocated by critics who seem to proclaim, "We are all *terrae filii*, all Philistines together." Ibid., 276.

104 Ibid., 282.

105 Ibid., 282–283.

106 Ibid., 283.

107 Ibid., 284.

108 Ibid.

109 Arnold used his expression several more times in *Culture and Anarchy*, drawn from lectures he had given in 1866 and 1867; once he demands that we get to know "whether through reading, observing, or thinking, the best that can at present be known in the world." Further I should mention, in fairness to Gertrude Himmelfarb, that when Arnold added a preface for the book publication in 1869, he wrote: "The whole scope of the essay is to recommend culture as the great help out of our present difficulties; culture being a pursuit of our total perfection by means of getting to know, on all matters which most concern us, the best which has been thought and said in the world." Yet, again, this does not make Arnold play a cultural past against the present. He explicates later in the preface, "If a man without books or reading, or reading nothing but his letters and the newspapers, gets nevertheless a fresh and free play of the best thoughts upon his stock notions and habits, he has got culture." Moreover, when he uses the familiar phrasing again in the "Sweetness and Light" section of *Culture and Anarchy*, it is to express his view that it must be the aim of culture "to do away with classes; to make the best that has been thought and known in the world current everywhere." The great men of culture carry, "from one end of society to the other, the best knowledge, the best ideas of their time," with a distinct focus on the contemporary context. Matthew Arnold, *Culture and Anarchy: With Friendship's Garland and Some Literary Essays*, ed. R. H. Super (Ann Arbor: University of Michigan Press, 1965), 191, 233, 529, and 113.

110 See Horace M. Kallen, *Judaism at Bay: Essays toward the Adjustment of Judaism to Modernity* (New York: Bloch, 1932), 8–9; Susanne Klingenstein, *Jews in the American Academy, 1900–1940* (New Haven, CT: Yale University Press, 1991), 43–45, 161–178.

111 Morris Dickstein, *Double Agent: The Critic and Society* (New York: Oxford University Press, 1992), 12.

112 Ibid., 15.

113 Ibid., 16.

114 Ibid., 16.

115 The term "*politically correct*" is pervasive in the multiculturalism debate. In a letter to the *New York Times Book Review* on May 31, 1992, Mark Kurlansky writes, "There was a time when I loved the phrase 'politically correct' as a wonderfully snide label for the safe conformism of the liberal establishment. But then it became a tedious cliché used to describe the tyranny of that same establishment, which tries to censor anyone who does not conform. Now we see another use. An idea can simply be dismissed by asserting that it is politically correct" (46). It was traced by Ruth Perry, "A Short History of the Term *Politically Correct*," in *Beyond P.C.*, ed. Aufderheide, 72–73, to 1970, to an essay by Toni Cade (who was yet to add Bambara to her name). Perry suspects that the term may come from Maoist rhetoric. Natalie Wexler has pointed out in "Goes Back to 1793" (letter to the editor, *New York Times*, December 15, 1993, A26) that the term was used once by Supreme Court justice James Wilson in *Chisholm v. Alabama*: "Is a toast asked? 'The *United States*,' instead of the 'People of the *United States*,' is the toast given. This is not politically correct." Wilson said this in 1793 in support of an argument in favor of the people rather than the states, but Wexler adds that it may have been an isolated occurrence. It is possible that the phrasing gained wider currency only in post–World War II critiques of totalitarianism. Thus when the protagonist of Ellison's novel *Invisible Man* (1952; New York: Vintage Books, 1972), 453, gets censored by the brotherhood he is questioned; and Brother Tobitt sarcastically asks, "You mean he admits the *possibility* of being incorrect?"

116 George Orwell, *Nineteen Eighty-Four* (New York: Harcourt Brace, 1949), 133. All Orwell quotes are from this first American edition.

117 Ibid., 311.

118 Walter Goodman, for example, reviewed one of the many new and politically correct dictionaries that are now on the market under the title "Decreasing Our Word Power: The New Newspeak," *New York Times Book Review*, January 27, 1991, 14." In a similar vein, Robert Lerner and Stanley Rothman complained about "Newspeak, Feminist Style," *Commentary* 89 (April 1990): 54.

119 Orwell, *Nineteen Eighty-Four*, 149.

120 Bérubé, "Public Image Limited," 139. See Orwell, *Nineteen Eighty-Four*, 45, for the occurrence of "*doubleplusungood*" in the novel.

121 Orwell, *Nineteen Eighty-Four*, 52.

122 Paula Rothenberg, "Critics of Attempts to Democratize the Curriculum Are Waging a Campaign to Misrepresent the Work of Responsible Professors," in *Debating P.C.*, ed. Berman, 268; Orwell, *Nineteen Eighty-Four*, 5.

123 Patricia Williams, "Defending the Gains," in *Beyond P.C.*, ed. Aufderheide, 197.

124 Journalists have used it again and again—in organs ranging from *Playboy* to *Reader's Digest*, in articles with such titles as "Campus Christians and the New Thought Police," "Thought Police on Campus," and "The Thought Police Get Tenure"—to describe the atmosphere of censorship in university life.

125 George Will, "Radical English," in *Beyond P.C.*, ed. Aufderheide, 112.

126 Michael Novak, "The New Ethnicity," *Center Magazine* 7 (July/August 1974): 18–25.
127 Camille Paglia, "The Nursery-School Campus: The Corrupting of the Humanities in the US," *Times Literary Supplement*, May 22, 1992, 19.
128 Quoted in Nat Hentoff, "Black Counterpoint," *Village Voice*, October 15, 1991, 27.
129 Hughes, "Fraying of America," 46.
130 Quoted in Searle, "Storm over the University," 110.
131 Todorov's review is—in the characteristic fashion of anecdote-retelling—cited by Kimball. Searle supplements it with the remark that "according to the literary theorists influenced by Derrida, there is nothing beyond or outside texts. So O'Brien is supposed to have triumphed over Winston after all." Searle argues that one cannot, within human linguistic practices, "intelligibly deny metaphysical realism, because the meaningfulness of our public utterances already presupposes an independently existing reality to which expressions in those utterances can refer." Ibid., 111, 113, 114.
132 Orwell, *Nineteen Eighty-Four*, 250–251.
133 Ibid., 251.
134 Ibid., 252.
135 Erich Fromm, afterword, in *Nineteen Eighty-Four* (1949; New York: Signet, 1961), 263–264.
136 Orwell, *Nineteen Eight-Four*, 128.
137 Daphne Patai, *The Orwell Mystique: A Study in Male Ideology* (Amherst: University of Massachusetts Press, 1984), 241; Orwell, *Nineteen Eighty-Four*, 12.
138 Orwell, *Nineteen Eighty-Four*, 210.
139 John Rodden, *The Politics of Literary Reputation: The Making and Claiming of "St. George" Orwell* (New York: Oxford University Press, 1989), 26–27.
140 Ibid., 16.
141 Ibid., 30.
142 Ibid., 37.
143 Reed, "America," 157–158.
144 Richard Polenberg, *One Nation Divisible: Class, Race, and Ethnicity in the United States since 1938* (New York: Viking, 1980), 70.
145 Philip Gleason, *Speaking of Diversity: Language and Ethnicity in Twentieth-Century America* (Baltimore, MD: Johns Hopkins University Press, 1992), 153–228.
146 Mann, *The One and the Many*, 142–143.
147 John Higham, *Send These to Me: Jews and Other Immigrants in Urban America* (New York: Atheneum, 1975), 220.
148 Stewart G. Cole and Mildred Wiese Cole, *Minorities and the American Promise: The Conflict of Principle and Practice*, Bureau for Intercultural Education Publication Series, No. 10 (New York: Harper and Brothers, 1954), 3.
149 Gleason, *Speaking of Diversity*, 93–94.
150 Donald R. Young, "Democracy and Group Relations," in *Civilization and Group Relations*, ed. Robert MacIver (New York: Institute for Religious Studies, 1945), 157.
151 Ibid., 158–159.
152 Ibid., 159.
153 Robert M. MacIver, "The Ordering of a Multigroup Society," in *Civilization and Group Relations*, 164.
154 Higham, *Send These to Me*, 221.
155 MacIver, "Ordering of a Multigroup Society," 165.

156 Ibid., 167.

157 Robin M. Williams Jr., *The Reduction of Intergroup Tensions: A Survey of Research on Problems of Ethnic, Racial, and Religious Group Relations,* Social Science Research Council Bulletin 57 (New York: Social Science Research Council, 1947), 63. Compare Higham, *Send These to Me*, 218n.

158 Williams, *Reduction of Intergroup Tensions*, 63 ("Simultaneous direct attack," drawing on Talcott Parsons); "[P]roblems of group conflict," "Where strong prejudice is present," citing Northern criticism of the American South as one example); 67 ("Propaganda which appeals," "An effective propaganda approach"); 72 ("Hostility is reduced"); 64 ("The likelihood of conflict").

159 Ibid., 64.

160 Cole and Cole, *Minorities and the American Promise*, 3.

161 Ibid., 152.

162 Ibid., 153.

163 Ibid.

164 Gottfredson, Nettles, and McHugh, *Meeting the Challenges of Multicultural Education*, 8.

165 Gordon, *Scope of Sociology*, 140–168.

166 Malcolm X, with the assistance of Alex Haley, *The Autobiography of Malcolm X* (1965; New York: Grove Press, 1966), 277–278.

167 But compare ibid., 372–373.

168 Explicitly in ibid., 341.

169 LeRoi Jones, "What Does Nonviolence Mean?," *Home: Social Essays* (New York: William Morrow, 1966), 149–150, writes:

> The German Jews, at the time of Hitler's rise to power, were the most assimilated Jews in Europe. They believed, and with a great deal of emotional investment, that they were Germans. The middle-class German Jew, like the middle-class American Negro, had actually moved, in many instances, into the mainstream of the society, and wanted to believe as that mainstream did. Even when the anti-Jewish climate began to thicken and take on the heaviness of permanence, many middle-class Jews believed that it was only the poor Jews who, perhaps rightly so, would suffer in such a climate.
>
> Like these unfortunate Jews the middle-class Negro has no real program of rebellion against the *status quo* in America, quite frankly, because he believes he is pretty well off. The blatant cultural assassination, the social and economic exploitation of most Negroes in this society, does not really impress him. The middle-class Negro's goal, like the rest of the American middle class, is to be ignorant comfortably.

The formulation "cultural assassination" in this context gives expression to the post-Holocaust parallel of genocide and racial assimilation that helps to tilt the scale in favor of difference. Jones pursued a similar strategy in his poetry, and he did not always focus on African Americans. In his poem "Black Dada Nihilismus," *The Dead Lecturer: Poems* (New York: Grove Press, 1964), 61–62, LeRoi Jones invokes the "ugly silent deaths of jews under / the surgeon's knife." Having thus suggested the image of a Dr. Mengele and the inhuman medical experiments that accompanied the Holocaust, LeRoi Jones continues in the same line: "(To awake on / 69th street with money and a hip / nose." Plastic surgery as the enactment of assimilation is thus put into the symbolic universe of genocide. Jones's "hip nose" may pun on "hypnosis," just as Malcolm had used the word "mesmerized"—and both would refer to "brainwashing"—to describe assimilation as a form of being taken possession of by a deadly alien force.

170 Richard Rorty, *Achieving Our Country: Leftist Thought in Twentieth-Century America* (Cambridge, MA: Harvard University Press, 1998).

Acknowledgments

I am grateful to Micah Kleit and Leslie Mitchner for asking me to put together and introduce this selection of essays for Rutgers University Press. It gave me a welcome opportunity to work with Leslie, who made excellent suggestions in the editing process. I also thank George Blaustein, Alide Cagidemetrio, and Glenda Carpio for reading and commenting on earlier versions of the introduction. Lauren Manoy and Marianna Vertullo copyedited the manuscript.

Chapter One, "Literature and Ethnicity." *Harvard Encyclopedia of American Ethnic Groups*, edited by Stephan Thernstrom, Ann Orlov, and Oscar Handlin (Cambridge, MA: Belknap Press of Harvard University Press). Copyright ©1980 by the President and Fellows of Harvard College. I am grateful to Daniel Aaron for recommending me as potential contributor to the encyclopedia and for discussions, and I thank the editors, the anonymous readers, and Harold Abramson and Philip Gleason for their comments.

Chapter Two, "National Identity and Ethnic Diversity: Of Plymouth Rock and Jamestown and Ellis Island: Ethnic Literature and Some Redefinitions of 'America.'" In *Immigrants in Two Democracies: French and American Experience*, edited by Donald Horowitz and Gérard Noiriel (New York: New York University Press, 1992). Copyright © 1992 by the New York University Press. Reprinted in *History & Memory in African-American Culture*, edited by Geneviève Fabre and Robert O'Meally (New York and Oxford: Oxford University Press, 1994), 92–121. I thank Catherine

Clinton, Geneviève Fabre, Donald Horowitz, Gérard Noiriel, Robert O'Meally, and Stephan Thernstrom for suggestions and comments.

Chapter Three, "Dedicated to a Proposition: 'All Men Are Created Equal' in American Culture." *America in the Course of Human Events*, edited by Josef Jařab, Marcel Arbeit, and Jenel Virden (Amsterdam: VU Press, 2006). Thanks to Josef Jařab for his kind invitation to deliver this paper at the European Association for American Studies meeting in Prague and for his permission to republish it here. Also thanks to Daniel Albright for his references to Declaration music, David Sollors for alerting me to *Hair*, Cambridge Ridley for her research assistance, and Marcel Arbeit for editing the essay for publication.

Chapter Four, "A Critique of Pure Pluralism." *Reconstructing American Literary History*, edited by Sacvan Bercovitch, *Harvard English Studies* 13 (1986). Copyright ©1980 by the President and Fellows of Harvard College. I am grateful to Sacvan Bercovitch for asking me to write this essay and for his suggestions for revision, and to Ann Waters for editing it.

Chapter Five, "De Pluribus Una / E Pluribus Unus. Matthew Arnold, George Orwell, Holocaust and Assimilation. The Multiculturalism Debate as Cultural Text." From *Beyond Pluralism: The Conception of Groups and Group Identities in America*, edited by Wendy F. Katkin, Ned Landsman, and Andrea Tyree (Champaign: University of Illinois Press, 1998). Copyright © 1998 by the Board of Trustees of the University of Illinois Press. An earlier version was presented in 1992 as Working Paper no. 53 of the John F. Kennedy-Institut, Freie Universität Berlin; and a German translation appeared in Berndt Ostendorf, ed., *Multikulturelle Gesellschaft: Modell Amerika* (München: Fink, 1994), 53–74. For their comments I am indebted to Daniel Aaron, Howard Adelman, Anthony Appiah, Sacvan Bercovitch, Nathan Glazer, Margaret Gullette, Lauren Gwin, John Higham, David Hollinger, Wendy Katkin, Stanley Lieberson, Jeffrey Melnick, Berndt Ostendorf, Maxine Senn-Yuen, Marc Shell, Winfried Siemerling, Brook Thomas, Stephen Toulmin, and Robin M. Williams.

Index

Page numbers in italics refer to figures

About the Author

Werner Sollors is a research professor of English at Harvard University, professor of global literature at New York University Abu Dhabi, and Fellow of the American Academy of Arts & Sciences. He has published the books *Beyond Ethnicity*, *Neither Black nor White yet Both*, *Ethnic Modernism*, *The Temptation of Despair*, and *African American Writing*.